GLOUCEST
AIRFIELDS
IN THE SECOND
WORLD WAR

David Berryman

COUNTRYSIDE BOOKS
NEWBURY, BERKSHIRE

First published 2005
© David Berryman, 2005

COUNTRYSIDE BOOKS
3 Catherine Road
Newbury, Berkshire

To view our complete range of books,
please visit us at
www.countrysidebooks.co.uk

ISBN 1 85306 949 3
EAN 978 1 85306 949 9

*For my son, Ben,
for his encouragement and support*

The cover picture is from an original by
Colin Doggett and shows Mark IV Blenheims
on flight test over the Gloucestershire countryside

Designed by Mon Mohan

Produced through MRM Associates Ltd., Reading
Typeset by Techniset Typesetters, Merseyside
Printed by Woolnough Bookbinding Ltd., Irthlingborough

CONTENTS

GLOUCESTERSHIRE'S SECOND WORLD WAR AIRFIELDS

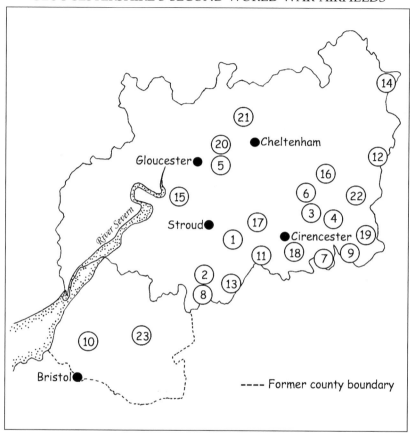

KEY TO MAP

1 Aston Down
2 Babdown Farm
3 Barnsley Park
4 Bibury
5 Brockworth
6 Chedworth
7 Down Ampney
8 Down Farm
9 Fairford
10 Filton
11 Kemble
12 Little Rissington

13 Long Newnton
14 Moreton-in-Marsh
15 Moreton Valence
16 Northleach
17 Overley
18 South Cerney
19 Southrop
20 Staverton
21 Stoke Orchard
22 Windrush
23 Yate

ACKNOWLEDGEMENTS

I would like to thank the following individuals and organisations that have assisted me in writing this book:

Colin Cruddas; Terry Heffernan; Nick Stroud and the team at *Aeroplane Magazine*; Jeanette Powell, MoD; Jean Buckberry, Senior Librarian, RAF College Cranwell; British Aerospace; Gloucestershire Museum and Library Service; Museum of Army Flying, Middle Wallop; National Archives, Kew; RAF Museum, Hendon; Wiltshire County Libraries; Alan Hartley, RAF Down Ampney Association; Nigel Clarke of Nigel J. Clarke Publications (for more information of their books and photographs, see www.njcpublications.co.uk); Michael Turner (for more details and information on Michael's work, visit www.studio88.co.uk).

I would also like to thank Nicholas Battle and his team at Countryside Books for their help and encouragement, and my wife Karen for her typing skills and her support in helping me compile this manuscript.

I
SETTING
THE SCENE

The County of Gloucestershire has played an important part in the development of aviation in Britain. It was not only home to two major aircraft manufacturers, Bristol and Gloster, plus a few smaller companies such as Parnall and A.W. Hawksley, but has a history of aviation that began with the very earliest hot-air balloons. The first of these was probably that built in 1784 by Doctor Edward Jenner, the discoverer of vaccination. He released it, albeit un-manned, from Berkley Castle, and it flew for two miles. More balloon flights followed in the county, and several attempts at heavier-than-air flight were made.

The first manned powered flight in Britain took place almost a century and a quarter after Jenner's balloon flight, on 16 October 1908 when Samuel Cody flew an aircraft of his own design from Laffan's Plain, Farnborough (later the site of the Royal Aircraft Establishment). Other aircraft designs followed, but one of the first aircraft manufacturing companies to be established was set up not long afterwards in Gloucestershire. This was in February 1910 when the Bristol and Colonial Aeroplane Company was established at Filton. By the end of the following year it had built over 120 machines and the popular Bristol Boxkite design was in service with several flying schools, including one opened by the company itself at Larkhill on Salisbury Plain.

The outbreak of the First World War a few years later (and then known as the Great War) would transform not only aviation, but Gloucestershire itself. The Bristol Aeroplane Company was already well-established, and soon entered into war production for the Royal Flying Corps and Royal Naval Air Service. They were joined by the Gloucester Aircraft Company at Cheltenham and the Parnall Aircraft

Training aircraft flown from Gloucestershire airfields during the Great War included Maurice Farman Shorthorns. (Aeroplane)

Company at Bristol. Airfields were built for the Royal Flying Corps (which amalgamated with the Royal Naval Air Service to become the Royal Air Force in 1918), such as those at Rendcombe, Leighterton and Minchinhampton for flying training and at Brockworth and Yate for the repair and overhaul of aircraft. The end of the Great War saw a contraction in the forces and a reduced requirement for equipment. Although Brockworth and Yate were abandoned by the RAF, they were taken over by the Gloucestershire Aircraft Company and Parnall Aircraft, respectively. These companies, along with the Bristol Aircraft Company, somehow managed to keep going, producing aeroplanes into the 1920s and 1930s.

During the inter-war years several private airfields were opened and an interest in aviation was sparked off by such personalities as Sir Alan Cobham, who toured the country with his 'Flying Circus' from 1920 onwards. His flying displays under the title 'The National Aviation Day Campaign' included aerobatics and crazy flying, and joy rides were offered to the public. Cobham's Circus received widespread publicity and popularised aviation. He encouraged local authorities to open their own airports and coincidentally, if not as the direct result, construction of an airport was started in 1934 at Staverton to serve Gloucester and Cheltenham.

On 14 June 1929, No 501 (County of Gloucester) Squadron had been formed at Filton as a Special Reserve Bomber Squadron. Such units were raised and maintained in specific localities to act as part of the air defence of Great Britain. This resulted from an initiative started by

Marshal of the Royal Air Force, Sir Hugh Trenchard, who envisaged a reserve air force to back up the regular RAF, organised along the lines of the Territorial Army. No 501 Squadron was the third such unit to be formed since the force was authorised in October 1924. Although it was administered by the County Territorial Association it was staffed by a cadre of regular RAF officers and airmen, with at least two thirds of its strength being made up by locally recruited personnel.

All of the officers had to hold a private pilot's licence, or be prepared to obtain one, and were compelled to receive flying tuition to qualify for RAF pilot's wings. They were required to attend regular training sessions and an annual two week summer camp. Initially equipped with the Avro 504N two-seat, single-engined biplane trainer, the unit received DH 9A bombers in March 1930, but these were soon replaced by Westland Wapitis and Wallaces. In 1936 the squadron became part of the Auxiliary Air Force, and received Hawker Harts.

Shortly after having been issued with Hawker Hind bombers in 1938 it was announced that the unit would be retrained as a fighter squadron, and in March 1939 the first of its Hawker Hurricanes arrived. No 501 was one of the 20 additional operational squadrons that were provided by the Auxiliary Air Force to supplement the front line strength of the RAF on the outbreak of war. All of these squadrons would acquit themselves well in the coming conflict.

British military aviation had revived during the 1930s as a result of the RAF Expansion Scheme. This was initiated in July 1934 by the government, prompted by the threat posed by the rapid increase in the strength of the German air force. At the time the RAF was still feeling the effects of the post-Great War cutbacks and the investment famine of the 1920s. It had a strength of 850 aeroplanes, the number being based on balancing the only continental air force that it was thought could pose a threat to Britain at the time – i.e. France. The rapid rearmament of Germany had come as an unpleasant shock. The fastest British aircraft in 1934 was the 207 mph Hawker Fury biplane fighter, and the most potent was the Handley Page Heyford biplane bomber, which had a bomb load of 3,000 lbs and a range of 500 miles.

Over the next few years, new airfields were opened at South Cerney for flying training, at Aston Down and Kemble for the storage of aircraft and at Little Rissington for both. Orders for new aircraft were placed with Gloucestershire aircraft companies, and soon Glosters were making Gauntlets, Gladiators and later Hawker Hurricanes, and Bristol were licence-building Hawker Audaxes as well as tooling up to produce their new Blenheim bomber. The result of this timely preparation was that on the outbreak of war the RAF had some 2,000 aircraft in front-line service and some 2,200 in reserve (many of them modern monoplanes such as the 300 mph Hawker Hurricane and Supermarine Spitfire fighters, and the Vickers Wellington and Handley Page Hampden bombers that could take a 4,000 lb bomb load far into Germany at well over 200 mph). The Luftwaffe facing it had over 4,000 first-line aircraft, with 1,000 in reserve, but although it was numerically superior, could not match the training, courage and spirit of the Royal Air Force.

More new airfields for the RAF were being planned or were under construction in the county just as the war started. With the outbreak of hostilities all general flying was stopped, and only authorised civilian flights were allowed to take place. The vast majority of civil aircraft were then requisitioned for service use. During the early stages of the war most of the airfields in Gloucestershire were too far from the Continent for the conduct of offensive operations, but they were nevertheless ideally suited for training and support. Aston Down, Little Rissington, South Cerney and Staverton became important training centres, and to these were later added Moreton-in-Marsh and Chedworth. Transport and communications aircraft were also flown from Staverton and the airfield later became an important flight test centre. As the tide of the war started to turn, airborne forces airfields were constructed at Down Ampney and Fairford, in preparation for the planned invasion of Europe.

Representative of the threat that prompted the RAF Expansion Plans, a Heinkel He 111 bomber being refuelled at its base before the war. (Aeroplane)

Examples of defences built during the Second World War still exist. This circular pillbox was photographed at Southrop airfield in May 1996. (Steve Lawrence)

The programme of airfield building required a huge amount of labour and materials. A typical airfield took at least seven or eight months to complete, employing a thousand men. The Minister of Labour, Ernest Bevin, was responsible for providing the workers for the programme, and also for other large defence and civilian projects. There was, for example, the need to repair civilian housing, as many thousands of houses had been damaged in air raids. The rubble from destroyed buildings was sometimes used as the hardcore for building airfield runways.

To give an idea of the scale of the airfield building programme, in December 1942, 510 airfields were in operation in Britain. A further 106 were under construction and 54 were at various stages between survey and commencement of work. Civilian contractors such as Wimpey, McAlpine, Taylor Woodrow, Costain and Laing, along with a host of sub-contractors, were busily engaged in this work. RAF Works Squadrons and US Army Engineers assisted with the construction of some of the airfields.

RAF airfields built in the late 1930s were provided with perimeter tracks and hard standings, but the landing and take-off areas were predominantly grass. The RAF refused to lay hard runways across its green turf, except in the case of heavy bomber stations and this was

11

later to result in problems. The layout of the operational and technical areas was excellent, however. The stations were usually provided with a number of spacious hangars, and buildings such as the headquarters and officers', sergeants' and airmen's messes were finished in brick or stone to a high standard, and designed, often in a neo-Georgian style, to blend with the local environment as far as possible.

The massive expansion in airfield building that came with the war meant that time and expense did not allow for such graceful pre-war buildings, and instead they became utilitarian and basic. Many of the technical buildings and communal messing sites were built of brick with cement rendering, but most of the domestic accommodation was provided by wooden or corrugated iron huts of various sizes. Due to the need for dispersed sites (to minimise the possibility of collateral damage in case of air raids), nowhere ever seemed close to anywhere else, and bicycles or road vehicles were essential! The airfields themselves grew in size during the wartime period. Standard runways (where they were provided) were normally of around 3,300 feet in length and 150 feet wide in 1939. By 1942, to cope with heavier aircraft, the RAF had accepted that concrete runways had to be laid as standard, and a main runway of 6,000 feet was more the norm, with two subsidiaries each of 4,200 feet. Extensive perimeter tracks were also built, deliberately provided with loop-type or pan-handle dispersals leading off them.

The need for supplementary airfields also developed, particularly for the Maintenance Units (MUs) and the flying training stations. Satellite Landing Grounds were soon needed by the MUs for the storage of aircraft as their main sites became overcrowded. These were usually just convenient fields, often with woods nearby in which to disperse and hide the stored aeroplanes. Relief Landing Grounds (RLGs) were required by flying training units to ease the congestion that often occurred at their main airfield. With as many as 100 trainers operating from a typical flying training station it is not difficult to understand the necessity! The RLGs were used for take-off and landing practice, and for circuit flying. They also provided convenient locations for night flying practice, not only so that any enemy bomber attracted by their flare paths would not cause any damage to the main base, but also so that the personnel sleeping there would not be disturbed by the noise!

Dummy airfields were also built to act as decoys and draw enemy attacks from the real ones. These were of two main types – K sites for day decoys and Q sites for night. The latter were easier to construct as they reproduced the lighting of an airfield at night, which was minimal anyway. They could be constructed anywhere, even in an undulating landscape as the lights were carried on poles. K sites were more difficult to build as they had to look like the real thing, including all the necessary buildings, installations and dummy aircraft. The sites were extremely successful. As more and more airfields were built, so too were decoys. Airfield decoy sites built in Gloucestershire included Farmington for Little Rissington, Shurdington (Brockworth) and Patchway (Filton). Eventually over 200 were in existence all over the country. By the end of 1941 the Luftwaffe had made 322 attacks on the decoys, as opposed to 304 on genuine airfields.

Other types of decoys were the Starfish and QL sites. These were designed so that trays of fuel could be lit and controlled from a bunker, as it was noticed that German bombers were attracted by fires. The sites were given the name SF (Special Fire) or Starfish. The QL sites consisted of special lighting effects that could be used on their own or with the SF sites to add realism. These included 'hares and rabbits', which were lights on a rig travelling along the ground to simulate an aircraft taxiing or taking off. Others replicated vehicles. Further features later added to the decoy airfields included dummy flare paths and Drem approach lighting (a system for guiding aircraft in the vicinity of an airfield in to land at night). These enhanced the apparent authenticity of the decoys, but unless Allied pilots knew of their locations, they too could be duped, and land in a field in the middle of nowhere! As well as simulating airfields, some Starfish/QL sites were built to protect industrial targets. A ring of ten such sites was built around Bristol, including a huge one in the Mendip Hills that simulated Temple Meads railway station and marshalling yards. A ring of four similar sites was built around Gloucester (at Longney, Standish, Brimpsfield and Coberley) to protect the city and docks.

In December 1941 the USA was reluctantly drawn into the Second World War following the Japanese attack on Pearl Harbour. As Germany was an ally of Japan, the Americans decided to demonstrate their opposition to both countries by establishing a military presence in Britain. Only seven weeks after the Japanese attacked, US troops were in the UK. The build-up that followed was, however, slow as a great many of the Americans made their crossing of the Atlantic by troop ship. For many the relief of their arrival in Britain after the long crossing was tinged with apprehension, as they were arriving in what was to them a war zone, and this was evidenced by the bomb-damaged buildings in the British ports of arrival, such as Liverpool.

There were problems of transport, logistics and accommodation, and these were addressed by moving the US Army ground units mainly to the western parts of the country away from the established British infrastructure of camps and supply routes. Soon US Army hutted camps could be found all over Cornwall, Devon, Somerset, Dorset, Wiltshire and Gloucestershire.

From a trickle, the US military build up in Britain turned into a strong flow during 1943, and by the beginning of the following year there were some 750,000 US Army personnel in the UK. Over the ensuing five months these numbers increased still further as the Allies prepared for the invasion of France. By May 1944 the number of US servicemen stationed in Britain was over 1.5 million.

In May 1942 advance elements of the US Army Air Force (USAAF) had begun to arrive in Britain. The US 8th Air Force was formed to join RAF Bomber Command in its strategic bombing campaign, from bases in East Anglia. There was therefore little sign of the USAAF in the West Country, until October 1943 when the US 9th Air Force was established in Britain. The 9th, with its HQ at Sunninghill Park, Ascot, was set up as the US tactical air force for the invasion of north-west Europe, planned for 1944/45. The formation was to include fighter, light bomber, medium bomber and troop-carrier squadrons. It was the aircraft of the 9th Air Force, particularly the Douglas C-47s of its troop carrier squadrons, that were to make their presence known in the South West.

Although US C-47s flew from Gloucestershire airfields on detachment, the only USAAF units that were based in the county were the Liaison Squadrons. These operated from Chedworth, but more usually flew from temporary airstrips. The latter included Beggars Bush Field, at Abbots Leigh on the north-west outskirts of Bristol, because of its close proximity to the HQ of the US 1st Army at Clifton College. Aircraft such as Piper L-4 Cubs and Stinson L-5 Sentinals of various units operated from the field, including the 153rd Liaison Squadron which was the 9th Air Force unit attached to the HQ for communications duties, flying despatches and general liaison.

Avonmouth docks near Bristol were reserved almost exclusively as one of the main arrival ports for the US Army. It was also the main receiving port for the 9th Air Force, and a massive Port In-transit Depot was established nearby at Wapley Common to store aircraft, spares and aviation-related equipment for onward distribution. The aircraft arrived on freighters or tankers that had been specifically modified to take deck cargo as well as their usual cargo of oil or petrol. Each vessel carried between 15 and 20 single-engined aircraft (less of the twin-engined types). They were usually shipped all in one piece, less propeller and tail units, but some, particularly the more fragile types, were crated.

From December 1943 the main destination for these aircraft was IX Base Aircraft Assembly Depot (BAAD) at Filton, until early June 1944 when the BAAD was closed and its constituent squadrons moved south, eventually to go forward onto the Continent. Avonmouth was especially busy in June, as it was one of the embarkation ports for the D-Day invasion fleet. Aircraft continued to arrive for the USAAF during the summer of 1944, and these were taken on to the BAADs at Burtonwood and Warton in Lancashire, by rail or by coaster. Monthly arrivals of aircraft were high throughout this period, with 294 in April 1945. In May, with the war in Europe coming to an end, shipments to Avonmouth stopped. A total of 2,167 US aircraft of all types had been shipped through the port by this time.

As well as airfields, there were other sites in Gloucestershire that had involvement with the RAF or aircraft operations. These included Innsworth, Quedgeley and Pucklechurch. Innsworth housed No 7 School of Technical Training, which was responsible for the training of ground crews. The station later became a Women's Auxiliary Air Force (WAAF) training depot, and the RAF Training and Receiving Centre for the South of England. Quedgeley was opened as No 7 Maintenance Unit on 15 April 1939. It was one of seven storage depots built under the final phase of the RAF Expansion Scheme. One of the depot's first tasks following the outbreak of war was to issue vehicles and equipment to 87 Squadron, which then deployed to France with its Hurricanes as part of the Advanced Air Striking Force, in support of the British Expeditionary Force. Located on eight sites, the MU covered an extensive area. It played a most important role, and was used for the receipt, storage and issue of a wide range of essential stores and equipment, including motor vehicles, clothing, paint, fabric, ground equipment, parachutes, gun turrets, weapons, medical items and aircraft spares.

Pucklechurch was opened as No 11 Balloon Centre on 9 August 1939. It was one of several that were established across the country to support the squadrons that flew barrage balloons as part of Britain's air defences. The balloon squadrons were part of the Auxiliary Air Force, formed to defend their local area. Each squadron operated 24 balloons and was sub-divided into three independent flights that could each operate eight balloons in different locations. No 11 Balloon Centre

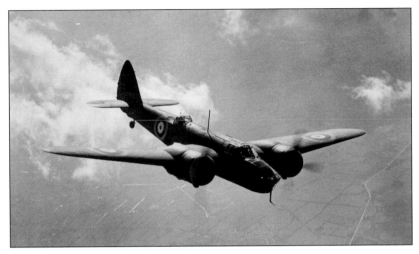

Evocative portrait of one of the most important products of Gloucestershire's wartime aircraft factories – the Bristol Blenheim bomber. (Aeroplane)

acted as a depot for the Bristol area, providing training for the local squadrons, and supplying equipment including their launch vehicles, gases and the balloons themselves, which had to be assembled and tested. Three units were initially supported from Pucklechurch – Nos 927, 928 and 929 'County of Gloucester' Auxiliary Air Force (Balloon Barrage) Squadrons. They were formed at the end of August 1939 to defend Bristol and Avonmouth. Shortly after the outbreak of war however, two of the squadrons were moved to other parts of the country, but were later replaced by other balloon units. As well as protecting Bristol and Avonmouth, the Pucklechurch squadrons maintained barrages over Filton and Brockworth airfields.

Although often deterring attacks by German bombers on their intended targets, the balloon units sometimes became targets themselves and during the Luftwaffe raids on Bristol during 1940 and 1941, several balloon sites were bombed, resulting in serious injuries and several fatalities of balloon crew members. The balloon units proved their worth during this time, and were maintained for the remainder of the war. In fact the last major raid by the Luftwaffe on Bristol was as late as 14 May 1944 (when 91 aircraft were despatched to bomb the city, but only one got through to its target). Shortly after this many of the squadrons based in South Wales and the West Country, including Bristol, were withdrawn and transferred to the south coast,

16

where they provided part of the layered defences under Operation Crossbow, against the V1 flying bomb attacks.

Although not initially in the front line at the beginning of the war, the airfields of Gloucestershire took on the role of training and support, and then defence against enemy air offensives. The county's aircraft factories kept in production throughout the period, despite heavy air attacks, and maintained the supply of aeroplanes to the squadrons of the RAF and Fleet Air Arm (FAA), enabling them to keep the Luftwaffe at bay. Later, as the Allies went over to the offensive, these airfields became the bases from which the war could be taken to the enemy and eventually helped to launch part of the expeditionary force that was to pave the way for the defeat of the Axis, and thus bring the war to an end.

2
ASTON DOWN

4 miles south of Stroud
SO 912010

Situated on the edge of the Cotswold Hills, overlooking the valley of the river Frome, Aston Down is sited on part of the former Downs Farm, an estate that was established during Tudor times. The airfield dates back to the First World War, when a training station was built on the site for the Royal Flying Corps. The first occupants were in fact the Australian Flying Corps (AFC), who established it as No 1 Station, under No 1 Wing of the AFC, the headquarters of which were at Tetbury in Gloucestershire.

The airfield, then known as Minchinhampton, had two runways laid out on the grass and a technical site consisting of four large Belfast truss hangars together with storage sheds, workshops and transport sheds. The first unit to arrive at the airfield was No 6 (Training) Squadron AFC, on 25 February 1918, closely followed by No 5 (Training) Squadron. With the two-seat Sopwith One and a Half Strutter and Avro 504, the units conducted basic and elementary training, then advanced training on the single-seat Bristol Scout, Sopwith Pup, and later Royal Aircraft Factory SE5a and Sopwith Camel, producing many pilots for the AFC Squadrons on the Western Front. However, this intense flying activity came to a sudden end in November 1918 with the Armistice. Both Australian squadrons were disbanded in January 1919 and the airfield was closed. The land was auctioned off in early 1920, and shortly afterwards the site was cleared of most of its buildings and the land returned to agriculture.

In less than two decades, however, the area would once again resound to the sound of aero-engines. Under the RAF's Expansion Plans of the mid-1930s the site of the former airfield of Minchinhampton was chosen as the location of an airfield-based Aircraft Storage Unit (ASU).

Work on the airfield began in 1937 by several companies including Wilson Lovatt and Sons Ltd. A technical and administrative site was built in the north-west corner of the airfield and eight large storage hangars were constructed at various points around its edge, connected by a concrete taxiway. Opened as RAF Aston Down on 12 October 1938, the airfield's first resident unit, No 7 ASU, was renamed No 20 Maintenance Unit (MU) a few days later under the command of Squadron Leader N.A. Tait. It wasn't long before aircraft started to arrive, the initial ones being newly completed airframes on delivery from their manufacturers. There was plenty of storage space and as well as aircraft, vehicles and bombs were kept in the new hangars. The latter were stored on the three most outlying sites, B, D and F, which were to the north-east, south and south-west, where the hangars were covered with earth banks.

During the summer of 1939, Fighter Command took an interest in Aston Down, as it needed new locations for its training units. On 23 August 1939, the Command's No 12 Group Pool was set up at Aston Down under Squadron Leader Fuller Good, its role being to provide advanced training to pilots prior to joining the operational squadrons of 12 Group. Its students were trained to fly modern front-line aircraft types and learned operational techniques such as fighter tactics. This method of providing advanced training to newly-qualified pilots was an innovation, as until then they would have gone straight from Flying Training Schools to front-line squadrons and would have trained 'on the job'. No 12 Group Pool was only the third one to be formed and, along with other such pools, later formed the basis of the wartime Operational Training Unit organisation.

To train its pupils the unit was issued with operational types such as Gloster Gladiators, Bristol Blenheims, Fairey Battles and Hawker Hurricanes, along with North American Harvard and Avro Tutor trainers. Accommodation at the station was at a premium, and so additional buildings for the Pool had to be specially erected. Until these were ready, its personnel were billeted in the local towns. The billets included the George Hotel at Nailsworth, where the dining room and anterooms were set aside as the unit's officers' mess.

The effect of the outbreak of hostilities was felt at Aston Down just three days after the declaration of war on 3 September 1939, when a dozen Wellington bombers of No 214 Squadron arrived. They had been dispersed at short notice for fear of attack on their base at Feltwell, and arrived at Aston Down without warning. When it became apparent

19

Fairey Battles were stored and maintained by 20 MU. (Aeroplane)

that their base was not in imminent danger the Wellingtons returned to Feltwell.

Because of the state of war, most civil flying was stopped. Some companies were allowed to retain their aircraft if they were operating services in the national interest. All remaining civil aircraft were requisitioned and taken to RAF collecting centres. One of these was 20 MU, where the aircraft were secured, to prevent unauthorised use, and inspected for possible use by the RAF. With the arrival of more aircraft, fields adjoining the airfield were used for the open-air storage and dispersal of aircraft coming from the main site. The majority of the MU's staff were civilian and, by the end of 1939, it employed 600 people, and had 400 aircraft in store including Hawker Audaxes, Harts and Henleys, Bristol Blenheims and Beauforts and Fairey Battles.

No 12 Group Pool's first fatality occurred on 19 November 1939 when Sergeant Linton was killed. He was collecting a Gladiator fighter from Little Rissington when the aircraft caught fire and crashed. A further loss took place a few days later on 21 November, when Pilot Officer Masterton of 12 Group Pool was killed in a Harvard. The aircraft went into a spin but failed to recover and crashed into the ground at Oakridge just to the north of the airfield.

In the New Year a new task was given to the 12 Group Pool when its Blenheim Flight was detailed to take part in aircraft delivery. The first

20

deliveries took place on 10 January 1940, to Aden. In February, Yugoslav personnel arrived on the station to collect Blenheims for their air force. The first flight departed on 1 March, when Wing Commander Dragic Hinco and his crews left with four aircraft for their homeland. More Yugoslav aircraft followed two weeks later.

In early March, 12 Group Pool personnel were involved in more ferrying work, this time taking Blenheims to Egypt. A few flying accidents occurred on the station in mid March; the first of these involved Beaufort L4470 up on a test flight from 20 MU, which force-landed in a field near the airfield due to engine failure. Then Blenheim I L9385 crashed on the 16th, killing its crew, and two Gladiators collided, fortunately without serious injury to either pilot on the 21st.

By this time (actually on 15 March) 12 Group Pool had become No 5 Operational Training Unit (OTU), and was flying Supermarine Spitfires, Boulton Paul Defiants and Miles Masters as well as its other types. Flying Officer Arthur Pease trained at 5 OTU in early 1940. After having graduated he was posted to 603 Squadron at Dyce that summer to fly Spitfires. He was involved in dogfights with the Luftwaffe during the Battle of Britain and shooting down a Heinkel He 111 on 30 July 1940 and a Messerschmitt Bf 109 on 3 September 1940. His aircraft was damaged by enemy fire on 7 September, but he managed to crash-land without injury. He was shot down again on 15 September 1940 but unfortunately was not so lucky the second time, and died in the resulting crash.

In March 1940 the first Hawker Hurricanes were received at 20 MU, followed by Armstrong Whitworth Whitleys and Handley Page Hampdens and Herefords. Les Freeman started working at the MU at this time, and remembers receiving these aircraft types. On arrival they were checked for condition before being put into store. There they were fitted with the equipment that had not been installed at the factory, such as guns, bomb racks, bomb sights etc.

For a time during the early years of the war, from 1940 onwards, Vickers had the use of one of the hangars on D site on the south-east side of the airfield. This was for repair work on Wellington bombers which had been shot up on operations or badly damaged in accidents. They were totally rebuilt by the Vickers team, and the MU staff were impressed with the standard of work that they could achieve in bringing hopeless-looking wrecks back as serviceable aircraft. Because of the Wellington's novel geodetic construction (devised by its designer Barnes Wallis), whole sections of the fuselage or wings that had been damaged could be cut out and replaced with new.

With the summer came the Luftwaffe's assault on mainland UK and several air raid warnings were received in late June. Fortunately Aston Down received little attention from the Luftwaffe, but on 27 July a Junkers Ju 88 appeared in the area. It was shot down by one of the OTU's Spitfires (that had been armed as a contingency against just such a threat), and came down near Oakridge. The four crew members bailed out and were taken prisoner, with the exception of one who was killed when his parachute failed to open.

Pilot Officer Jan Zurakowski was newly arrived in the UK in the summer of 1940. An ex-Polish Air Force fighter pilot, he joined the RAF and was posted to 5 OTU at Aston Down to train on Spitfires. When he graduated in August 1940 Jan was posted to 234 Squadron at Middle Wallop. He was shot down over Southampton during the Battle of Britain, but escaped uninjured from his aircraft. He spent the remainder of his wartime service on fighters, and stayed in the RAF after the war. He later graduated as a test pilot and specialised in aerobatics, perfecting a manoeuvre of his own on the Gloster Meteor: the Zurakowski roll.

During the Battle of Britain the preparation of fighter aircraft took priority at 20 MU, Spitfires and Hurricanes being the main types that were turned out. Part of the work involved aligning the aircraft's guns and sights. As with the OTU's aircraft they were armed before their RAF ferry pilots took them away in case they came across any enemy aircraft during their delivery flights. Fighter aircraft were also returned to Aston Down for repair or salvage following accidents or battle damage. Between July and October 1940, 20 MU repaired 257 Hurricanes, an average of 64 per month, which made a great difference to the front line fighter strength at a critical time. Unfortunately, 20 MU didn't have to look far for repair work – customers often appeared on their doorstep! As a few examples during the summer of 1940, on 13 May Hereford L6065 of 14 OTU crashed on approach to the airfield and three days later Spitfire P9514 struck a wall on take-off; on 8 June Harvard P5870 crashed on the approach; on 3 July Blenheim K7112 crashed on take-off; and on 13 July Battle L5133 crashed on landing at Aston Down (the latter four aircraft were home-based, with 20 OTU).

Meanwhile the site contractors, Walter Lawrence & Son, had been busily working on the airfield's accommodation. From September 1940 they undertook work on lecture rooms, an armoury annexe, WAAF accommodation, enlarged stores, the sergeants' mess, and a fuel compound. These were followed by an officers' mess, MT sheds, airmen's dining hall, officers' quarters and, in November 1940, a new station headquarters. November also marked the renumbering of 50 OTU to No 55 OTU in a reorganisation of the fighter OTUs. The unit's task remained that of the advanced training of aircrew for Spitfire and Hurricane day fighter and Blenheim night fighter squadrons.

Because of the intense use of Aston Down by the MU and units such as 55 OTU, and the increased all-up weight of aeroplanes, it had been decided to lay concrete runways. Work started in early 1941, but slow progress was made mainly due to the weather and also because of the high level of flying activity. However, this changed in the spring, when orders came for the transfer of 55 OTU. Movement started in late February, and by 14 March all of the unit's aircraft had gone to its new base at Usworth. (No 55 OTU was later disbanded at Annan in January 1944, but was subsequently reformed at Aston Down.)

Enemy bomber activity had continued sporadically during the winter of 1940 and the spring of 1941. Although Aston Down had not received any further attention, one of its Q decoy sites at Horsley, three and a half miles to the south-west, was bombed on the night of 29 March.

With the lower level of flying following the departure of 55 OTU, and a general improvement in the weather, the runways were completed. This was very timely, as in August 1941 No 52 OTU moved in. There was a perceived renewed danger of invasion by the

Curtiss Tomahawks were flown by 52 OTU from Aston Down in 1941. (Aeroplane)

Germans and as a result all of the vulnerable fighter OTUs were moved to safer locations. As 52 OTU was based at Debden in Kent, it was relocated to Aston Down and brought along a variety of aircraft including the Curtiss Tomahawk and Bristol Blenheim (although it was gradually standardising on the Miles Master and Hawker Hurricane). This move also resulted in a more general separation of UK airspace into operational and training areas.

Operational training was a hazardous affair and almost immediately, on 3 August, 52 OTU suffered its first casualties whilst flying from Aston Down, when two Hurricanes collided near the airfield during a simulated combat. Sergeants Fleming and Cheyne were both killed. On 7 August a further collision occurred, this time on the ground, when a landing Hurricane swerved off the runway and collided with another. Two US pilots flying with 52 OTU were involved in another mid-air collision on 18 August. Pilot Officer Williams had to abandon Hurricane V7179 by parachute, but Pilot Officer Gallo managed to bring V7002 back to Aston Down with a damaged wing. An indication of the intense flying activity and number of accidents at Aston Down during 1941 is illustrated by the fact that 21 fighter aircraft were involved in incidents at the airfield, resulting in many injuries and two deaths.

The ferrying of aircraft to and from 20 MU had been undertaken by service pilots resting between postings but, in order to release them to fly operationally, during 1941 most ferrying was taken on by the Air Transport Auxiliary. This organisation had been formed in 1939 under the administration of British Airways and the control of the Air Ministry, and later in 1941 it was transferred to the Ministry of Aircraft Production. Initially its pilots ferried trainers and transports between the factories, the ASUs and the squadrons, but later fighters and bombers were also flown by them. The demand for ferry pilots was such that women were recruited into the ranks of the ATA, and soon proved themselves to be most capable fliers; one of the first was Amy Johnson, already a world-famous, record-setting endurance pilot. With its HQ at White Waltham, the ATA was organised into Ferry Pools, based near aircraft factories. By 1942 there were 14 Ferry Pools, including No 9 based at Aston Down (formed under the command of Captain Hugh Bergel in October 1941). Eventually the ATA would have 22 Ferry Pools, each having a number of Avro Ansons to act as taxis to position pilots.

ATA pilots were trained to fly a variety of aircraft types at the organisation's Conversion School and later the RAF's Central Flying

School at Upavon. They were categorised according to their training and flying experience into six aircraft classes, ranging from trainers to flying boats, and one of the most experienced of the female pilots, Lettice Curtis, was a Class 5 pilot. This meant that she was expected to fly any one of 147 different types of aircraft, and on one day ferried a Harvard (single-engine trainer), a Spitfire (single-engine fighter), a Mitchell (twin-engine bomber), a Mosquito (twin-engine fighter bomber) and a Stirling (four-engine bomber). Each ATA pool had its own ground staff and engineers, but to supplement them they often employed Air Training Corps cadets to help out in such tasks as cleaning aircraft. The cadets were taken flying as a reward, often in types such as the Avro Anson that required an extra crew member to wind the undercarriage up and down. Cadets were also later given more responsible jobs such as acting as motor cycle despatch riders for urgent messages, and as couriers to deliver urgent aircraft spares by road or air.

In mid 1942, Les Freeman remembers F site on the south-west side of the airfield being put out of bounds to all but a few staff because 'a secret weapon' was being produced in the hangars there. This turned out to be the Hurricane IID, a ground attack version of the aircraft, which was being fitted with two x 20 mm underwing cannon for attacking armoured vehicles. Some of the aircraft were also fitted with

One of the Hurricane IIDs that were converted at 20 MU in 1942. (Aeroplane)

tropical filters and painted in sand and brown camouflage as they were intended for the Desert Air Force in North Africa.

Meanwhile the work of No 52 OTU carried on, its Hurricanes and Masters being supplemented by Spitfires. All were flown hard by pupils and staff. The OTU was organised into six flights, each one covering a different stage of the training syllabus. By the very nature of the training and tuition being undertaken, and of the powerful types being flown, especially the Spitfire, accidents occurred, both on and off the airfield. During the first two months of 1942 alone at least seven of 52 OTU's aircraft were involved in serious incidents. These included Spitfire X4162, which made a forced landing near the airfield on 24 January due to engine failure, and a similar affliction brought P9326 down four days later. Both pilots were unhurt. Unfortunately on 6 February Sergeant B.H. Cassidy, a Canadian, died when Spitfire X4932 crashed at Aston Farm. Two days later Sergeant S.R. Pierce was also killed, when Spitfire R7135 dived into the river Severn near Oldbury Sands. A US pilot, Sergeant Arn died on 10 February following the crash of Master AZ311 while he was flying near Berkeley. Another Canadian pilot, Sergeant G.A. Davies, died when Spitfire P9546 broke up in the air on 11 February, and on 27 February Spitfire X4240 overshot on landing at Aston Down and crashed, fortunately with only minor injuries to the pilot. Although the Master was a dual-control aircraft, the Spitfire was never produced in a trainer version, meaning that all tuition in the air had to be by radio.

In April 1942 Chedworth near Cirencester was opened as a satellite of Aston Down, and 52 OTU used it for flying training, as a useful alternative to the busy main airfield. In August two of the OTU's flights were moved to Chedworth and on 15 January 1943 these became the Fighter Leaders School. They were not to remain at Chedworth for long as on 9 February 1943 the school left for Charmy Down, and Chedworth became a satellite of South Cerney.

Aircraft types being processed by 20 MU during 1942 included the North American Mitchell. One of these was being test flown on 29 July by Warrant Officer W. Cappleman, an experienced pilot who had completed a 32-operation tour on Wellingtons with Bomber Command. His crew included two air cadets as authorised passengers. After returning to base having completed the test flight, the pilot found that the starboard undercarriage leg would not lower. He decided to make a forced landing, but before doing so he flew around the local area, burning off as much fuel as possible. When they returned over the airfield, watchers on the ground saw the ventral escape hatch jettisoned and two bundles drop from the aircraft. Two parachutes opened, and the air cadets landed safely on the edge of the aerodrome. The pilot brought the Mitchell in to land, while ambulances and fire tenders stood by. The starboard undercarriage was still retracted, but Warrant Officer Cappleman kept the starboard wing up until the last moment, and when it finally stopped the aircraft was found to be practically undamaged apart from the crumpled starboard wing tip.

The 15th of October was a bad day for 52 OTU. Spitfire P7966, flown by a New Zealander, Pilot Officer Beage, inexplicably dived into a storage shed at RAF Quedgely, killing a civilian worker as well as the pilot. Later in the day Spitfire X4059 collided with Master AZ364 in the circuit at Aston Down, killing both pilots.

On 16 October 1942 the first Horsa gliders appeared, by road, at Aston Down. Transported in sections – the nose, centre section, tail and wings – they were taken to D site on the south-east side of the airfield for assembly in the hangars there. Tail sections were made locally by Taylors Ltd of Griffins Mill, Bowbridge.

Once the Horsas were assembled they had to be flight-tested, just as with powered aircraft. The glider was towed out onto the runway by tractor, where the Whitley V tug aircraft would be taxied into position in front of it. The towrope was laid out between the two aircraft, checked, then hitched on. The Whitley would start to roll, taking up the

Horsa on flight test behind a Whitley. (Aeroplane)

27

slack in the towrope, then the Horsa moved off down the runway. The Horsa lifted off before the tug then, when the tug lifted, the aircraft could together fly off to a spot away from the airfield where the Horsa would be tested. Once the glider pilot was happy that his aircraft was flying satisfactorily and that the controls were effective, he would cast off, then put the Horsa through a few basic manoeuvres before heading back to land. The landing of a Horsa was exciting, as the pilot would, as in all gliders, make a steep dive on the approach to keep up speed, then flatten out to land on the runway at the required spot. Later, in April 1943 Aston Down would be nominated as one of the storage sites for gliders in preparation for the D-Day invasion.

The accident rate for 52 OTU remained fairly high during 1943. Losses included a Spitfire which stalled and crashed near the control tower on 2 January, killing its Trinidadian pilot, Sergeant Britto. On 26 January two Spitfires from the unit collided over the river Severn: Sergeant Clark managed to land P8207 on the shore, but Sergeant Caldwell was killed when P8208 hit the water. Sergeant Burdan, a Canadian, was injured when his Spitfire crashed following a glycol leak which filled his cockpit with flames on 6 February. Another Canadian, Sergeant Callinan, was killed on 7 March when he hit power cables while low-flying near Slimbridge in his Spitfire. On 4 July, Spitfire P7918 flown by Sergeant Adams of 52 OTU collided with Mustang AG489 of 20 MU. The Mustang pilot, Flying Officer Coker, parachuted and was injured on landing. Unfortunately Adams' parachute did not deploy in time and he was killed.

During late 1942 and into 1943 the main types that 20 MU were concerned with were the Spitfire and later the Hawker Typhoon. As well as being produced at the main Vickers Supermarine shadow factory at Castle Bromwich, Spitfires were also manufactured at smaller production units in southern England, such as Winchester in Hampshire, and Trowbridge and Salisbury in Wiltshire. These were established when the main Supermarine factory at Woolston was bombed by the Luftwaffe in 1940. The aircraft were test flown from airfields near the factories, then delivered by ATA pilots to Aston Down. In 1943 the Mk V was being produced, but later this was replaced by more developed Merlin-powered Spitfires, such as the Mk IX, and the first of the Griffon-powered versions, the Mk XXI.

Most of the Typhoons that joined the Spitfires at Aston Down were not actually produced by Hawkers, but under a sub-contract arrangement by Glosters in their factory at Brockworth. The Typhoon was a promising design. Although it had its teething troubles, these

Spitfires of various types passed through 20 MU. These Mark Vs are from 243 Squadron. (Aeroplane)

were eventually sorted out and the Typhoon became a powerful and manoeuvrable fighter that could challenge the best aircraft of the Luftwaffe. Its rugged construction also enabled it to be used as a ground attack aircraft, carrying rockets and bombs on hard-points under the wings.

The first Lancasters to arrive at Aston Down were received in late 1941. Once checked and equipped they didn't stay in store for long as they were urgently needed for operations by Bomber Command. In 1944 a new type of Lancaster was arriving at 20 MU, a Canadian-built aircraft that had to be fitted out for squadron service. These were fitted with US-built Packard Merlin 28 and 38 engines and, to give them the extra range across the Atlantic, extra fuel tanks were fitted into the bomb bay. As the bomb bay doors could not be fitted with the tank in position, one of the first jobs was to fit replacement doors that had been collected by road from another MU at Bracebridge Heath, Lincolnshire. Armstrong Whitworth Albemarles were also brought to the MU, for the incorporation of fittings to undertake their role as Airborne Forces Support aircraft. These included the installation of glider towing and parachute dropping equipment.

No 52 OTU continued its training role using Aston Down's airfield. It had assumed some responsibility for the teaching of tactics to potential fighter squadron and flight commanders, and this resulted in the formation of the Fighter Leaders School within the OTU at Chedworth in January 1943. Although the School had moved to Charmy Down shortly afterwards, due to the re-allocation of its new base to the USAAF, it was moved again in early August, this time to re-join the OTU at Aston Down. Shortly after the move, the parent unit itself was renamed, as 52 Operational Training Unit (Fighter Leaders School) on 16 August 1943. A few months later, in October 1943, it was retitled 52 Operational Training Unit (Fighter Command School of Tactics) although its role remained much the same. Towards the end of January the unit was moved to Milfield in Northumberland, where on 26 January 1944 it was disbanded to become part of the Fighter Leaders School.

No 84 Group Support Unit (GSU) was formed at Aston Down on 14 February 1944. This was a mobile unit whose role was to provide replacement aircraft for the front line squadrons that were to be based in France following the planned invasion. No one knew, of course, that the D-Day landings were to take place on the Normandy coast four months later, but the establishment of the unit at Aston Down at this time is an example of the long-term and complex planning that lay behind Operation Overlord. No 84 GSU was accommodated in tents on the south side of the airfield. During the build up to D-Day, more and more aircraft arrived at Aston Down for storage. As the hangars were full they were stored in the open, with every available piece of flat ground seemingly covered in aircraft parked wingtip to wingtip.

One of the main types dealt with by 20 MU during 1944 was the Hawker Tempest. Developed from the Typhoon and designed by Sydney Camm, the Tempest became one of the most effective fighters of the Second World War. It was one of the few aircraft capable of catching the V-1 flying bombs, and of defeating the Messerschmitt Me 262 jet fighters (at least eleven Me 262s were shot down by Tempests, the highest total for any Allied fighter). The aircraft was also successfully used as a fighter bomber and in ground attack.

Hawker Tempest Mark V JN751 was but one example of the many aircraft of the type that passed through 20 MU. It was built at Hawker's Langley factory and delivered to Aston Down on 20 February 1944. It was issued initially to 486 Squadron which along with Nos 3 and 56 Squadrons formed No 150 Wing. This was the first Tempest Wing to be formed, at Newchurch in Kent, in preparation for the forthcoming invasion. After transfer to 3 Squadron, JN751 became the personal mount of Wing Commander Roland Beaumont (later to become a legendary test pilot), the Officer Commanding of 150 Wing. The Wing provided air cover for the Normandy landings, and during a sortie on 8 June, Beaumont shot down a Bf 109G, the first enemy aircraft to be downed by a Tempest. JN751 was holed in the starboard wing by a cannon shell in this combat. With the arrival of V-1 missiles over southern England following D-Day, 150 Wing were assigned to the defensive role. From June to August, JN751 was flown on many V-1 patrols and shot down over 30 of them. Following an engine failure on 1 September the aircraft made a forced landing, but was repaired and collected by the Wing Commander from the Langley factory on 5 September 1944, who brought it back to Newchurch. This was his last flight in the aircraft. The aircraft was returned to 20 MU at Aston Down on 3 October 1944, probably for modifications or a repaint, and was re-issued again a few months later to 287 Squadron at Hornchurch, an anti-aircraft co-operation unit. It was with this unit that the aircraft was being flown by Flight Sergeant D.C.A. Redstone on 18 May 1945 over the Isle of Sheppy. JN751 crashed, killing the pilot, while he was trying to avoid a fogbank.

No 1311 (Transport) Flight arrived at Aston Down in May 1944, equipped with Anson Mk I ambulance aircraft. This unit had been formed at Llandow the month before, also as part of the invasion preparations, to undertake the rapid transfer of casualties from the battlefront to the UK. In early June, eight squadrons of the RAF Regiment also arrived, swelling the population of the station to 3,500, including 2,500 under canvas. The Regiment squadrons had been moved forward from their bases to be nearer their ports of embarkation. The units were to follow up the main seaborne landings and secure areas that had been identified as advanced landing grounds in Normandy. They were then to defend these areas with armoured cars and AA guns to allow fighter-bombers and fighter-aircraft to operate from them without interference from the enemy. No 8 General Hospital, a forward RAF field hospital, also formed at Aston Down at this time in preparation to move ahead with the landings.

After the Normandy landings had taken place, No 1311 (Transport) Flight moved to Thruxton to be nearer the Continent. There it was joined by 84 GSU, which absorbed it as the GSU's Transport Flight. On 21 July, No 84 GSU acted as a forward delivery unit for replacement aircraft to be delivered from Aston Down and the other MUs to front line fighter squadrons. The unit moved to France later that summer, to fulfil its role in-theatre.

During this time, the ATA was given the task of ferrying aircraft for the Continent. At first this was only as far as Aston Down or White Waltham, where they were handed over to the RAF pilots to take on to France. Later, from September, as the front-line moved further inland, ATA pilots delivered aircraft to airfields in France and Belgium. The ATA Ansons also flew to the Continent. As well as acting as taxis to bring the crews back to Aston Down, on their outward journeys they took food, medical supplies, mail, small arms and ammunition, in addition to passengers.

No 3 Tactical Exercise Unit (TEU) was moved to Aston Down after the departure of 84 GSU. The unit was previously based at Annan, and consisted of two squadrons flying Typhoon IBs and Hurricane IIAs for the training of fighter pilots in the close support of ground troops. This included the destruction of targets on the ground using rocket projectiles and other ground-attack weapons, and in strafing, dive-bombing and other fighter-bomber techniques. By the end of August the unit had 64 Typhoons on strength alongside a few Hurricanes, Mustangs, Masters and Martinets. On 18 December 1944, 3 TEU was disbanded to reconstitute 55 OTU at Aston Down. Upon formation, the unit had a strength of 134 aircraft. The Chief Flying Instructor Typhoons in January 1945 was Wing Commander Robin McNair, DFC and bar, an ex-Battle of Britain fighter pilot who had flown Typhoons during D-Day and the operations that followed, as Officer Commanding 247 Squadron.

The majority of flying accidents during 1944 were to 3 TEU aircraft, although a Mustang of 306 (Polish) Squadron did crash during take-off on 4 April and Typoon MN488 of 84 GSU overshot during an emergency landing on 20 June. On 14 July Typhoon JR127 stalled recovering from a dive and crashed near the airfield, and on 4 August Typhoon MN286 went through the boundary fence after an engine failure during take-off. Other Typhoon accidents during this time included JR516, which dived into the ground following an engine fire on 5 August, killing its pilot, Sergeant Brightwell; MN207 which stalled and crashed on the approach, fatally injuring Flight Sergeant Cameron; and EK151, which crashed on take-off, its pilot being only slightly injured.

Aircraft continued to arrive at 20 MU into 1945, to support the squadrons that were fighting to defeat German forces on the Continent and those that were moving in on the Japanese forces in the Far East. Newer types and later versions of existing designs of aircraft maintained the edge of technology as well as numbers over the enemy. The later, Griffon-engined Spitfires were steadily coming though 20 MU and, in preparation for the final assaults against the Japanese, a new type of four-engined bomber, the Avro Lincoln, was appearing. This was a development of the Lancaster, designed to succeed it in service with Bomber Command, with more powerful Merlin 85 engines, redesigned wings and a lengthened fuselage.

No 55 OTU continued with its training courses into 1945 still flying their Typhoons, along with some Mustangs, inevitably with the occasional accident. One of the Typhoons crashed into a dispersal hut near B site on the north-east side of the airfield on 25 March 1945. It burst into flames, trapping several airmen and airwomen inside, 15 of whom were injured and two killed, as well as the pilot.

The end of the war in Europe came amid joyous celebrations at Aston Down. The main impact was felt when the lights could come on again at night time! The war carried on in the Far East of course but it was decided that the RAF had more than a sufficient number of trained pilots for its squadrons. It therefore started to reduce the flying training programme, and the number of units involved. No 55 OTU was therefore disbanded on 14 June 1945. Other changes at Aston Down included the closure of the dispersals, with the outlying fields handed back to their owners and the aircraft brought back onto the main site. Despite there being over 1,000 aircraft on the airfield, aircraft still came and went in support of the war in the Far East.

Following the disbandment of 55 OTU, control of the airfield reverted once again to 20 MU. Towards the end of 1945 the ATA too was disbanded and in their place, on 1 December 1945, No 2 Ferry Pool was formed at Aston Down with Ansons, Oxfords, Tiger Moths and Proctors, along with Spitfires and Mosquitos. During the wartime period the ATA had delivered over 300,000 aircraft of 51 different types, and at its height had 1,318 pilots on strength (1,152 men and 166 women). However, this came at cost, as 129 men and 20 women pilots of the ATA were killed in service.

With the end of the war in the Far East, Aston Down became a collection site for surplus aircraft. As squadrons were disbanded, their aircraft were flown in and taken on charge. The majority were stripped of their equipment and put aside for disposal. The newest and best of the aircraft were retained in store until, as they were replaced by more modern types, they too were disposed of.

In November 1945 41 Group Training Flight formed at Aston Down to undertake ferry training with Harvard and Mosquito. It disbanded on 6 March the following year to become 1689 (Ferry Pilot Training) Flight, then flying Hornets, Wellingtons, Lancasters, Tempests,

Aerial view of the main site of Aston Down in 1995. (MoD)

Spitfires, Vampires and Meteors. On 9 April 1953 it moved to Benson to become part of a Ferry Training Unit. It had been joined at Aston Down by 2 Ferry Pool. Disbanded on 1 February 1953, this unit became 187 Squadron which, still based at Aston Down, ferried aircraft in the UK and Germany before being disbanded on 2 September 1957.

Other post-war residents included No 83 Gliding School which arrived in October 1946 on transfer from Moreton Valence, to train Air Cadets. They remained until disbandment in September 1955. With the reduction of Maintenance Units, 20 MU was finally closed on 30 September 1960. The hangars were then used by 5 MU at Kemble for additional storage.

Although Aston Down was to continue temporarily as a Relief Landing Ground for the Central Flying School at Little Rissington, the closure of 20 MU saw its end as a viable RAF station, and it was transferred to the Ministry of Aviation on 1 April 1963. It then became the Ministry's main depot for the storage of aircraft production jigs and special tools. Under the MoD, the depot continued in this role for almost another 40 years, until in 2002 the Ministry sold the hangars for industrial use, and they still stand today. The airfield has since been sold to the Cotswold Gliding Club, who maintain it in everyday use.

3
BABDOWN FARM

3 miles west of Tetbury
ST 845938

This airfield was established as a Relief Landing Ground (RLG) for 9 Service Flying Training School (SFTS) at Hullavington and came into use in July 1940. The first flying accident at the airfield, however, occurred on 17 April 1940, when the school's Audax K7308 crashed on landing – presumably trying out the RLG for size?

Babdown Farm was used mainly for night flying training by the school's Hawker Harts, Audaxes, Airspeeds and Oxfords. When night flying was scheduled, a ground party would be sent to set out a flarepath of goose-neck flares and to man the basic runway control and support facilities. The aircraft would then be flown over from Hullavington late in the afternoon, and at the end of the night-flying session all personnel and aircraft would return to Hullavington, usually in the early hours of the morning. The ground crews had to be on standby, ready to douse the flares if enemy aircraft were detected in the area. The importance of this was illustrated during the night of 3 August, when a German bomber pilot spotted the flarepath and dropped several bombs on it, fortunately without damage or injury.

The RLG was used occasionally by other units, such as 16 Operational Flying Unit, Upper Heyford. One of their Hampdens crashed there on 1 August 1940 when its undercarriage collapsed. Other units included the Overseas Despatch Flight at Kemble who used the RLG for night flying training before undertaking ferry flights overseas. Martin Marylands were present, for example, in November 1940.

Pupil and instructor with their Hawker Audax. (Aeroplane)

Babdown Farm was heavily used by the trainees of 9 SFTS during 1940 and this was reflected in the number of accidents that occurred there, usually on landing. Hart Trainer K6541 crashed on the approach on 7 August, for example. Audax K7447 crashed during a night landing on 11 October, as did K7412 on the 23rd, while K7452 came down on the approach in daylight on 1st November. Three Hart trainers crashed at Babdown Farm in November (K6496 on the approach on the 17th; K6438 on take-off on the 28th and K6447 on landing on the 29th).

More flying accidents took place at Babdown Farm during 1941. On 18 March, Master T8374 of 9 SFTS spun in and crashed near the airfield. On 24 March, Hurricane P3603 also spun in, this time on the approach, and on the same day Master T8443 struck a shed while flying in the circuit! Another Master crashed on take-off on 22 April, and this was followed by a spate of Hurricane accidents. Between 25 April, when L1867's undercarriage was retracted by its trainee pilot whilst taxiing, and 30 September when L1695 undershot and hit a wall, twelve Hurricanes were seriously damaged in separate incidents. Most of these involved an undercarriage collapse after being subjected to a heavy landing by their student pilots, although in August N2402 stalled and crashed on landing.

On 26 July Master N7992 crashed during a night take-off, while on 17 August Master N7780 suffered an engine failure on take-off and went into the trees. Three more Masters crash-landed or overshot later in August and, on 16 October, T8317 crashed on a night approach, followed by T8670 on 11 November.

No 9 SFTS was redesignated No 9 (Pilots) Advanced Flying Unit ((P) AFU) in February 1942, and the change in its training regime, to that of advanced flying training, probably resulted in the need to upgrade the facilities at Babdown Farm. The airfield was brought up to full RLG standard by the laying of runways of steel Sommerfield tracking, the erection of blister hangars so that aircraft could be kept under cover, and the construction of accommodation and administration buildings. While the upgrade was underway, 9 (P)AFU used Castle Combe for training, but in the event they never returned to Babdown Farm, having been transferred to Errol in Scotland at the end of July 1942. They had been replaced by No 3 Flying Instructors School (Advanced) (FIS(A)) at Hullavington, and when Babdown Farm was reopened for flying in August, it was this unit's Magisters, Masters, Oxfords and Harvards that appeared in the circuit. Two of the unit's flights were detached to the RLG and their personnel moved into the accommodation. Although 3 FIS(A) used the RLG mainly at night, flying Oxfords, it was also used during the day and by other units, such as 52 OTU which flew Spitfires from Aston Down and Chedworth.

Miles Magister, as flown by 9 (P)AFU. (DGB)

37

North American Harvard. (Aeroplane)

One of 3 FIS(A)'s Oxfords, N4728, caught fire and crashed on take-off on 9 September 1942. On 14 October two Spitfires of 52 OTU crashed at Babdown Farm: P8381 while on approach to the airfield, and AR227 nearby, killing its pilot, Sergeant Morton. Another Spitfire, P7543, crashed one mile north-east of the airfield, while making its approach in bad visibility. On 3 January 1943 Oxford X7261 of 3 FIS(A) hit a haystack on take-off from Babdown Farm.

A Standard Beam Approach system was installed at Babdown Farm in the spring of 1943, on the main (east/west) runway, and in June the Oxfords of 1532 Blind Approach Training (BAT) Flight moved in from Hullavington. The BAT Flight were seconded to 3 FIS(A) to assist the unit's students in night flying techniques, especially in the use of the Beam Approach landing system. Other improvements during the year included the construction of three Teeside hangars as part of a technical site on the south-east of the airfield. When No 3 FIS(A) moved away in September 1943, No 1532 (BAT) Flight remained, and continued flying in the area.

Later in October new residents at the RLG arrived in the form of part of 15 (P)AFU, which had relocated from Ramsbury to make way for the USAAF. The other flights of 15 (P)AFU moved to Castle Combe. The unit's equipment included Ansons and Tiger Moths as well as Oxfords.

Electric runway lighting was installed at Babdown Farm during early 1944, and it seemed to be this that attracted a single German raider on the night of 15 May. Two bombs were dropped, but no damage was done to the airfield or equipment. No major accidents had occurred at Babdown Farm since the end of January 1943, but this was to change on the night of 28 August, when Oxford N6322 of 15 (P)AFU struck trees on the approach. Later that evening another Oxford, N6322, of the unit crashed on a night approach straight into the runway controller's caravan, killing the duty controller. A further flying accident on 12 October involved Anson AW910 of 15 (P)AFU which overshot on landing and crashed when its undercarriage collapsed.

Heavy rainfall during the autumn of 1944 restricted flying from Babdown Farm, and the situation barely changed through the winter. Similar problems at Long Newnton and 15 (P)AFU's main airfield at Castle Combe didn't help matters. While conditions improved during the late spring of 1945, so flying training started to run down as the end of the war in Europe was in sight. What later turned out to be the last flying accident at Babdown Farm took place on the eve of VE Day, Oxford LX142 hitting V4080 during a take-off on the night of 18 May 1945.

In May 1945 all of the 15 (P)AFU flights transferred to Babdown Farm, and on 19 June the unit disbanded there. No 1532 (BAT) Flight had disbanded at the RLG four days earlier. Within a few days the aircraft were ferried away to Maintenance Units, and the airfield was effectively closed. No 7 MU Quedgeley used hangars at Babdown as a stores area until January 1948, when the airfield was de-requisitioned and sold off. The site has since been returned to agriculture, although some of the airfield buildings remain in position today as a reminder of its past.

4
BIBURY

6½ miles north-east of Cirencester
SU 123075

A landing ground near the village of Bibury in the Cotswolds was picked out by passing pilots, probably from South Cerney, in April 1939. The fields, at Bibury Farm on the edge of Ablington Down, proved to be a useful spot for practising take-offs and landings, and the site was commandeered as a Relief Landing Ground (RLG) by 3 Service Flying Training School (SFTS) based at South Cerney in the spring of 1940. The school's Oxfords were regular visitors during April and May. However, following the German Blitzkreig in France, and the fear of invasion of the British mainland, Bibury airfield was closed and covered in old cars to prevent landings by German Junkers Ju 52 transports, or gliders.

Flying resumed at Bibury in July 1940, mainly at night, with ground parties travelling from South Cerney each evening to lay out a goose-neck flare path to illuminate the airfield and its approach. Bibury, being in a relatively remote location in the countryside, was chosen for night flying as any raiders attracted to the flarepath would cause far less damage there than they would to the main base at South Cerney. However, night flying at Bibury was no less risky to the pilots than if the Germans did attack, as the occasional flying accident did occur. The first of these was on 7 July 1940, when North American Harvard N7070 of 15 STFS visiting from Kidlington crashed on landing. A couple of weeks later, on 20 July, Oxford R6320 of 3 SFTS also crashed on landing at the RLG.

The first fatal accident at Bibury occurred the following month when on 5 August another 15 SFTS Harvard, P5793, undershot on landing, killing its pilot, Pilot Officer D.J. Young. The next evening, Oxford R6332 of 3 SFTS crashed just after take-off on a night-flying exercise.

With the Luftwaffe making night raids in August 1940, it was decided to use Bibury for the deployment of night fighters to protect Cheltenham and the area south of Birmingham. Accordingly on 7 August, A Flight of 87 Squadron flew their Hurricanes in on detachment from their base at Exeter. The pilots didn't have to wait long for action, as the following night they intercepted a Heinkel He 111 while on patrol, and it was shot down by Pilot Officer Conilly.

The flight was replaced by a detachment of Spitfires of 92 Squadron, which arrived on 19 August, escorting in the three Bristol Bombay transports that brought their ground crews and equipment. While the squadron personnel were settling into their new temporary home, German raiders were in the area. One of these, a Junkers Ju 88 of III/KG5, found Bibury and came in fast and low over the airfield, machine-gunning and dropping bombs. One Spitfire was destroyed and another badly damaged. Two of the Spitfire pilots reacted quickly, jumped into their fighters and took off in pursuit of the raider. After a long chase they caught the German bomber over the Solent and shot it down into the water. The Junkers went down fighting, and damaged one of the Spitfires, which had to crash-land along the coast. Its pilot, Flight Lieutenant T.W. Wade (who later became a test pilot for Hawkers), escaped from his burning aircraft in the nick of time, just before it blew up.

No 92 Squadron's tenure at Bibury ended on 3 September, when the detached flight rejoined the main unit and was transferred to Biggin Hill. They were replaced by another detachment of No 87 Squadron, represented this time by B Flight. The weather on the evening following B Flight's arrival was perfect for night flying, with bright moonlight and good visibility. A patrol was put up, and Flying Officer 'Bee' Beaumont (later Chief Test Pilot of the British Aircraft Corporation) intercepted and damaged a Ju 88 near Bristol in his Hurricane V7285. The following night he was on patrol with Pilot Officer Jay when they spotted two Junkers Ju 88s. Both were attacked, but the raiders escaped. This unit remained at Bibury until mid-December 1940, with A and B Flight being detached to the RLG in rotation.

The Hurricane pilots didn't find Bibury the easiest airfield to fly from, especially at night; one of B Flight's aircraft crashed on 10 September, during landing. An Oxford of 3 SFTS crashed on 26 September, when its student pilot landed with the undercarriage up, extensively damaging the aircraft. Another 87 Squadron Hurricane, this time of A Flight, crash-landed at Bibury on 11 October. The weekly rotation of the two 87 Squadron flights continued, but B Flight's return to Bibury on 24 October was tragically marred when two of the arriving Hurricanes collided in the circuit. Pilot Officer Cook managed to land his aircraft, but the other aircraft went out of control and when Pilot Officer Jay bailed out, his parachute failed to deploy in time and he was killed. The Hurricanes of 87 Squadron continued to mount night patrols from Bibury over the following weeks, but the only other night action that took place during this time was on 24 November, when Flying Officer Rayner attacked a Heinkel He 111 that was lit by searchlights. He fired a six-second burst of machine-gun fire at the enemy bomber but the results were inconclusive.

The squadron was transferred to Colerne in Wiltshire on 28 November, but its detachments to Bibury continued. On 18 December however, the week after a further move to Charmy Down in Somerset, the detachments were stopped, as the need for them had passed. Bibury was left to the Oxfords of 3 SFTS, which continued their night flying routines. Oxford N6330 of 3 SFTS had crashed on the approach to Bibury on 28 November and another Oxford, P6807, overshot while attempting a night landing on 23 December.

Intense flying activity by the aircraft of 87 Squadron and 3 SFTS had had an adverse affect on the airfield's surface, and following an inspection by the Air Officer Commanding from HQ Training Command on 10 February 1941, an improvement programme was ordered. While the work was planned, flying carried on, but the intense routine of landings and take-offs continued to wear the surface and

Several Airspeed Oxfords came to grief at Bibury. (Aeroplane)

flying accidents were not uncommon. During the first half of 1941, six Oxfords crashed, two on take-off (in February and March) and four on landing, which was the most critical period of the flight, especially for 3 SFTS students. One Oxford crashed during a night landing in March, and three others on landing during June, one stalling on the approach, one on landing, and one on overshooting. Another five Oxfords crashed during the second half of 1941, four involving landing. Unfortunately the fifth, which occurred on take-off, resulted in another fatality, when Flying Officer Willoughby hit the trees in AP396 just after having got off the ground.

Nonetheless, improvement work started later that year and carried on steadily through 1942 into the following year. The airfield was extended and two Sommerfield tracking runways were laid on it, along with a perimeter track. Six hangars (one T type and five blisters) and various buildings were erected to provide accommodation for personnel on four dispersed sites around the airfield. An instructional and technical site was also provided. While this construction work was going on, the Oxfords of 3 SFTS, which became No 3 (P) AFU in March 1942, carried on training at Bibury. Only three Oxfords crashed here during 1942: N6429 hit the trees whilst attempting to land in the fog on 21 March, and AT674 came down one mile north of the airfield after experiencing engine failure during an overshoot practice, while AP401 crashed on overshooting on 13 October.

The airfield was further upgraded in the spring of 1943 with the installation of a Standard Beam Approach system, which enabled aircraft to land at night, in bad weather, or on instruments. On 13 July 1943, No 1539 (Beam Approach Training) Flight, which had formed at South Cerney two months earlier, moved to Bibury to undertake training using the Beam Approach equipment. This unit, which also flew Oxfords, gradually took over Bibury as its operating base, although 3 (P)AFU also continued to use it. Two Oxfords crashed at Bibury during 1943. The first was V3603, which caught fire on the approach and crash-landed on the airfield on 16 February. The second incident occurred some time later, on 26 November, when V33592 suffered an engine failure on the approach. This tragically resulted in both pilots, Flying Officer Cunningham and Sergeant Mackay, being killed. Another aircraft crash-landed at the airfield during the year – this was Master DL520 of 3 GTS that had flown in to pick up a force-landed glider. Unfortunately the aircraft overran and was seriously damaged.

Training at the RLG continued into 1944, but continual rain during January and February caused severe water-logging which limited flying operations. Tricky surface conditions proved to be a recurring problem at Bibury for the rest of the year. The only aircraft accident for 1944 in fact did not occur in flight but on the ground, when on 19 August, Oxford AT742 caught fire in the dispersal area. However, flying operations at Bibury were not to continue into 1945. No 1539 (BAT) Flight vacated its accommodation at the airfield on 15 November and returned to South Cerney. A limited amount of flying by the aircraft of 3 (P)AFU then continued over the next few weeks, but this had ceased by the end of November.

On 1 December 1944 responsibility for Bibury was transferred to 40 Group, Maintenance Command, and allocated to 7 Maintenance Unit Quedgely. It was then used as a sub-store for furniture and domestic equipment for another year or so, before being sold off sometime in 1950. Remains of the airfield facilities can still be seen at Bibury, in the form of derelict huts and until recently at least one blister hangar, which was being used for farm storage.

5

BROCKWORTH
(Hucclecote)

½ mile south of Brockworth
SO 882160

Brockworth airfield will forever be associated with the Gloster Aircraft Company for it was home to the company for many years. The site had its origins in the early part of 1915, when a field near the village of Hucclecote was selected for an Aircraft Acceptance Park by the Air Board, the government authority for aircraft production during the First World War.

Amongst the aircraft tested at Hucclecote were the Bristol F2Bs and Nieuport Nighthawks manufactured under sub-contract by the Gloucestershire Aircraft Company at Sunningend in Cheltenham. This company was formed in June 1917 as a joint venture by H.M. Martyn and Co Ltd and the Aircraft Manufacturing Company (also known as Airco). H.M. Martyn was a high quality woodworking company located in Cheltenham that was renowned for its wood-panelling and fittings in prestigious buildings and ocean liners. It was also a sub-contractor for the manufacture of aircraft spares, components and sub-assemblies to Airco, a London-based company producing a range of aircraft under licence for the Government, in addition to its own types devised by its chief designer, Geoffrey de Havilland. The Gloucestershire Aircraft Company was formed to take over Airco's sub-contract work by renting H.M. Martyn's factory in Cheltenham.

For flight testing the finished aircraft, minus their wings, were towed by lorry to Hucclecote, which was some seven miles away from the factory. There they were assembled in Belfast truss hangars built there for the Air Board, checked, then flown.

By the spring of 1918 the Gloucestershire Aircraft Company was building 45 aircraft per week, including Airco DH6 and DH9 fuselages as well as Royal Aircraft Factory and Bristol designs. However, the Armistice that came eight months later brought with it a cessation of orders. Although limited production of the F2B and Nighthawk continued for a while the company, like the rest of the British aircraft industry, faced an uncertain future. Then the Aircraft Manufacturing Company went out of business (although Geoffrey de Havilland was later to form his own aircraft company) and similarly the Nieuport and General Aircraft company closed. However, in November 1920 the Gloucestershire Aircraft Company managed to acquire the rights to the Nieuport designs, and also secured the services of the company's chief designer, Harry Folland, famous for the SE5 and SE5a, probably the finest single-seat fighters of the Great War.

The company obtained an order from the Japanese Government for the supply of 50 modified Nieuport Nighthawks in 1921. It also developed racing biplanes, and test flew them from Hucclecote using a hangar rented from the Air Board for assembly, servicing and maintenance. One of these designs, the Bamel (conceived and built in under four weeks), won many air races and captured the World Air Speed Record at 212.15 mph in December 1921. The development of fighter biplanes by the company resulted in the Grebe, and following evaluations for the Air Ministry this design was ordered for the RAF. A total of 130 Grebes were built between 1923 and 1927. Two of these aircraft were modified to be carried under the Airship R-33 in 1926. The Gamecock followed in 1926, an aeroplane that was also sold to the Finnish Air Force.

The company's enthusiasm for building racing aircraft extended to seaplanes, and between 1924 and 1929 they designed and built a complete series of racing seaplanes to compete for the world famous Schneider Trophy. The most successful of these were the Gloster IIIA, which came second in 1925, and the Gloster VII, the company's first monoplane, which attained the World Speed Record of 336.3 mph in October 1929. A lot of interest in the products of the Gloucestershire Aircraft Company was then coming from abroad, but overseas buyers found the company's name difficult to pronounce. Therefore in November 1926 it was decided to change the name to the simpler 'Gloster Aircraft Company Ltd'.

Although the company had used Hucclecote since 1921, at first it had

Gloster Gauntlets in formation in the mid-1930s. (Aeroplane)

only the limited use of one hangar for servicing and maintenance. This capacity increased in 1925 when another hangar was rented for fabrication work, and a couple of years later some work was moved from Cheltenham into other hangars and office space that had been rented. Eventually it was decided to move all production to Hucclecote, and to buy the site. This took place in 1928, when the entire 200 acre site including hangars and office accommodation was purchased for £15,000.

The move also marked the transition from the building of traditional wooden aeroplanes to all-metal construction. This meant that Glosters could now bid for sub-contracts from other manufacturers. As a result, from 1927 to 1929 the company produced the Armstrong Whitworth Siskin, which was the first time they had built complete all-metal aeroplanes to another manufacturer's design.

This was followed by a contract for all-metal wings for the Westland Wapitis. A total of 525 sets of wings were built at Hucclecote and delivered to Yeovil from 1929 to 1932. This was important work for Glosters, and helped the company to stay in business during a lean period due to lack of orders for its own machines. Other work taken on at the time included the manufacture of milk churns, car bodies and fish fryers. Glosters secured an order for a developed version of their SS19B design (later to become the Gauntlet) in September 1933, but this was only for 24 aeroplanes, not enough to fill the factory with aviation work.

In May 1934 Hawker Aircraft Ltd made a takeover proposal to the Gloster Aircraft Company's board. Hawker had a large order book that they were unable to fulfil with their own production facilities, and needed more capacity. It was clear to the directors of Glosters that such work was needed if Hucclecote was to remain open as an aircraft factory, and so they accepted Hawker's offer. Thus ended the existence of the Gloster Aircraft Company as an independent company, although its name was to remain, under Hawker's ownership. Work soon arrived from Hawker in the form of production of various versions of the Hawker Hart family of biplanes. These included the Hardy reconnaissance/bomber, the Audax Army co-operation aircraft and the Hart itself in bomber and trainer versions. While this work was in hand between 1934 and 1937, extensions were made to the Hucclecote facilities, increasing the factory floorspace to one million square feet.

Harry Folland must have been asking himself whether any of his designs would ever find favour with the Air Ministry in the early 1930s, as he had presented a number of designs to the Ministry that had not resulted in any orders. With the placing of the contract for a development of his SS19b design in late 1933 he must have perked up. Things got better as the Gauntlet, as it was to be known, received excellent reports from the RAF's test pilots, and follow-on orders were received. Eventually 228 Gauntlets were built for the RAF, equipping 14 fighter squadrons. From 1935 to 1937 they were the fastest fighters in RAF service, and the aircraft was also exported to Denmark and Sweden.

As the first Gauntlets went into production Harry Folland was already working on a development, refining the basic design to effect major improvements in performance. The result of this was the SS37, which flew on 12 September 1934. The new design incorporated, like the later Gauntlets, Hawker methods of construction, but was more streamlined and had a revised undercarriage and four machine guns (there were two in the Gauntlet). Although not fitted to the prototype, it also had provision for a cockpit canopy. The aircraft was ordered into production by the Air Ministry in July 1935 as the Gloster Gladiator.

Nice study of Gloster Gladiator on test flight. (Aeroplane)

The first RAF squadron to take delivery of the new aircraft was 72 Squadron in February 1937. More powerful engines were later fitted, and three-bladed propellers replaced the earlier two-bladed ones. In September 1938, at the time of the Munich Crisis, there were 96 Gladiators equipping six squadrons of Fighter Command defending the UK alongside nine squadrons of Gauntlets. There were another 44 Gladiators in RAF service overseas. The aircraft was an export success, with 14 overseas customers including Latvia, Lithuania, Eire, Greece, China, Sweden, Norway, Portugal and Finland. Total production of the Gladiator was 748 aircraft.

The first Gladiators to see action were those purchased by the Chinese, who in 1937 were resisting the Japanese. Thirty-six aircraft were supplied to China and, although the accident rate was high initially, the remaining Gladiators gave a good account of themselves against the Japanese fighters. RAF Gladiators were used in Palestine in early 1938, in support of the Palestine Police against insurgents. Gladiators of the Swedish Air Force went into action alongside Hawker Harts when the Russians invaded Finland in January 1940. The Finns also had Gladiators and lost 13 to more superior Russian fighters, but

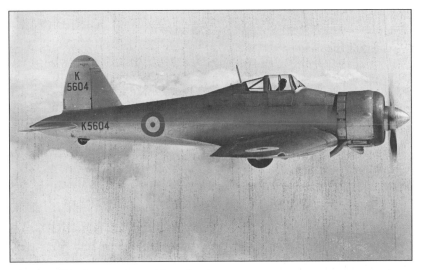

Gloster F5/34, first prototype. (Aeroplane)

the remainder were still in service when the two countries agreed peace terms in March 1940.

Largely replaced in Fighter Command by the outbreak of war, RAF Gladiators were nonetheless sent to France with 607 and 615 Squadrons to support the British Expeditionary Force. Gladiators flew during the Battle of Britain with 247 Squadron to protect Devonport dockyard and overseas, Gladiators operated by 263 Squadron flew from a frozen lake in Norway against the Luftwaffe, while others took part in actions in the Western Desert and Greece. The Sea Gladiator, a naval version of the aircraft, was developed with the addition of an arrester hook, catapult points and a ventral fuselage dinghy pack. It went to sea on carriers during the early war period and fought in the North Sea and in the Mediterranean; four Sea Gladiators provided the sole air defence of Malta in June 1940. The Gladiator flew with 41 RAF units and 7 FAA squadrons.

Although Harry Folland was responsible for the Gladiator's success, he felt restricted by the Hawker takeover and left Glosters in 1937 to start up his own company at Hamble – Folland Aircraft Ltd. His last Gloster design was a single radial-engined monoplane fighter against Air Ministry specification F5/34. With the factory concentrating on the development of the Gauntlet and Gladiator, progress on the Gloster F5/34 contender was slow. By the time the

50

Final production work on Hawker Hurricanes and Henleys at Brockworth. (Aeroplane)

prototype flew in December 1937, the Spitfire and Hurricane, which had also been produced to meet F5/34, were both in production, and Gloster's design failed to win an order.

Gloster's last piston-engined design was against specification F9/37 for a twin-engined fighter. The company's new chief designer, W. G. Carter, revised an earlier design for a twin-engined bomber that had been suspended, and a prototype was produced. The aircraft first flew from Hucclecote on 3 April 1939 and showed great potential. Unfortunately the prototype was badly damaged in a landing accident at Boscombe Down. Although it was repaired and a second prototype was produced, the type was not selected for production.

Production of the Gladiator at Hucclecote lasted from 1937 to 1939 but mid-way through that period another type appeared on the shop floor. This was the Hawker Henley, the planned manufacture of which had been transferred from Hawker's Langley plant due to shortage of space. The Henley had originally been developed as a high-speed single-engined light bomber using Hurricane components, but the Air Ministry withdrew its requirement so the design was changed to the new role of target training. A winch was fitted into the aircraft, which wound the target drogue cable in and out. Henley production ended in

51

September 1940, but alongside it in October 1939 the manufacture of Hurricanes had also started. This was in fact a logical step since both types showed the same outer wings, tail surfaces and undercarriage units. The first Gloster-built Hurricane I, L2020 was completed on 27 October 1939, and by the end of October 1940 the 1,000th example had been completed.

Hurricane production at Hucclecote had in fact been planned before the war. Glosters had been instructed to build a shadow factory and this had been started on 19 August 1938 using space on the eastern side of the airfield, across from the main works. The new factory was completed in November 1940 giving some 24 acres of factory floor area. It was entitled the No 2 Shadow Factory, but more generally known as Brockworth, lying as it did on the other side of the parish boundary from Hucclecote. The roof of the new factory was camouflaged to blend in with the local countryside, as was the main factory. A concrete runway was built at this time, to provide a good all-weather surface to fly from. The airfield was also camouflaged with paint and creosote, to give the impression of hedged fields, and dummy hedges were built, mounted on wheels so that they could be moved away during flying. Defence was provided by the local units of the Home Guard, who used a variety of strongholds that included a First World War tank parked on the edge of the airfield.

On 10 February 1940, while the new Shadow Factory was being constructed, HM King George VI and Queen Elizabeth visited Brockworth. They inspected the production lines and were shown progress on the new factory.

One of the first occupants of the factory was a new company, A.W. Hawksley Ltd. This had been created within the group that owned the Hawker Aircraft Company, Hawker Siddeley, and other companies including Armstrong Whitworth (AW). The name was concocted from the initials of Armstrong Whitworth, the first syllable of Hawker and four letters from Siddeley. It was set up at Brockworth to manufacture the AW Albemarle. The aircraft had originated as a Bristol design for a reconnaissance bomber, and was twin-engined with a tricycle undercarriage (the first such British aircraft to see squadron service), but responsibility for the design had been transferred to Armstrong Whitworth, who built the two prototypes before production started at Brockworth.

The first 32 aircraft were produced as bombers, but it was decided to change the aircraft's role to that of glider tug and special transport, in which it would become very successful. In order to conserve strategic materials, the Albemarle was made largely of wood. This meant that its components and major assemblies could be produced by firms dispersed around the country that were not part of the aircraft industry, such as furniture manufacturers and cabinet-makers. In all over 600 Albemarles were to be built at Brockworth. The aircraft played a significant role as a transport and in the airborne operations over Sicily, Normandy and Arnhem.

Some Hurricane production was also undertaken in the new factory at Brockworth. Components were assembled from 43 local manufacturers, and in 1940 1,211 Hurricanes were produced. This was followed by 1,359 in 1941 and 180 in 1942, a total of 2,750 aircraft. At its peak, six aircraft were produced each day, along with an average of four wing sets as spares.

Glosters had been trying to obtain extra capacity throughout 1940 in order to meet demands. By the end of the year it had taken over 32 other premises in the local area and converted them for use as design offices, stores and workshops. By the end of March 1941 six new dispersal factories were also to be built, at Ledbury (wing assembly), Uckington (fitting shop and presses), Bentham (experimental design office and factory), and Newent (sheet metal fabrication), along with

Armstrong Whitworth Albemarles outside the final erection hangars at Brockworth. (Aeroplane)

Hawker Typhoon, the majority of which were produced by Glosters. (Aeroplane)

two factories at Stoke Orchard for assembly and flight testing. Within 18 months of the start of the war, Glosters therefore had an aircraft production area of almost 1.75 million square feet. Just as importantly, the company had a workforce of some 14,000 employees, recruited at a time when skilled and unskilled labour was in great demand across Britain in industry and the armed forces.

Sydney Camm started work on the successor to his Hurricane design (to be known as the Typhoon) in 1937. However, the decision to proceed with it was delayed by officialdom. When the need for the aircraft was belatedly realised it was rushed into service too early, before its teething problems could be resolved. In the event the new fighter would have great success, not in the role of interceptor for which it was designed, but as a close-support fighter bomber. Ten months before the last Hurricane left the Hucclecote factory, the Typhoon was appearing on the Gloster production line.

Unlike the Hurricane, which was built by Gloster in parallel with several other companies, the Typhoon (apart from the initial prototypes) was built by Glosters alone. The first production aircraft, R7576, flew on 27 May 1941. Unfortunately it was dogged with problems with its Napier Sabre engine and with structural defects, which resulted in numerous engine failures and the loss of the prototype. Because of this only 28 Typhoons were completed in the latter half of 1941. During the following year 677 were built, but more structural problems were encountered that resulted in the loss of several aircraft due to the tail unit separating from the fuselage when under stress. When the engine problems were eventually solved and the fuselage strengthened, the Typhoon evolved into a thoroughbred. Production peaked at 130 per month in December 1942; the following year 1,460 aircraft were produced, and 1,164 in 1944. The final aircraft were built in 1945 making a total of 3,330 Typhoons produced, all at the Hucclecote factory.

Typhoons were fast – they were the first 400 mph fighters in the RAF and were invaluable in combating the 'hit and run' raids being mounted in mid-1942 by Focke Wulf Fw 190 fighter bombers over the UK. The aircraft were later used as fighter bombers and took the war back to the enemy by attacking their airfields, communications and transport; Typhoons were soon renowned as 'trainbusters', destroying as many as 150 locomotives per month by the middle of 1943. They were heavily engaged in the operations leading up to D-Day, 18 squadrons of the Tactical Air Force then being equipped with the type. Their offensive armament had steadily increased, from the original 500 lbs to 1,000 lbs, then 2,000 lb of bombs, and the aircraft had also been fitted with rocket rails and could fire eight 60 lb rocket projectiles. Rocket-firing Typhoons put German radar stations off the air just before D-Day, and were employed after the landings in the destruction of enemy armour and defences. The Typhoon squadrons followed the Allied armies into Holland, frequently changing their bases at short notice. They sometimes flew alongside other RAF squadrons equipped with the Typhoon's successor, the Hawker Tempest. Both aircraft continued in service performing their important role until the end of the war.

Although the Gloster factories were seen as prime targets for the Luftwaffe, there were relatively few attacks by German bombers on Hucclecote – three attacks were made in daylight and several more during the night time. Of the 60 or so bombs dropped, only a few landed within the perimeter of the works. During a daylight raid in October 1940 an oil and several HE bombs were dropped. The oil bomb hit the roof of No 7 machine shop and toolroom, which caused a good deal of damage and injuries to the staff working inside. Fortunately the HE bombs landed on open ground nearby and exploded harmlessly.

Then, on 17 June 1941, a pair of Heinkel He 111H-2s of KG100, the

Luftwaffe pathfinder squadron, were despatched to raid the Gloster factory. They followed electronic guidance beams directed at the factory from stations in France. They were intercepted by a Beaufighter of 604 Squadron based at Middle Wallop when Pilot Officer Crossland, flying his third operation, engaged the first aircraft, which flew into the ground between Stourton and Kilmington in Wiltshire, making a crater 20 feet across. The second Heinkel escaped. However, on Easter Saturday 1942, 4 April, another attack on the factory resulted in injuries and fatalities. Five bombs were dropped in the late afternoon, as a shift-change was taking place. HE bombs straddled the airfield, factory and adjoining houses. One of the bombs hit the bus park killing 13 people. Many more were injured.

While Hurricane production was being busily undertaken at Hucclecote in the spring of 1941, an important event occurred on the airfield. Because of its secret nature, it was not observed by many, and those that did watch probably didn't realise its significance. This was the first time that Britain's jet aircraft, the Gloster E28/39, had left the ground.

The project had started on 3 February 1940 when the Air Ministry issued a contract to Glosters for the design and construction of an aeroplane to specification E28/39, the primary object of which was to flight test a jet engine designed by Frank Whittle. He had come up with the idea of using a gas turbine for the jet propulsion of an aircraft to take it to speeds of over 500 mph. He started work on his idea while studying at the RAF College, Cranwell, in the 1920s and came up with some firm proposals in 1930. The RAF was not interested, so he patented the project and set up his own company, Power Jets Ltd, in 1936 to build an experimental engine. This was ready by 1938, when its potential was at last officially recognised and the Air Ministry ordered some prototypes for flight.

Glosters had been selected for the project because they had the capacity and the capability of undertaking the task. The design of the aircraft was conceived by George Carter, with the close co-operation of Frank Whittle, there being a mutual understanding of their requirements. The layout of the aircraft was for a low-wing monoplane with a single fin and rudder. The engine was to be mounted in the fuselage aft of the cockpit and fuel tank, with a single jet pipe exiting at the rear of the fuselage. The undercarriage was of a tricycle arrangement, to keep the jet pipe parallel to the ground and aid take-off. Air for the engine was taken in through a large intake in the nose and through ducts either side of the cockpit to the rear.

Gloster E28/39 prototype at Brockworth. (Aeroplane)

Initial construction of two prototypes took place in the experimental department at Hucclecote, but to maintain security and due to the threat of enemy attacks on the airfield, the first aircraft due to be completed, W4041, was dispersed to Regent Motors in Cheltenham. There the airframe was finished and the engine fitted in great secrecy. W4041 was returned to Brockworth by road on 7 April 1941, where that evening the company test pilot, P.E.G. Sayer, began a series of runs with the engine set to 13,000 rpm. These were satisfactory, and were repeated the following day, with the engine revolutions increased to 16,000 rpm. During the third taxiing run the aircraft made three short hops about six feet off the ground, varying in length between 100 and 200 yards.

The aircraft was then taken to Crabtree's Garage in Cheltenham, which was another site used by Glosters as a dispersal factory. There it was dismantled and then taken by road to Cranwell where Power Jets, the engine manufacturers, were based. Flight trials could take place there from a bigger but more secluded airfield. The aircraft was reassembled ready for flight on 14 May 1941, when it was checked and taxied once more. On the following day the weather was not very good, but at 7 pm the clouds cleared. P.E.G. Sayer took the aircraft out onto the runway and at 7.45 pm he opened the throttle to 16,500 rpm and took off. That official maiden flight lasted 17 minutes, but it was enough to show Sayer that the aircraft handled and performed well, and had great potential. After a series of flight trials over the next two weeks, W4041 returned to the Experimental Department at Hucclecote. It was fitted with a more powerful engine but it would be some months before it would fly again.

Flight testing was continued in February 1942 at Edgehill in Warwickshire, which was conveniently placed for Gloster and Power Jets personnel. Sayer continued with the test flying programme of the E28/39, but was killed on 21 October while flying a Typhoon. His deputy, Michael Daunt, carried on with the test programme.

The second aircraft, W4046, had meanwhile joined the programme and was fitted with an engine made by Rover, the W2B. This aircraft made the first cross-country jet flight in Britain, from Edgehill to Hatfield, where a demonstration was put on for Winston Churchill. The aircraft was later lost on a test flight while being flown by Squadron Leader Douglas Davie, an RAF pilot. The ailerons jammed and the aircraft went into a flat spin from which the pilot could not recover, so he baled out, the first pilot to do so from a jet aircraft. W4041 continued to fly until after the war. In April 1946 it was put on display at the Science Museum, South Kensington, where it still resides.

During 1943 every part of Glosters' technical, production and administrative facilities was working flat out: work was proceeding on the F9/40, the Typhoon was in production, development of the E28/39 continued and its successor was being brought into production. A workforce of over 14,000 men and women worked in 40 factories dispersed over a wide area of Gloucestershire to achieve this, under the co-ordination of the Hucclecote management. In October 1943, due to the size of Hucclecote airfield and the danger to housing nearby, it was decided to move all flight test work to Moreton Valence, a larger airfield some eight miles to the south-west.

Well before the E28/39 flew, plans were in hand at Glosters to produce an operational successor. Due to the limited power developed by the jet engines then available, a twin-engined layout was selected for Britain's first jet fighter. As in the E28/39, it was of a low-wing, tricycle undercarriage configuration, this being straightforward and well-proven. The engines were to be mounted mid-way along each of the wings. Eight prototypes were built, and the production contract for 20 further aircraft was placed in September 1941, four months after the first flight of the E28/39.

Originally the Gloster F9/40 was to be known as the 'Thunderbolt', but this was changed to 'Meteor' in March 1942. The first one to be completed was powered by two Rover W2B turbojets but, as the engines failed to produce enough thrust, it undertook taxiing trials only. It was the fifth prototye, DG206, that became the first Meteor to fly, from Cranwell on 5 March 1943. This aircraft was powered by Halford H1 engines, forerunners of the de Havilland Goblin that was to power the Meteor's contemporary, the de Havilland Spider Crab, or Vampire as it was later called. Other prototypes had Halford H1s or Whittle W2 and W2B engines. The actual turbojet engine that Frank Whittle originated later went to Rover, then to Rolls-Royce during its lengthy development, and eventually became the W2B Welland, which developed 1,700 lbs of thrust.

The first production Meteor Mk I, EE210, first flew on 12 January 1944, but was exchanged for a US Bell YP-59 Airacomet under an agreement between the UK and US governments. The YP-59 was the first US jet fighter, and was fitted with General Electric type I turbojets, developed using British technology. The exchange aircraft was flown from Moreton Valence in September 1943. The Meteor was the only Allied turbojet-powered aircraft to see operational service during the Second World War. It was first issued to No 616 Squadron, then based at Culmhead in Somerset, the first pair being delivered there on 12 July 1944. The squadron later moved to Manston in Kent and flew missions to intercept V-1 flying bombs. The first enemy 'aircraft' to be brought down by a jet fighter was a V-1, by Flying Officer Dixie Dean of 616 Squadron on 4 August 1944. While flying EE216 near Tonbridge he spotted the rocket and closed in to attack but his guns jammed, so he flew alongside at 365 mph and positioned one of his wingtips under one of the V-1's. When he brought his wing up it lifted the V-1's wing, which upset the guidance system, causing it to crash into the ground.

There was no Meteor Mk II but the next version to see service, the Mk III, re-equipped 616 Squadron at Colerne in Wiltshire in January 1945. They were joined by a second Meteor III squadron, No 504 that started forming in April. The Meteor III had increased fuel capacity, and a sliding cockpit canopy (the Mk I's was hinged). The first 15 Meteors were fitted with the Welland engine and the remaining 265 had Derwents.

One flight of 616 Squadron flew to Belgium to join 84 Group of the 2nd Tactical Air Force in January 1945. Despite familiarisation flights over Allied airfields the Meteor pilots found themselves to be targets

Gloster Meteor first prototype DG202, now in the RAF Museum, Cosford. (DGB)

for trigger-happy gunners, so the aircraft were painted white overall to aid recognition. With the constant change of bases as the Allies moved forward, the Meteors had to operate from grass or metal-plank surfaces, but the design proved to be a rugged one, and the aircraft adapted well to these conditions. One aircraft even landed in a ploughed field to refuel and took off again. The Meteors met few enemy aircraft in the air, and were mainly engaged in strafing ground targets. One of the last engagements of the war was on 2 May 1945, six days before VE Day, when a Meteor came across a Fiesler Storch observation aircraft. The German pilot evaded the Meteor for a while, but eventually put his aircraft down in a field and managed to jump out before the Storch was destroyed by the Meteor's cannon fire.

In 1944 Glosters began building two new prototypes against specification E5/42, later reissued as E1/44 and known as the Gloster GA1. Neither was completed, as attention was instead focused on an improved design, the GA2, known unofficially as the Ace. This aircraft was gradually developed as time elapsed and methods improved, in versions to be fitted with Rolls-Royce Nene and de Havilland Ghost engines. Although production of the aircraft was considered in 1946, it was not proceeded with, as the GA2 was not sufficiently in advance of the Meteor to warrant the investment. Both prototypes later flew successfully however, and were used as trials aircraft by the Royal Aircraft Establishment Farnborough into the 1950s.

The Meteor III was the last variant to see service in the Second World War. It was later developed into the Mk IV, which made its first flight on 17 July 1945. This version had a pressurised cockpit, armour protection for the pilot, and a strengthened airframe to take the stresses of a 20% increase in speed, made possible by the fitting of the improved Derwent 5 engine which developed 4,000 lb of thrust. Shortly after production of the Mk IV was started at Hucclecote, the wings were reduced in span and the fuselage was increased in length, to improve handling characteristics. Eventually 657 Mk IVs were to be built, 192 of which were sold overseas. Most of these were manufactured by Gloster, although a small number were built by Armstrong Whitworth, who also made some Meteor components.

The next version of the Meteor, and the last pure single-seat fighter version of the aircraft, was the F8. This was produced as an urgent requirement in 1947 due to the appearance of other jet fighters in US and Russian service that could outclass the Meteor F3 and F4 in performance. The F8's airframe was strengthened and had the more powerful Derwent 8 engines, giving it a top speed of almost 600 mph at full war-load. The F8 also had Martin Baker ejection seats and a gyro gunsight fitted, and a fully transparent canopy for all-round vision. The Meteor F8 became the RAF's main front line jet fighter in the early 1950s and flew in combat during the Korean War with the Royal Australian Air Force. It was built in greater numbers than any other Meteor variant, and inspired a number of other developments as night fighters and trainers.

Jet-powered flight opened a new era of aviation, and Glosters was firmly a part of that. The company's design team had experimented with higher speed Meteors in 1944, and in August 1945 an F3 fitted with Derwent 5 engines had proved to be faster than any others tested to date. With the end of the war the team decided to make an attempt on the World Air Speed Record. This stood at 469.22 mph, set by Fritz Wendel in a Messerschmitt Me 109R on 26 April 1939. Although aircraft flew faster than this during the war, none was ratified as an official record. With official backing from the Air Ministry, two Meteors were prepared for an attempt. With armament and radios removed, and the machine gun ports faired over and a gloss finish applied to both aircraft, they were ready. Flying from Moreton Valance on 7 November 1945, Group Captain Hugh Wilson established a new record, flying an officially ratified 606.38 mph in

Meteor F3 EE454 named *Britannia* (he actually reached 611.20 mph in an unratified run that day).

Having regained the world record Glosters and the Air Ministry were keen to retain it for the UK as long as possible. A High Speed Flight was therefore formed at Tangmere on 14 June 1946. Four Meteor F4s were allocated to the Flight before being prepared for further attempts. All unnecessary equipment was removed, the external surfaces were smoothed and sealed, with extra fuel tanks installed and ballast in the nose inserted. On Saturday, 7 September, Meteor EE549 flown by Group Captain Teddy Donaldson achieved a new World Air Speed record of 615.78 mph. Several more attempts were made to increase this speed, but without success and the RAF High Speed Flight was disbanded on 26 September 1946, the day Geoffrey de Havilland junior was killed in a DH108 whilst practising for an attempt on Donaldson's record.

Glosters, however, continued to seek further records, which helped to publicise the Meteor and was good for sales. Squadron Leader Bill Waterton flew EE549 to 618.4 mph on a flight from Paris to Croydon on 16 January 1947, and many other time, distance and time to height records followed, with probably the fastest Meteor being RA476, a standard F4 flown by Squadron Leader J. Lomas from Turnhouse to Bovingdon at an average speed of 627 mph. These records confirmed the basic soundness of the Meteor's design, but its straight wing layout meant that it would never exceed Mach 1. Breaking the sound barrier and flying at supersonic speeds would require swept wing designs.

The following ten years were to be a successful period, with steady production and full employment of the workforce. The Meteor was built for the RAF in many variants and flew with 14 export customers. The last Meteor, Mark F8 WL191, left the Hucclecote factory on 9 April 1954, and this ended 19 years of production of the Meteor, which was built in 34 sub-types fitted with 21 different types of engines.

With the end of the war, the Gloster Aircraft Co was involved in another massive reorganisation to dispose of the dispersal factories and centre production at the main Hucclecote/Brockworth site. Experimental design and construction was to continue at Bentham, a site acquired during the war, and flight testing would continue at Moreton Valence.

The Meteor was succeeded on the Gloster production lines by the Javelin, a two-seat, twin-engined, all weather fighter. It was the first twin-jet delta wing aircraft in the world and was designed to have long endurance and high performance, its role being to intercept incoming bombers at high altitude and high speed, in all weathers, by day and night. The Javelin first appeared as the GA5, making its maiden flight from Moreton Valence on 26 November 1951. It was ordered into production in July 1952 and the first aircraft entered service with No 46 Squadron at Odiham two years later. Javelin production totalled 430 in eight versions over the next eight years, the last one, an FAW8, leaving the Hucclecote factory on 8 April 1960. This aircraft, XJ5128, proved to be the last Gloster-built aircraft to fly from Hucclecote, as no further Gloster designs were planned. (Javelin FAW9s were in fact later produced, but these were FAW7s converted by Glosters at Moreton Valance.)

Gloster, with no new aircraft designs in the pipeline, put diversification schemes in place to manufacture vending machines and agricultural harvesters. Fire appliances and emergency vehicles were also later produced along with road semi-trailers. Following a rationalisation of the Hawker Siddeley Group between 1961 and 1963, the Gloster Aircraft Company eventually became part of the Avro Whitworth Division of Hawker Siddeley Aviation. The Gloster name reappeared in a new company, Gloster Saro Ltd, which continued to produce vending machines, road tankers and refuellers. The Hucclecote factory was sold to Gloucester Trading Estates in April 1964.

Gloster Saro continued to produce vehicles at Hucclecote, although by the mid-1960s the airfield was no longer in use. The factory has since closed and the site developed for housing. Despite plans to preserve some of the historic buildings at Hucclecote this unfortunately never happened, and all were demolished. Throughout its history, the Gloster Co and its predecessors produced over 6,000 aircraft of all types at its Hucclecote and Brockworth factories. The presence of the company is today marked by a full-scale replica of a Gloster E28/339 placed on a roundabout at the entrance to the factory's former location.

6
CHEDWORTH

8 miles north-east of Cirencester
SP 042131

Situated on a plateau in the Cotswold hills, Chedworth was named after the picturesque village a mile away. The airfield was constructed during the winter of 1941/42, after farmland was requisitioned and a minor road that crossed the site was closed, and opened as a satellite of Aston Down in April 1942. The layout was unusual, in that it consisted of two runways almost at right angles to each other, a main one of 1,400 yards and a secondary one of 1,300 yards. A taxiway ran all the way round the airfield, punctuated by 25 dispersals.

Two blister hangars were later built to provide undercover storage and maintenance facilities, while a control tower and flight office were also added on the edge of the airfield. An administrative area included an armoury, stores and offices, while a semi-underground battle HQ was constructed nearby. Air raid shelters were also provided around the station and, in and around Withington Woods to the north-west, a number of living sites were built of wood and brick construction.

The first main users of Chedworth were No 52 Operational Training Unit (OTU) equipped with early marks of Spitfire and Master advanced trainers. The OTU had moved from Debden to Aston Down in August 1941, and used Chedworth as a useful training location away from the OTU's busy main airfield. The level of activity continued at Chedworth over the following year, and in August 1942 two of 52 OTU's flights moved in. This saved a lot of transit time by road and air, as the two flights were already spending most of their training time at Chedworth rather than Aston Down. In the spring of 1942, under the codename 'Saracen', the day fighter OTUs had been allocated squadron numbers, in case they needed to

Supermarine Spitfire Vb, of the type flown by 52 OTU. (Aeroplane).

be used operationally. No 52 OTU was given the 'shadow' title of 552 Squadron.

Towards the end of 1942 HQ Fighter Command had decided to form a new training organisation for potential fighter squadron flight and unit commanders, to teach them basic combat tactics and to evolve and explore new tactics. This resulted in the formation of the Fighter Leaders School (FLS) within 52 OTU, using the two flights based at Chedworth that dealt with the more advanced training. The first FLS course started at Chedworth on 15 January 1943, and lasted for three weeks. During the first week, individual section tactics were taught, on week two it was squadron and wing tactics, and on week three close support to ground forces. However, Chedworth had insufficient space or accommodation for the new school, and on 9 February, following completion of the first course, the FLS left for Charmy Down in Somerset.

Ten days later Chedworth came under the control of South Cerney. It was then used as a training landing ground by the two South Cerney-based flying training units, Nos 3 and 6 (Pilots) Advance Flying Units ((P)AFUs). The Oxfords of the two units were regular visitors to Chedworth during the spring and summer of 1943, and a detachment of No 6 (P)AFU was based there for a period. This continued into the autumn, but on 18 October responsibility for Chedworth changed once more when Honiley (in Warwickshire) took over as the parent station.

D H Mosquito, as flown by 60/63 OTU. (Aeroplane)

No 2 (Air Gunnery) squadron of No 63 OTU moved in from Honiley and was joined by the Air Gunnery Squadron of 60 OTU, from High Ercall in Shropshire. A combined 60/63 OTU Gunnery Squadron was formed and flew DH Mosquitoes, Bristol Beaufighters and Miles Martinets from the airfield. This continued for the next few months, until January 1944 when the squadrons returned to their home bases.

Like other RAF training stations, Chedworth had its fair share of flying accidents. The first to occur at the airfield was in fact to a visiting aircraft. On 1 June 1943, Armstrong Whitworth Whitley Z9479 of 24 OTU based at Honeyborne in Warwickshire developed engine trouble but its pilot, Flight Sergeant Gillon, managed to crash-land at Chedworth without injury to the crew. On 6 December Bristol Beaufighter T3024 of 63 OTU crashed on landing and on 28 December DH Mosquito H5826 of 60 OTU came down near Abingdon; the aircraft caught fire and the crew, Flying Officers Marcus and Rogers, were both killed. One of 63 OTU's Beaufighters, R2304 caught fire and crashed near Berkeley on 1 January, and in the same period Mosquito HJ814 of 60 OTU was wrecked after overshooting at Chedworth following an engine failure.

Chedworth remained quiet during early 1944, with no units in residence, but the Oxfords of No 3 (P)AFU started to revisit the station in March 1944 for flying training practice. This was because the airspace around South Cerney was becoming very busy due to the station's close proximity to Fairford, Down Ampney, Blakehill Farm and Broadwell, these four airborne forces' support bases being

Bristol Beaufighters were also seen in the circuit at Chedworth. (BAe).

heavily involved in training and preparation for what was to be Operation Overlord, the invasion of Europe. Their squadrons' Dakotas also used Chedworth for training, and it was during a night navigation exercise on 10 April that Dakota KG369 of 512 Squadron, based at Broadwell, struck trees while overshooting and crashed. The crew of four were killed.

Following the successful completion of the Normandy landings the USAAF briefly used Chedworth when the HQ Squadron of the 9th Air Force was based there between 19 June and 9 July 1944. During that time it and the 125th Liaison Squadron flew their Cessna L-4 Cubs and Stinson L-5 Sentinels for communications and liaison work from the airfield.

On 17 July 1944 control of Chedworth was transferred once again, this time back to Aston Down. There, No 3 Tactical Exercise Unit (TEU) was in residence, and the unit started to use Chedworth for flying practice. Within a few days C Squadron of No 3 TEU was detached to Chedworth to be based there; the squadron flew Mustangs for fighter-bomber training. On 18 December 1944 No 3 TEU became 55 OTU, although its role remained that of close support to the Army, specialising in the training of fighter-bomber pilots. Hawker Typhoons were added to the unit's strength and soon over 120

Mustangs and Typhoons were on its complement. This period was probably the busiest for Chedworth, supporting a very busy and active flying training programme, and the station's strength in late 1944 stood at 672 officers and other ranks.

No 3 TEU's debut at Chedworth was accompanied by its first accident there on 28 July, when Mustang FZ138 collided with a truck on take-off and crashed, injuring the pilot. The following day Mustang FB200 was seriously damaged when its undercarriage collapsed on landing. The next Mustang accident on the airfield however, was fatal, when, on 30 July, the engine of FX934 cut out just after take-off, and the aircraft crashed nearby, killing Pilot Officer Walsh. Another undercarriage collapse occurred on 23 September, to Mustang SR414, just before take-off, seriously damaging the aircraft but not the pilot. The last recorded accident at Chedworth was on 18 March 1945 to Typhoon MN146, which overshot on landing, the pilot escaping without injury.

Training continued into the spring of 1945, there being a steady demand for fighter bomber pilots to fly with the front-line squadrons supporting the steady Allied offensive in North-West Europe. However, when the war in Europe came to an end in May 1945, so did the need for more pilots. Flying training at Chedworth ceased on 29 May 1945 and the personnel and aircraft returned to Aston

One of the airfield buildings still in place at Chedworth in 2001. (Steve Lawrence).

Down. The airfield was then placed onto a Care and Maintenance footing.

The Admiralty took an interest in Chedworth in December 1945 and reopened the station for storage. The airfield was also later used by the Central Flying School located at Little Rissington, as an emergency landing ground on which to practice forced-landings away from their main base. A gliding club was established at the airfield in the late 1960s. Chedworth was used for the occasional tactical exercise by Wessex helicopters in the mid 1970s, but by the mid 1980s agriculture was the sole activity at the former airfield. There are still substantial remains of its past in place. A good proportion of the buildings still exist, including one of the two hangars, the battle headquarters, flight office, the armoury, and several buildings on the communal site in Withington Woods.

7
DOWN AMPNEY

6 miles south-east of Cirencester
SU 100965

Although Down Ampney is a quiet Gloucestershire village today, one of its claims to fame is that it was the birthplace of one of Britain's foremost composers, Ralph Vaughan Williams. He named a hymn tune after the village, a setting to the words of *Come Down O Love Divine*. Another of Down Ampney's claims to fame is of a very different nature, that it was the site of an important operational airfield during the Second World War. In 1943 the Government requisitioned farmland at Down Ampney to build a new airfield. This was one of three (the others being Blakehill Farm in Wiltshire and Broadwell in Oxfordshire) to be constructed north of Swindon to house units of No 46 Group, the RAF formation created to bring together the tactical air transport squadrons that were to support the Army in the planned invasion of Europe.

The main contractors for the site, Wimpey Construction, soon got to work. Hedges were removed at Down Ampney and the area cleared of trees so that three runways could be laid down in the traditional 'A' shape typical of many wartime airfields. Aircraft dispersals were arranged all round the site with a T2 squadron hangar to the south of the runways and another, along with a control tower, operational buildings and technical site, on the north-west side. In contrast, the headquarters and domestic buildings seemed, to the new arrivals, to have been jumbled up with the village! The officers' mess was in the orchard behind a farmhouse and the sergeants' mess and accommodation for the various other personnel were provided by Nissen huts arranged in fields around the village.

An opening-up party arrived at Down Ampney on 7 February 1944 from Broadwell and the following day convoys of barrack stores (beds, wardrobes, etc) arrived from the RAF Depot at Newport. Group Captain J. Bradbury, DFC, arrived on 14 February to assume command of the station, and later that day an officer and 50 personnel from 4843 Works Flight, detached from 5019 Airfield Construction Squadron, moved in to carry out the construction of glider marshalling areas. These were laid out at each end of the runway and alongside the dispersals at the western end of the technical site using Pierced Steel Planking (PSP) to protect the ground surface.

The first aircraft to land at the new airfield on 18 February 1944 was the Percival Proctor that brought Air Commodore Fiddament, Air Officer Commanding 46 Group, for a visit. Work rapidly progressed to get the station opened for business and, on 24 February, the advance party of the first flying unit to be based at the new station, No 48 Squadron, arrived by road. The advance party of the second squadron, No 271, came the following day. Both squadrons' main parties, bringing with them their Dakota aircraft, flew in on the 29th. On the same day the fire section opened, with one crash tender!

No 48 Squadron had been a Coastal Command squadron with Lockheed Hudsons, based in Gibraltar until it was recalled to the UK in February 1944. There it was transferred to Transport Command as an airborne forces support squadron with Dakotas. No 271 Squadron was formed at Doncaster as a transport unit in 1940 with Handley Page Harrows, along with Bristol Bombays and a mix of civil aircraft including de Havilland Albatrosses and a Ford Tri-motor.

Handley Page Harrow of 271 Squadron's 'Sparrow Flight'. (Aeroplane)

The Harrow was a high wing, twin-engined monoplane that first flew in 1935. Originally designed as a transport, it was adapted as a bomber due to a shortage of suitable offensive aircraft. It went into service with 214 Squadron at Scampton, Lincolnshire in 1937, but with more purpose-built designs coming along such as the Vickers Wellington, it was replaced in front line service by December 1939. The Harrow was then employed in the role for which it was originally intended, as a transport. With gun turrets and bombing equipment removed, the aircraft would carry 20 troops or 3,000 lbs of freight. The transport version of the type was widely known as the Sparrow. In January 1944, No 271 Squadron also received Dakotas and became an airborne forces support squadron, but a number of Harrows were retained for ambulance flights.

The Dakota was the name used by the RAF for the US C-47 Skytrain, the military version of the Douglas DC-3 airliner. One of the first all-metal, stressed-skin transport aircraft, it was powered by two Pratt and Witney Twin Wasp radial engines. Flown by a crew of four, it could carry 28 fully-equipped troops. Of the 10,123 military DC-3s eventually built, some 1,900 were supplied to the RAF, who used them on every battle-front that it was engaged in during the Second World War. The aircraft was renowned for its toughness and versatility and was well-loved by its crews. The Dakota flew with 30 RAF squadrons during the war, and went on to serve with many more afterwards. The last RAF Dakota was eventually retired in 1970.

After conversion onto the Dakota, the crews of both squadrons undertook continuous flying, including cross-country navigation exercises. They then started training to tow gliders and, as part of this process, pilots were sent to the gliding school at Brize Norton to experience the sensation of flying in a Horsa glider and see things from the glider pilot's point of view. One of the pilots of 271 Squadron was Flight Lieutenant Jimmy Edwards, later to become a well-known comedian. He remembered flying in Horsas as very educational, giving him an appreciation of a glider pilot's problems, but after having had four launches it was not an experience he wanted to repeat! Jimmy Edwards was a member of C Flight, and his flight commander was Pier Joubert, a Major in the South African Air Force. 'Jouby' had flown for many years as a commercial pilot in southern Africa before the war and, although he could have had a quiet time as a flying instructor at home, volunteered for a front line squadron in the UK. He was a good pilot and inspiring leader, well respected by his crews.

On 1 March 1944 Down Ampney was officially opened as a station within 46 Group. Its declared function was, according to the RAF Form 540 (the station's Operations Record Book), no secret – it was 'to be in the air assault role to deliver onto Drop Zones (DZs) and Landing Zones (LZs) part of the airborne force of men and equipment in the forthcoming second front, to deliver reinforcements in the air trooping role, to deliver by air supplies to forward landing grounds and to drop supplies by parachute or free; these tasks to be carried out by day and night'. Although at that stage the airfield was still incomplete, it was to be operational within twelve weeks. Form 540 comments that 'the buildings were only half finished, the runways and roads cut out of virgin farmland barely recognisable, but the urgency of the times decreed that Down Ampney, along with its sister stations, was to have first priority with its demands for weapons, equipment and personnel'. And so, with that typical British way of giving of its best when hard pressed, Down Ampney with its handful of pioneers was soon to become a hive of activity.

Practice flying had started shortly after both squadrons' arrival in order to keep men and machines in peak condition. However, several taxiing accidents occurred on the airfield due to the presence of mounds of earth and contractors' vehicles on the runways and taxiways. A Station Flight was set up with a number of Airspeed Oxfords, which as well as general communications was also used by the Dakota squadrons for navigation and radar training. The first gliders arrived at Down Ampney on 15 March, and on the following day so did No 91 Staging Post. This unit was to establish medical facilities at the airfield that were capable of being taken into the field for the treatment and evacuation of casualties from the battle front. A few days later the station's team spirit was shown when its football team's first game was played against another station – although it lost 1-0 to Aston Down. On 22 March the first ground defence personnel arrived, from 2727 and 2605 Field Squadrons of the RAF Regiment.

By mid-March 1944 there were some 3,500 personnel stationed at Down Ampney. Both squadrons were up to full strength, No 271 having 38 Dakotas and 19 Horsa gliders on inventory. However, having taken them on charge, the Dakotas had to be sent away again in batches to Hendon where they were modified with the required glider-towing and paratroop-dropping fixtures and fittings. Night flying practice started on 24 March using goose-neck flares to illuminate the runways and approaches.

The first accident to one of Down Ampney's aircraft occurred shortly afterwards, on 25 March, when two Dakotas collided near Blakehill

Farm. One aircraft managed to return to base but the other crashed, killing its crew. Two days later an Oxford of the Station Flight crashed. It was flying near Little Rissington in bad weather and had to make a forced landing but hit a building – there were no survivors. One of the first visiting aircraft from the USAAF arrived at Down Ampney on 30 March. This was a Republic P-47 Thunderbolt with undercarriage problems, but its pilot was able to make a successful belly landing on the grass beside the main runway.

The squadron crews spent much time on glider towing training and, to acquire the required skills, travelled to the Operational and Refresher Training Unit at Hampstead Norris, north-east of Newbury. They learnt that there were several tricky moments during take-off with a Horsa in tow. The first of these was when the slack in the tow cable had to be taken up very gradually until it was taut. This would be indicated by a marshall with signalling flags and by the glider pilot, who talked to the training tug pilot by intercom wire in the cable. The tug pilot then had to open his throttles gradually but steadily until, on full power, the Dakota's tail lifted. If he accelerated too quickly, the tow cable could snap or be pulled out of the glider. The glider would be airborne before the tug, and its pilot would have to keep his aircraft about 20 feet above the tug to avoid its slipstream (if he flew higher, the glider could lift the tug's tail, so that the tug's nose dropped and it wouldn't get off the ground). The glider would then take up station behind the tug, but above its slipstream. On reaching the LZ the glider pilot released the cable and proceeded in to land. The tug could then either drop the tow cable at a pre-determined dropping point alongside the LZ, or take it back to base.

To learn how to drop paratroops the crew visited RAF Netheravon, one of the airborne forces training centres. There they dropped sticks of experienced paratroopers over established training DZs. Paratroop-dropping presented different problems. The main requirement was that the aircraft had to be brought over the DZ at the correct height (usually 500 feet) and at the right speed (about 70 knots for a Dakota). The aircraft also had to be at the correct attitude, which was nose-down, so that as the paratroops jumped out of the door, they went under the tailplane and not into it. This called for precise flying by the pilot and nerves of steel, particularly under fire as the Dakotas presented an easy target from the ground. Accidents happened during training and during C Flight's time at Netheravon, one trooper, the last of his stick, got his static line caught. He fell through the door and was left dangling. As luck would have it, the aircraft was carrying extra crew members and together they were able to haul the unfortunate man back inside. The paratrooper turned out to be the unit padre, and rather than be returned to earth by Dakota, he asked the pilot to go round again, so that he could join his flock! The pilot was taken aback but obliged the padre, who made a successful jump.

Major exercises took place in April, the first on the 9th when 35 Dakotas towing gliders flew a navigational exercise around central England. The Down Ampney squadrons also took part in a major paratroop-dropping exercise on 21 April involving more than 700 aircraft. On 25 April a mass take-off demonstration was given to AOC 46 Group, with 40 Dakotas towing 40 Horsa gliders. It took 27 minutes for the whole formation to manoeuvre into position and take off, but that time was soon to be bettered.

That evening the Down Ampney crews took part in the first of a series of exercises code-named Bullseye, which were intended to improve their night navigation skills. They flew from Down Ampney to Salisbury in Wiltshire, then to Boscastle in Cornwall before returning to base. At various stages they made prearranged passes over searchlight batteries to experience searchlight coning (i.e. being picked up in a number of searchlights, working together with AA batteries) and how to evade them.

The squadrons flew their first operational missions in late April. These were code-named 'Nickelling' sorties, which involved crossing the Channel and dropping propaganda leaflets over occupied France. They gave useful opportunities to practice night navigation over enemy-held territory in a relatively low risk fashion.

However, Nickelling was not without its moments! The Dakotas used the Gee system to navigate their way around. This employed radio transmissions to produce a pattern of signals that would give the receiving aircraft its position. On the evening that Jimmy Edwards and crew set off in Dakota KG444, named *The Pie-eyed Piper of Barnes*, all went well after take-off and they crossed the French coast. Flying at 8,000 feet and heading for Tours in the Touraine, Harry Green, the navigator, reported to Edwards that the Gee was jammed and that he couldn't get any signals. Jimmy decided to press on and when they thought that they were in the vicinity of their target, they dropped the pamphlets and turned back. They headed north on the basis that they must hit England eventually and flew on in silence.

After a couple of hours the lights of an aerodrome appeared. The whole place was lit up and the searchlights around the perimeter made a cone at 2,000 feet, which was standard practice in the UK as an indication to aircraft which had lost its radio or bearings. The airfield looked very inviting but Jimmy Edwards was uneasy, because no code signals were being flashed by the control tower. Edwards transmitted on the Darky frequency – an emergency request for bearings or landing information, but got no response. Despite the protests of his crew, Jimmy Edward decided to head north, until he was positive that they were over England. After they had been airborne for six hours, the horizon began to lighten and they could make out the coastline ahead – but where were they?

Once across the coast they found an airfield and having spotted the code letters 'TR' beside the control tower, realised that they were over Tarrant Rushton in Dorset. From there they easily found the way back to Down Ampney and landed with great relief. It transpired that the wind had swung round 180 degrees and sent them further south than they had intended – they had delivered the leaflets to the Pyrenees! Edwards was criticised for not turning back when his Gee was declared unserviceable but complimented for not landing at the first aerodrome that he saw, as it was German base near Cherbourg, lit up to lure Allied pilots in to land.

Training continued into May and intensified with exercises such as Confirmation II when, on the night of the 5th/6th, 15 aircraft of 48 Squadron and 15 of 271 Squadron, together with aircraft from Broadway and Blakehill Farm took part in practice pinpoint drops. Each was to drop a container at a given DZ in moonlight but without drop aids, such as flares or lights. Later that day a massed take-off of 20 Dakotas and gliders was laid on for Air Chief Marshal Sir Leigh Mallory, Commander-in-Chief, Allied Expeditionary Air Force. A major exercise was then mounted every few days throughout May, and interspersed with these were squadron night-flying, cross-country or navigational sorties.

Flying was occasionally curtailed because of the weather and once, on 15 May, because of advance radar warnings of enemy aircraft movements near the coast. On 20 May the flying was interrupted by the arrival of a Whitley at Down Ampney that made an emergency landing with its port engine on fire. The next day Exercise Consternation involved taking 75 Horsas to Netheravon, where they had to be landed within ten minutes. The Dakotas then returned to base to drop their tow ropes before continuing on Exercise Gulliver, a cross-country and wireless transmission exercise taking them to Warminster, Newquay, the Isles of Scilly, Isle of Man, and Rhyl

Douglas Dakota of 271 Squadron. (Aeroplane)

before returning to base. Medical orderlies were taken on these exercises to give them experience of long flights.

On 27 May 1944 training was considered complete and all flying training from Down Ampney ceased. The tension at this time must have been palpable, as all squadron and station personnel must have been aware that momentous events were about to unfold. Suspicions that something was going on were confirmed in early June when an instruction was issued that all aircrew moustaches were to be shaved off. The station intelligence officer had arranged for photographs to be taken of all personnel who might be captured behind enemy lines so that they could be quickly pasted into false identity papers supplied by the French Resistance. It was felt that moustaches looked too British, especially the 'handlebar' ones that typified RAF officers. Jimmy Edwards had a splendid example of such a one (as he did later, as a comedian) and with due ceremony, it was shaved off.

On 2 June at 14.00 hours all living-out personnel were brought onto the station, which was then sealed by armed guards who were told to let no one in (or out!). Briefings were then given to squadron personnel on Operation Tonga, the airborne landings that were to take place in

Normandy as part of the invasion of occupied Europe. The Down Ampney squadrons were part of a wider plan entailing the attack by parachute and glider borne troops on selected objectives inland from the invasion beaches. British paratroops were to land to the east, and US paratroops to the west, in order to protect the flanks from German counter-attacks so that a beachhead could be established and consolidated. These landings were originally to take place on the night of 4 June but with 24 hours' notice were postponed because of the bad weather until the following night. On the morning of Sunday, 4 June church services were held and in the afternoon a gramophone recital of *The Pirates of Penzance* was held in the NAAFI.

The air over southern England, the Channel and northern France was going to be full of aeroplanes and to ease identification, orders were issued for all Allied aircraft to be painted with black and white stripes on the rear fuselage forward of the tail plane and on the wings outboard of the engines (or on the outer-wing panels in the case of gliders). This had to be kept secret until the last possible minute and was not therefore made known until the evening of 3 June, which gave little time for all of Down Ampney's aircraft to be painted. Volunteers were called for, and so all available personnel, including the aircrew, rallied round to help. Armed with large paintbrushes, everyone headed out to the dispersals. While someone measured out the areas to be marked, others stirred the paint, boarded the ladders and got to work, sploshing liberal amounts of black and white paint onto the airframes (and not a few uniforms).

To keep aircrews occupied during the delay period, they were taken by coach to Netheravon, Headquarters 38 Group. There in the operations room they saw the large-scale model of the Normandy coastline used for planning the build-up to D-Day (as it was to be called). Every farm or hamlet was shown, along with the German defences. The crews of both squadrons were addressed by the Commander in Chief of Transport Command, Air Chief Marshal Sir Frederick Bowhill, who wished them well.

A transit camp of bell tents and marquees had been set up beside the airfield at Down Ampney to house the troops of 6 Airborne Division who were to be flown into battle by 48 and 271 Squadrons. On returning from Netheravon, the aircrews found that even more tents had appeared between their Nissen huts and the airfield. Troops were everywhere, preparing their weapons and equipment ready for action.

Leading Aircraftsman Alan Hartley, an engine-fitter with 271 Squadron, remembers the preparations for D-Day and painting the black and white stripes on the aircraft. At about 06.00 on the 6th, while on the dispersal preparing for take-off, someone cried, 'Here, look at this lot,' as marching around the perimeter track to board their aircraft came troops of the 1st Canadian Parachute Battalion. They had cropped their hair like Cherokee Indians and daubed black and white paint on their faces. As well as their equipment, many carried large knives. They looked fearsome and Alan and the rest of his crew were happier to help them depart rather than have them arrive!

As the villagers and townsfolk of north-east Wiltshire, north-west Oxfordshire and southern Gloucestershire prepared for bed on the evening of 5 June, the silence was broken by the sound of 216 Dakota engines starting up on the three airfields of 46 Group. Aircrews went through their pre-take-off checks as their aircraft taxied into position. Operation Tonga began from Down Ampney at 22.48 hours that night, as the first 46 Dakotas of 48 and 271 Squadrons took off carrying paratroops of the 1st Canadian Parachute Battalion and Headquarters troops of 3rd Parachute Brigade. Because of the congestion at Down Ampney some of 271 Squadron's Dakotas (A Flight) were deployed to Blakehill Farm, and flew from there. The first wave of seven Dakotas to take off were towing Horsa gliders. These were followed at 23.20 hours by 39 Dakotas carrying paratroops.

The Headquarters troops of 3rd Parachute Brigade under Brigadier J. Hill were to be landed on DZ 'K', to secure the area and set up their headquarters. Troops of the 1st Canadian Parachute Battalion were to land on DZ 'V', then to capture and destroy the two bridges to the east, over the river Devre at Varaville and Robenhomme, to prevent the Germans crossing the river onto the beachhead. Pathfinders had been dropped ahead of the main airborne landings to mark out the DZs and LZs with lights and radar beacons. Unfortunately, some of the equipment was lost during the drop, and some DZs were wrongly marked – DZ 'N' was marked up as 'K' for example.

The gliders started to arrive overhead at 00.45 hours, and were released successfully onto their LZs. With the gliders safely on the ground, they were followed by the main contingent of paratroops, who started to jump at 00.56 hours. Although the majority of the paratroops made it onto the correct DZs, a good number were scattered, including Brigadier Hill who landed two miles away from his DZ in a marshy area that had been flooded by the Germans. The troops with him had to ditch their heavy equipment to avoid drowning, and it then took them several hours to reach their Rendezvous (RV) at the DZ.

Meanwhile, the Canadians had been scattered. Lieutenant Norman

Roseland of B Company, 1st Canadian Paras, gathered his men and stragglers from other units and, with the assistance of a French girl who acted as a guide, made his way to Robenhomme Bridge. There they met some sappers, but they had lost most of their equipment. Together the troops managed to find enough explosives to blow up the bridge. C Company 1st Canadian Paras, whose target was Varaville, had gathered on their DZ, but suffered casualties when the area was hit by Allied bombers. Major Murray McLeod and his remaining men headed towards the village. Collecting supplies on the way, they reached Varaville but when they tried to get to the bridge, were pinned down by enemy fire. Eventually a section led by Captain John Hanson managed to get through to the bridge and demolish it. Later that morning, despite being outnumbered by enemy troops in prepared fortifications, the remnants of C Company took the village. Sadly, Major McLeod was killed in the process.

Jimmy Edwards' part in the operation was to tow one of the seven Horsas (carrying a contingent of Canadians) with his Dakota. Having got to the vicinity of the LZ they couldn't locate it, but when the two aircraft came under enemy AA fire, the glider pilot pulled the release and headed for the ground. Edwards returned to base, but on the approach to Down Ampney found that the ground fire had damaged the Dakota's hydraulics. The crew had to pump the undercarriage down and he made an emergency landing without flaps on the grass beside the main runway.

Along with the other crews returning in the early hours of the 6th, Edwards' crew was debriefed, fed and rested, while their aircraft was checked and refuelled ready for the next phase of the assault. This was Operation Mallard, which was a mass uplift of gliderborne troops for a landing to the east of the river Orne bridge to protect the eastern flank of the beachhead. At 18.40 hours, 15 Dakotas from 271 Squadron and 22 of 48 Squadron started taking off, towing 37 Horsas carrying two companies of the 1st Royal Ulster Rifles and troops of 6 Air Landing Brigade. The weather was fine and the visibility good, so that the troops could enjoy the impressive sight of the invasion fleet as they crossed the Channel.

As they neared the French coast, the Orme river and the Caen canal that ran alongside it could easily be seen, pointing towards their LZ. The gliders were released at 21.00 hours, and all but a few landed successfully on target. One of the 48 Squadron aircraft was hit by flak and had to ditch (the pilot and co-pilot escaped successfully but unfortunately the wireless operator did not).

The third mission of D-Day was Operation Rob Roy, a re-supply to the troops in the beachhead. Ten Dakotas from 271 and 48 Squadrons took off in the evening, at 22.25 hours to drop supplies by parachute. They arrived over the DZ at 23.50 hours, dropped the supplies without any interference from ground-fire or enemy fighters, and were back in the circuit at Down Ampney by 01.19 hours.

After the intense activity and excitement of the D-Day operations, the most extraordinary thing happened at Down Ampney on the 7th – nothing! Apparently, because everything went so well on the day and the objectives were achieved without reinforcements or additional equipment being required, the Down Ampney Dakotas weren't to be needed. There were no operations on 7 June, and on the 8th both squadrons were stood down until 13 June.

When landing strips had been established in Normandy, the Dakota squadrons started to fly supplies in; they then brought casualties out, thus beginning their 'cas-evac' role. The first casualties were flown back to Down Ampney on 18 June when 183 patients arrived from Normandy. The next day crews based at Blakehill Farm brought back 90 injured men, and eleven Down Ampney aircraft were tasked to collect RAF personnel from Tangmere and take them to Airstrip B4 at Beny-sur-Mer, one of the temporary landing strips in the Allied beachhead. On the return from B4 the eleven aircraft were carrying 183 battlefield casualties for treatment in the UK. Ninety more arrived on 21 June and this set the pattern for the next few weeks, with cargo and passengers being transported to Normandy and casualties brought back on the return flights. Nursing orderlies were carried on the aircraft and, on arrival at the forward airstrips; they supervised the loading and securing of their patients, each plane being able to carry 18 stretcher cases and six sitting casualties. The men would have had emergency treatment in the field for their injuries, and during the flight home the nursing orderly would monitor their condition.

On arrival at Down Ampney the men were taken to the Casualty Air Evacuation Centre (CAEC). One of these had been set up at each of the three 46 Group airfields to unload, attend to, classify and reload the casualties received. The Centres were staffed by medical personnel who would assess the injuries on arrival before allocation to the appropriate specialised hospital. All the soldiers were recently wounded and many were in urgent need of surgery, having received only basic treatment in the field hospitals. Casualties with burns were then taken to Odstock, near Salisbury, head injuries went to St Dunstan's, near Oxford, and spinal or serious skin injuries went to

RAF Dakotas flew on transport schedules between Down Ampney and other UK stations such as Croydon (above) as well as to the Continent. (Aeroplane)

Stoke Mandeville, near Aylesbury. Others, whose condition had stabilised or improved, were taken to various hospitals or Casualty Clearing Stations (CCS) for more routine treatment.

Of the first batch of casualties received (on 18 June), half were sent to Wroughton RAF hospital and half to Swindon CCS. On 27 June, 233 casualties were received but, by 17 July, the numbers stabilised to around 100 per day, arriving on three Dakotas at 12.30 and three at 19.00. Casualties often arrived back in the UK within 24 hours of being wounded (sometimes within twelve hours) and if seriously ill were in a hospital ward two hours after touching down at Down Ampney. The knowledge that such swift and reasonably comfortable evacuation to England by air awaited a man should he be wounded must have been a potent factor in the maintenance of morale. The alternative journey by land and sea would have taken three to seven days and probably resulted in many of the casualties dying on the way.

On 24 June, ten aircraft from Down Ampney moved personnel and equipment of 122 Wing, a Typhoon unit, from Ford in Sussex to B6 airfield at Coulombs in Normandy. The Dakotas returned to Ford the following day, when eleven aircraft picked up the personnel and stores of No 125 (Spitfire) Wing and took them to B11 at Longues. The next day 16 aircraft flew to Hurn to collect stores for B9. On each return trip the Down Ampney aircraft brought casualties home.

On 2 July 1944 a daily shuttle service was set up between Down Ampney and Northolt to collect passengers from Normandy, the aircraft leaving Down Ampney at 11.00, collecting at Northolt and flying to Normandy where it overnighted before returning at 08.00 the following day for Northolt, and return to Down Ampney. This pattern of scheduled flights, freight shuttles and casualty evacuations continued throughout the rest of July and August. The destinations in France increased as the Allied footholds increased. On 22 August Jimmy Edwards was the first to land at Carpiquet (Caen Airport), although he had to overfly the runway to frighten away the cattle before he could touch down. On 27 August the squadrons flew into Orleans.

With all the routine flying going on, it was obviously felt that the pilots' skills at glider-towing should not be lost. On 4 July Exercise Balbo was mounted at Down Ampney. This entailed the towing and release of gliders by 20 Dakotas (ten from each squadron). Normal services also took place on this day, with two aircraft of 271 Squadron taking medical supplies and plasma to B8, returning with 18 and 22 casualties, and one aircraft of 271 Squadron taking 3,700 lbs of mortar ammunition and supplies to B8 and returning with General Browning and six of his staff, along with one stretcher case.

By mid July all blood and most of the penicillin required by the British field hospitals in Normandy was flown in by the RAF, most of it from the cold-rooms of the CAECs, where medical supplies were stored. The 3,000th wounded man to be landed at Down Ampney arrived on 20 July. The first US casualty was received at the CAEC on 25 July – an American soldier who had been knocked down by a British vehicle outside the RAF hospital in Normandy!

No 1697 Flight started operating from Down Ampney on 25 July, having moved from its base at Northolt. This unit was originally set up as an Air Despatch Letter Service Flight, to carry confidential orders and correspondence, flying Hurricanes and Beaufighters. It also flew Ansons on a VIP passenger service to the Continent. A couple of days later, more Ansons appeared at Down Ampney, with 48 Squadron, to start a passenger and freight service to Airfield B14 Amblie. The Ansons were also used on the occasional casualty evacuation flight.

On 29 July the 10,000th casualty to be evacuated by 46 Group from Normandy reached Down Ampney. He was Trooper F.H. Davis of the Inns of Court Regiment, Royal Armoured Corps; he had landed in

Normandy with his regiment by sea on 1 July and was wounded at Creuilly almost a month later. Navigation exercises continued during this time; on 3 August, for instance, Exercise Extraction involved a flight to Netheravon. There paratroops were picked up and flown to Thame, where they were dropped on a DZ, whereupon the Dakotas returned to base.

As the Allies moved forward the re-supplies by air followed them not only to forward airfields such as B14, but also by parachute to such locations as Vannes and Chamboise. On 21 August, six aircraft from 48 Squadron and four from 271 Squadron flew to Chamboise with 48,462 lbs of artillery ammunition. As they flew toward their objective the weather conditions were poor, with rain from a cloud base of 400 feet and visibility dropping to a quarter of a mile. They also encountered moderate flak, but it was inaccurate and didn't impede their progress.

The pilot of the first aircraft (KG421), Wing Commander Sproule (OC of 48 Squadron) spotted flares on the DZ and made his run in. As he did so the flak intensified and the slow-moving Dakota started to receive hits. Several bursts exploded through the cabin windows and the floor, damaging the engines. Every member of the crew was wounded by shell splinters and with the engines losing power, Sproule decided to make for B14. With the rudder put out of action, he tried to maintain his course by varying power between the engines, while the despatchers pushed the supply containers out of the cargo door. After taking further bursts of flak the aircraft hit the tops of some trees, but Sproule managed to bring the aircraft safely down into a field on a hilltop to the west of Jurques. Fearing an explosion, the four aircraft despatchers, who were the least wounded, assisted the rest of the crew to get away from the aircraft. They made for the trees where they built a shelter from the rain. Having rested up, the crew managed to make their way towards Allied lines, and after three hours they made contact with British troops who took them to Airfield B14.

Casualty evacuations continued and by early August, some 20,000 had been brought back to the 46 Group CAECs at Broadwell, Blakehill Farm and Down Ampney. On 8 August, due to a major action, the stations were warned to receive 1,000 casualties that day. By 18.00 hours, 527 wounded were already at Down Ampney, completely filling the available accommodation. The loading of ambulances to get the men away for treatment continued through the night, until 03.00 the following morning.

On 27 August a Servicing Wing was established at Down Ampney to improve the serviceability of the station's aircraft. The new Wing included the station's workshops, Nos 4808 and 4271 Servicing Echelons, one to look after each Dakota squadron, and Nos 12 and 13 Glider Servicing Echelons to support the Horsas. At the beginning of September an Allied logistics crisis occurred, when the fuel supply through the Pipe-Line Under The Ocean (PLUTO) was interrupted due to a fault. This pipeline supplied fuel across the Channel for the Allied armies, which would be brought to a halt unless something was done. The Down Ampney squadrons, along with the rest of 46 Group, were therefore immediately switched onto fuel delivery and, while the fault was being rectified, spent several days carrying jerrycans of petrol to Evere and Moelsbrook airfields near Brussels.

Transport and casualty operations continued throughout early September but on 15 September these were stopped and the station was closed to outgoing flights and passengers, and to incoming casualties. This was because the station's squadrons were to prepare for their next major venture, Operation Market, the airborne phase of the Allied thrust across the Rhine at Arnhem in Holland, Operation Market Garden.

The plan involved simultaneous airborne assaults on the bridges at Eindhoven, Grave, Nijmegen and Arnhem. US Airborne forces were to take the first three; while British paratroops were to take the most northerly objective, the Arnhem bridge. An Allied Armoured thrust was to then link up with the paratroops and cross the Rhine, leaving the gateway open to Germany. The plan was to relieve the British Airborne force within four days.

On 17 September 1944, 49 aircraft took off from Down Ampney, towing Horsas to LZs to the north-west of Arnhem. It took 34 minutes for the force to take-off. Before setting course the aircraft climbed to 10,000 feet, but then had to descend as they flew south due to heavy cloud. As they approached Oxford, five of the gliders released themselves and another was released by the tug captain when his Dakota was forced into an uncontrollable dive. These gliders all made successful emergency landings although there was one fatality amongst the crews.

As the formation appeared over Arnhem there was no enemy air opposition and little flak. The remaining gliders were released over the LZ at 2,500 feet and 39 of them landed successfully. A total of 542 troops, 19 jeeps and trailers, a 15 cwt truck, four 6 pdr AT guns, 34 motorbikes and other equipment was successfully landed on the LZ, a lift of 261,560 lbs in weight. The second lift made the next day involved 50 aircraft from Down Ampney towing Horsas to the same LZs. The weather was hazy and slight flak was experienced near the cast-off point, but the gliders were released successfully. This time they landed 285 troops, 30 jeeps, 50 trailers, ten 5 cwt cars, 20 motorbikes, two 6 pdr AT guns and other equipment (a total of 326,154 lbs in weight).

On day three of the operation, 19 September, 32 Dakotas took off from the station with 16 panniers in each aircraft and headed to Arnhem DZ 'V' with a supply of ammunition and food for the troops. One aircraft towing a Horsa left over from the previous day's roster also flew across (the glider subsequently landed successfully, although the tug was damaged by gunfire). The weather was poor, with 10/10th cloud cover for most of the flight over, improving towards the target, but with thick haze. Medium flak was experienced as the formation neared the DZ (which by then was occupied by German troops, although the RAF crews didn't realise this at the time). On the run-in the aircraft captained by Flight Lieutenant Hollom was hit in the port engine and badly damaged to the extent that it needed to make an emergency landing at B56 (Brussels Levere) on the return flight. Seven other aircraft were also damaged and five were shot down, three from 271 Squadron – Flight Lieutenant Lord, Flight Lieutenant Wilson and Flying Officer Mott – and two from 48 Squadron, captained by Pilot Officer Christie and Flying Officer Pattee.

Flying Officer Pattee of 48 Squadron was flying KG401. After making their way through heavy cloud and avoiding other formations of aircraft, he and his crew arrived over the DZ at 5,000 feet. Due to flak they were forced to weave, then turned to starboard and completed an 'S' turn to approach the DZ. As visibility was poor down to 2,000 feet they couldn't identify the DZ until it was too late, so tried to rejoin the stream to try again. Encountering small arms fire, they managed to maintain a height of 1,200 feet and dropped their panniers. As they pulled away, the aircraft came under intense enemy fire. The tail unit was hit, jamming the rudder and damaging the port elevator. The port engine was hit, and the starboard fuel tank. Most of the cockpit instruments were then knocked out as the fuselage was raked with machine gun fire. One of the despatchers was mortally wounded.

Flying Officer Pattee pointed the aircraft's nose down and managed to level the aircraft at 800 feet, flying at 95 mph. He opened up the throttle and got up to 1,500 feet but KG401 was hit by flak again, in the port wing and the fuselage, and a fire started in the starboard engine. Pattee coaxed the aircraft along, trying to avoid landing in enemy territory. With some twelve miles to go, more hits resulted in smoke, and then fire, in the cockpit and cabin. At last he spotted the Albert canal, which marked the limit of Allied lines. Once across the canal, enemy fire ceased. Flying Officer Patee tried to gain height for the crew to parachute out but no one wanted to leave the aircraft, so he descended through the mist to select a suitable landing area. Houses started to appear, but he pulled the nose up and managed to avoid them as he put KG401 down in a field. The crew evacuated the cabin in seconds as flames enveloped the aircraft. They had landed on the outskirts of Kesel at about 16.10 hours, and soon many helpful Belgians arrived, followed by Allied troops. Despite receiving medical attention the wounded despatcher died. The remaining crew returned to Down Ampney the following day.

Meanwhile, running into the DZ zone at 15.00 hours that afternoon, the aircraft flown by Flight Lieutenant David Lord of 271 Squadron was hit as heavy AA fire tore into his formation of Dakotas. Two hits on the starboard wing caused the engine to burst into flames as the despatchers were preparing to push the cargo out of the main door. Lord would have been justified in abandoning his run at that point, but he refused to do this and maintained his course, descending to 900 feet for the three minute run-in to the DZ. Despite more hits on his aircraft, and having made his run, Lord was informed that due to damaged rollers, two panniers remained in the aircraft. Aware that the paras on the ground were desperately short of supplies, and in spite of the fact that the aircraft was badly damaged he turned in for another run.

The Dakota took more hits on the second run, so with the remaining panniers finally dropped, Lord ordered the crew to bail out. However, a few seconds later the starboard wing collapsed and the aircraft ploughed into the ground in flames, just north of Reijiers-Camp Farm on the edge of the DZ. There was only one survivor of the crew (the navigator, Flying Officer Harry King), who was thrown out of the aircraft's cargo door as he was assisting the crew members into their parachutes.

David Lord and his crew's selfless act of bravery was witnessed by many troops on the ground, who stood up in their trenches to will them on, moved by this tremendous display of courage on their behalf. For his act of supreme valour and self-sacrifice, Flight Lieutenant David Lord was posthumously awarded the Victoria Cross. The award was not in fact made until after the war as Flying Officer King and many other witnesses of the event were taken prisoner by the Germans. It was only when Harry King made his delayed report to the Officer

The action over Arnhem is depicted in this atmospheric painting by Michael Turner, which shows a Dakota dropping supplies over the DZ under fire. (M.Turner)

Commanding 271 Squadron in 1945 that the decoration was recommended. Flight Lieutenant David Lord is buried in the Commonwealth War Graves Commission cemetery at Arnhem, close to his crew (Pilot Officers Medhurst and Ballantyne, along with RASC Air Despatchers Corporal Nixon, Private Harper and Drivers Ricketts and Rowbotham). He remains the only member of Transport Command to have been awarded the VC.

Later on the 19th, 20 of Down Ampney's Dakotas flew petrol to D56 and D58, but the following day they were rostered to fly another re-supply mission to Arnhem. The plan called for 32 aircraft to drop 512 panniers to 1st Airborne Division on DZ 'V'. All of the aircraft reached the DZ successfully and dropped their panniers from 1,000 feet right on target. A fighter escort had been provided but no enemy aircraft were sighted. There was light opposition from the ground in the form of machine guns and flak. Several aircraft were hit and one suffered the loss of an engine, but all returned safely to base.

The Down Ampney crews were not so lucky on 21 September when a further re-supply drop was mounted. This time 25 crews flew again to DZ 'V' to drop panniers, but experienced heavy flak on the run-in from the north-east. Unfortunately there was no fighter escort in the vicinity of the DZ and it was at this point that several Focke-Wulf Fw 190s and Messerschmitt Bf 109s appeared. The Dakotas were easy targets, and KG340, flown by Pilot Officer Cuer of 271 Squadron, was immediately shot down.

Shortly after the drop, as Warrant Officer Webb took his aircraft up to 4,000 feet, it was hit by cannon fire. When a Fw 190 flew past the starboard wing he realised that his Dakota was being pursued by fighters. The navigator got into the astrodome and spotted a gaggle of 15 Fw 190s on the port quarter, some of which were coming in to attack. There were another ten Fw 190s to starboard and 1,000 feet above in line astern, and the first of these was also peeling off to attack. The Dakota pilot immediately took evasive action, turning towards the fighters as they made their approach, with the result that only a few hits were registered. However, these started a fire under the wing centre section.

Warrant Officer Webb managed to find some cloud cover but this soon evaporated and ten of the Fw 190s were again seen 1,000 feet above on the port side. As they dived in to attack, the Dakota again took evasive action but two of the fighters scored hits, causing the fire to extend to the starboard engine. The aircraft went into a steep dive with the pilot fighting the controls. The navigator, Pilot Officer Clarke, ordered the wireless operators and air despatchers to bail out, informed the pilot, then fought his way to the door of the diving aircraft and bailed out himself. The Fw 190s continued to attack the Dakota as it dived and six of the fighters turned their attentions to the descending parachutists. By hauling in the lift webs, Pilot Officer Clarke realised that he could swing violently to one side and in this way managed to survive two passes by the Fw 190s. On the third pass the fighter's wing-tip passed within two feet of his parachute and Clarke could clearly see the German pilot laughing.

The aircraft's slipstream caused the parachute to collapse and Clarke dropped like a stone until at 500 feet above the ground it redeployed and he landed safely. While disengaging from his harness he saw four of the Fw 190s returning and he rolled to one side as cannon shells tore into the grass five yards away. The German fighters departed when Allied AA guns opened up on them. Clarke was taken by local Dutch civilians to a farmhouse and later reunited with the survivors of his crew. The air despatchers had all been wounded by the Fw 190s and one of them died shortly afterwards. The wireless operator, Warrant Officer Birlinson, had also been killed in the attack. The Dakota's pilot, Warrant Officer Webb and co-pilot, Flight Sergeant Plear were killed when the aircraft dived into the ground.

As Flight Lieutenant Mott flew in over the DZ he saw two other aircraft on fire and being abandoned by their crews. Having successfully dropped his panniers, his Dakota was hit in the tail by tracer, but he managed to clear the area and headed for Nijmegen. He was then attacked by two Fw 190s, resulting in loss of control and a rapid reduction in power from the engines. As the aircraft descended it was attacked again, so Mott ordered the crew to bail out. He followed the others out of the door and his parachute partially opened and was damaged by the tail, but all the crew landed safely in Allied territory and returned to Down Ampney within a couple of days. Three other crews weren't quite so lucky.

Flight Lieutenant Jimmy Edwards climbed away to 8,000 feet in his aircraft KG444, having successfully made his drop, and settled down on a course for home. He had just passed over Eindhoven when the aircraft was attacked from behind by Fw 190s. Jimmy immediately took evasive action and tried to find some cloud cover, but was attacked again from the port side and behind, resulting in the loss of control. When the starboard engine burst into flames, he ordered the crew to bail out. The co-pilot and navigator jumped but as Edwards made his

Dakota of the Battle of Britain Memorial Flight in 2003, marked up as David Lord's Dakota of 271 Squadron. (DGB)

way through the cabin he found that three of the air despatchers were wounded and that the wireless operator and fourth air despatcher had remained in the aircraft to help them. Jimmy returned to the flight deck and decided to crash-land the aircraft in order to give the others a chance of survival.

By this time flames were enveloping the cockpit and Jimmy couldn't see through the windscreen. He yanked open the escape hatch in the roof, stood in his seat and stuck his head out so that he was able to judge his height above the ground. He pulled the aircraft's nose up as it was heading towards some trees, then it crashed into the forest. As luck would have it, the Dakota had landed in an area of saplings, and their progress was slowed. As the aircraft came to a stop Jimmy was thrown from the hatch and landed beside the fuselage. The wireless operator and one of the air despatchers also managed to get out of the aircraft but the three wounded men died in the crash.

The survivors ran for cover as the Fw 190 returned to finish them off, but the German fighter only fired four cannon rounds before running out of ammunition and flying off. After hiding in the forest and avoiding capture by German troops searching the area, the three airmen were picked up by the Dutch Resistance. Jimmy's wounds were treated by a local doctor and they were taken by their rescuers to the

Allied lines. After treatment Jimmy eventually rejoined the squadron at Down Ampney and was awarded the Distinguished Flying Cross for his actions.

Flight Lieutenant Finlay's aircraft was also intercepted in the same area as that of Flight Lieutenant Edwards. He was flying north of the Eindhoven area at 4,000 feet when he heard on the radio that other aircraft had been attacked by enemy fighters, then saw three Dakotas being pursued by eight Fw 190s. Several of the German fighters broke off and headed towards him. As they neared, Flight Lieutenant Finlay started taking evasive action, but the fighters scored several hits on the transport aircraft. Its starboard fuel tank then caught fire, followed by the starboard wing, then the fuselage. The air despatchers couldn't remain in the fuselage, so they bailed out.

With both engines now on fire, Finlay ordered the remaining crew members to crash positions, and looked for a suitable landing site. He found a field, but a large tree loomed into view and the Dakota hit it about 20 feet from the ground. The nose caved in and the burning aircraft dropped to the ground. However, the crew all escaped successfully from the wreckage and were picked up by troops of the 11th Armoured Division who were in the area. They were given initial treatment for their wounds, then taken to the nearest field dressing station, where they were reunited with the four air despatchers who had jumped. The crew returned to Down Ampney on a 48 Squadron Dakota from B56 (Evere) the following day.

The aircraft flown by Squadron Leader Duff-Mitchell was severely damaged by flak, but the pilot managed to nurse it back to B56, where he crash-landed, without injury to the crew. Another Dakota, flown by Flight Lieutenant Beddow, was hit by flak in the tail and starboard engine over the DZ, when turning after completion of the drop. The engine stopped, but Beddow managed to keep the aircraft flying at 1,500 feet. When the Dakota took more hits he decided to head for B56; he reached the airfeld safely and made a successful emergency landing.

The Dakota flown by Captain Campbell failed to return, and presumably crashed into the Channel on the return flight, as five aircrew bodies were picked up by a ship two days later, including the aircraft's navigator, Flying Officer Mudge.

Based at Down Ampney at the time, Leading Aircraftsman Alan Hartley remembers being depressed by the setback at Arnhem and the appalling sight of the battered Dakotas returning with gaping holes in their wings and smoking engines. Another 271 Squadron aircraft was lost on 21 September. This was flown by Flying Officer Hartley, but was not involved in the Arnhem mission. It was flying cargo to B66 (Blankenberg) and failed to return to base.

A further re-supply mission was flown on 23 September, when 26 crews were detailed to drop more panniers on DZ 'V'. There was a strong fighter escort, and no enemy aircraft were seen. Some flak was experienced north of Arnhem and several Dakotas were damaged. Despite this they made their approach and run-in to the DZ and successfully dropped 122 panniers and 34 medical bundles. However, the Dakota flown by Warrant Officer Felton was hit by flak in the tail immediately after dropping his panniers. There was a blinding flash, the aircraft's cabin filled with smoke and Felton lost rudder control and elevator trim. He managed to maintain his speed at 110 mph, and by moving the air despatchers as far forward in the cabin as possible, kept the aircraft straight and level. He eventually made B56 and brought the damaged Dakota in successfully, although on impact the port prop hit the fuselage and the starboard prop sliced into the wing. However, none of the crew were hurt.

Another aircraft of 48 Squadron, flown by Warrant Officer McLaughlin, was also hit by flak, this time in the port engine. Although the engine surged, the pilot managed to maintain a reasonable speed but gradually lost height. He decided to head for the nearest friendly airfield, and landed safely at Eindhoven, despite having a damaged undercarriage. Two other aircraft of 48 Squadron failed to return, flown by Pilot Officer Pring and Flying Officer Wills, and were presumed lost to enemy fighters.

Despite the valiant efforts of the beseiged airborne troops on the ground and the airmen who fought to protect and sustain them, with such heavy losses the Arnhem operation could not be sustained. It was decided to withdraw British troops from the north bank of the Rhine. On the night of 25 September, the remnants of 1st Airborne Division were ferried back across the river. Of the 10,005 men of the division landed at Arnhem, 2,163 escaped, the remainder being killed or captured. Despite official acceptance that the operation was ultimately unsuccessful, Market Garden was in fact a considerable feat. During the first four days of the operation the RAF flew 660 gliders, 95 guns, 544 jeeps and carriers, and 10,005 paratroops and glider-borne troops 60 miles behind enemy lines. This made it the most successful airborne operation to that date. The lightly-armed force was meant to hold out for four days – they eventually held out for nine days despite heavy enemy opposition from seasoned troops, including armoured units.

The fact that the operation ultimately ended in withdrawal does not detract from that tremendous achievement.

Because of their vulnerability, the Harrows of 271 Squadron (of D Flight, also known as 'Sparrow Flight') had not taken part in the Arnhem operation, but had maintained some of the scheduled transport services. They concentrated on taking blood and medical supplies out to the battlefront and bringing casualties back. They had by then been designated the Ambulance Flight to recognise this, and with the conclusion of the Arnhem operation the Dakotas of 48 and 271 rejoined them in the transport role.

The Down Ampney squadrons soon dropped back into their pre-Arnhem routine of taking passengers, equipment, ammunition, blood and medical supplies out to mainland Europe and bringing casualties and passengers back to the UK. Sometimes the odd urgent operational requirement would arise, such as on 9 October when 19 aircraft were detailed to fly special ammunition to B56. The week before, on 1 and 2 October, a need for extra fuel resulted in 37 sorties to B56. Although on the return flights a total of 566 casualties were brought back, casualty returns were gradually dropping by this time to an average of 250 per day. One of the main reasons for this was that good medical facilities were by then being established on the Continent, supported and made possible by the constant and reliable delivery of blood, plasma and medical supplies by the Allied transport squadrons such as 48 and 271.

Warrant Officer Robert Pearson flew with 271 Squadron during 1944. He remembered the delight of flying the Dakota, its large size (the flight deck being 20 feet off the ground and the aircraft's span at 95 feet being not far short of the four-engined Short Stirling) and the marvellously reliable engines. He flew the aircraft on many delivery flights from Down Ampney to forward bases in France and Holland, carrying anything that would fit through the Dakota's double freight doors. On a good proportion of these flights his aircraft returned with wounded for UK hospitals, carried in its cabin in tiers of stretchers, accompanied by medical orderlies who cared for their patients in transit.

There were few encounters with the enemy during this time, but these trips were not without their hazards – for example, on 27 October a Dakota crashed on take-off from B17 (Capiquet) due to an elevator lock being left in (the crew escaped with minor injuries). More seriously, shortly after take-off from Gatwick on the evening of 10 December KG584, captained by Pilot Officer E. Gibson, crashed

Royal Army Service Corps freight reception area at an airfield on the Continent in October 1944. An Anson used for light freight and medical supplies stands alongside a USAAF C-47, P-51, and RAF Hudson. (Aeroplane)

into Leith Hill near Dunsfold, killing the crew. The aircraft was empty, having just dropped off the passengers that it had brought back from B56 (Evere).

Typical tasks during the latter part of 1944 included taking spare engines, freight and ammunition to B58 (Melsbroek) on 13 October, the movement of 137 Wing from Hartford Bridge to B50 (Vitoy-en-Artois) on 15 October, taking tank spares, ammunition and battery acid to B70 (Duerne) on 19 October, winter clothing to B78 (Eindhoven) on 2 November, and Pierced Steel Planking (PSP) from Lyneham to B51 (Lille) on 15 November. From 29 November, newspapers and mail were being regularly carried. By this time the Down Ampney Dakotas had also been making frequent internal flights between airfields in the UK, e.g. taking freight to Northolt, dropping it off, then picking up passengers or stores for France. They were performing these tasks on the Continent as well, making it easier for military units to move equipment in the rear logistics areas and up to the battle-front.

Although the average casualty arrival rate at Down Ampney had dropped, numbers and types of wounded varied considerably. In early October 1944 they consisted mainly of US Airborne troops from the Eindhoven area; during the second half of the month they tended to be Canadians wounded in the battle for the Channel ports. On 8 December the Duchess of Kent visited the station, where she met the 20,000th casualty to be brought to Down Ampney by air. Return loads to the station were not always wounded – passengers were often carried, and mail, too. Other items included, on 7 December, for example, captured German maps and radio equipment.

On 13 and 14 December 1944 the weather severely affected the flying programme, and it got so bad that on the 19th flying was cancelled for three days. Sporadic flights were made over the next couple of days, but by Christmas Eve most of those aircraft that had got to their destinations on the Continent were weather-bound. One Dakota that did manage to beat the weather took clothing to B78 (Eindhoven) on the 24th. On its return flight that evening, it was attacked by a twin-engined night fighter, some 40 miles from Brussels. As four streams of tracers shot past his wings, the Dakota pilot took such violent evasive action that the enemy fighter broke off its attack, and the transport managed to escape safely across the Channel.

The weather over the following days was atrocious and, although eight aircraft flew to the Continent on Boxing Day, four became fog-bound at their destination and couldn't return. More followed gradually and, by 28 December, 25 Down Ampney Dakotas were stranded at Continental airfields, their crews waiting for the weather to lift. It was because of this that some of the station's aircraft were definitely in the wrong place at the wrong time on New Year's Day 1945.

A few Allied fighter patrols were up early that morning, but the vast majority of Allied air force personnel were taking it easy, and were in for a nasty shock. At 09.20, in a co-ordinated mission (codenamed *Bodenplate* – 'Breastplate'), over 300 Luftwaffe combat aircraft, including Fw 190 and Bf 109 fighter-bombers, Messerschmitt Me 262 jet fighters and Arado Ar 234 jet bombers, attacked 15 forward Allied air bases in Belgium and Holland.

At B56 (Evere), near Brussels, a warning had been radioed by the pilot of an Auster observation aircraft that had flown straight through one of the enemy formations heading towards the base. As a result, two Spitfires of 416 Squadron were just taking off to join two others already airborne when the German fighters appeared overhead. A further twelve Spitfires taxiing out were immediately attacked by the incoming

Fw 190s of JG26. The first one, flown by Flight Lieutenant Dave Harling, managed to get away, but the remainder were destroyed. Harling turned over the airfield, he then shot down one of the attackers, only to be bounced by two Fw 190s and shot down in turn. He was killed in the crash. Three of the Spitfires that had taken off earlier then joined the melee, and despite overwhelming odds, shot down eight of the attackers. However, the German pilots were able to remain over Evere for 30 minutes, causing extensive damage to the airfield buildings and installations, and destroying some 60 aircraft of various types.

Although the Dakotas of the Down Ampney squadrons escaped undamaged, seven Harrows of 271 squadron were destroyed in the attacks and one member of the squadron, LAC Highams, was killed. The remaining Harrows were to continue in service with the squadron until 10 February 1945, when the last one, K7000, was damaged beyond repair at Evere. Although the Allies were surprised by the Bodenplate attacks, a significant number of the attacking aircraft were hit by AA fire from the ground and by fighters that were on standing patrols or that had managed to take off in time. Although the German attack was successful in that it caused shock and a set-back to the Allies, its effects were short-lived. The Allied losses in aircraft were quickly replaced – some 300 aircraft were destroyed and 190 damaged. The RAF lost 30 personnel killed on the ground, and nine in the air. The US losses were similar. German losses were, however, significant – the 232 aircraft destroyed could not be replaced easily and, more seriously for the Luftwaffe, 168 pilots were killed and 73 became PoWs. These were mostly experienced personnel that could not be replaced; the Luftwaffe never recovered from these losses, and from that day ceased to be the considerable threat that it once was.

When the weather improved the marooned Down Ampney aircraft could return to base and take part in the resumed transport and 'cas evac' service. Passengers (or 'talking freight') became an increasing proportion of the loads, so in early February three Dakotas were fitted with seats obtained from 7 MU at Quedgeley, and used exclusively for passengers. Although the squadron's aircraft and crews were busy, they still found time to host a party of Air Cadets from Swindon ATC Squadron on 4 March and to take them flying in Dakotas.

On 22 March, 60 of Down Ampney's Dakotas were deployed to Gosfield in Essex for a special mission. Gosfield was a USAAF base that had been vacated by the A-20s of the US 9th Air Force. It was used by 46 Group to position the Dakotas nearer their objective – for they were to fly into Germany. With the Allies drawn up on the borders, Operation Varsity, as it was to be known, was to establish a bridgehead on the east bank of the river Rhine, north of Wesel. A crossing was to be made by 12 Corps of the British 21st Army Group on the night of 23 March, and Allied airborne troops were to be landed by parachute and glider the following day to consolidate the bridgehead. In order to achieve surprise the operation was to be a 'single lift', which meant that all the gliders and paratroops would land on the one day. The British force was to be lifted by 17 RAF squadrons of 38 and 46 Groups towing gliders, with the US Ninth Transport Command dropping the paratroops. They were to be joined by US aircraft towing gliders and lifting paratroops from bases in France. A total force of 1,600 transport aircraft and 1,330 gliders were to lift some 21,700 troops in this huge airborne operation.

At Gosfield the ground crews prepared and refuelled the aircraft during the afternoon of 23 March. On the following morning they performed the last inspections and checks, then stood by as the airborne troops loaded the last items of equipment into their gliders which were ranged at the end of the runway ready for take-off. With the go-ahead order given, the Dakotas moved into position, hooked up their gliders and accelerated down the runway. As they took off a vast armada of Stirlings (also towing gliders), Lancasters, Halifaxes, Mosquitos, Marauders, Mitchells, Mustangs, Lightnings and Typhoons roared overhead heading eastwards.

Over the DZs and LZs, the aircraft received some opposition from the ground and a few aircraft were hit, some going down. However, the Down Ampney Dakotas released their gliders without incident, before returning to base. Once on the ground, the landing force received a mixed reception. In some areas there was little opposition but in others they faced determined resistance (including some from armed civilians) and suffered heavy casualties. Most of the airborne troops had taken their objectives by late afternoon, however, and linked up with Allied ground troops. Operation Varsity was the largest and most successful airborne operation of the Second World War, and the last.

After their return from the Rhine crossings, the pressure on the Down Ampney squadrons did not let up. They carried on with scheduled transport and 'cas evac' runs, and with special requests. In April the first repatriated British prisoners of war started arriving at Down Ampney, having been released from their camps in Germany by the advancing Allies, and this began a steady flow of arrivals.

Freed Allied prisoners of war walk to RAF Dakotas that wait to take them home in May 1945. (Aeroplane)

Casualties were still being brought back and, during April, the total number of cases evacuated to the UK by air from Europe exceeded those by sea for the first time. As the war drew to a close, the operations of the Dakota squadrons became more formalised and following VE Day, 8 May 1945, scheduled services were set up.

In early July, No 48 Squadron was ordered to fit glider snatch gear to its Dakotas. This system using a cable and winch enabled grounded, but flyable, gliders to be retrieved by low-flying tug aircraft, and was most successful. Glider snatching was practised at Down Ampney in preparation for operations against the Japanese. During the following month the squadron moved to the Far East, where it was immediately involved in the Burma campaign, and flew freight and food into Burma and East Bengal, as well as evacuating casualties.

Meanwhile No 271 Squadron continued with its scheduled services, extending its routes to Germany, Italy and Greece in the absence of civil airlines immediately after the war. On 30 August the squadron moved to Odiham and continued with its services. Later it returned to Down Ampney's neighbouring airfield, Broadwell, where it effectively ceased to exist on 1 December 1946, being renumbered as No 77 Squadron.

Despite the departure of 271 Squadron, Down Ampney remained active as a Dakota base, as in early September 1945 Nos 435 and 436 Squadrons of the Royal Canadian Air Force arrived. These units had been withdrawn from Burma, where they had operated in support of the 14th Army. From Down Ampney both squadrons operated on Transport Command's scheduled services to the Continent, flying troops and freight to Germany, Czechoslovakia and Norway. This continued until the spring of 1946, when it was decided to wind down the operation and close Down Ampney. On 31 March, 435 Squadron disbanded and its personnel returned to Canada. It was followed by 436 Squadron, which left Down Ampney with its Dakotas on 22 April 1946. The last aircraft off the runway was KN256, its pilot Pilot Officer Hadfield. As the sound of the last departing Dakota disappeared, the closing down party went about their work before the last RAF personnel left the site.

Today the site of Down Ampney remains unspoilt, although there is little remaining to indicate its past importance. A memorial at the end of one of the former runways reminds those that care to look for it of the station's past. In the churchyard of All Saints' church the remains of several Down Ampney aircrew lie, and in the church itself a stained-glass window commemorates the RAF and Airborne personnel that flew from the station during its brief but remarkable existence.

8
FAIRFORD

2 miles south of Fairford town
SP 150990

Fairford was originally planned as a transport station for the USAAF but, by the time construction started in the summer of 1943, it was no longer required by the Americans. The airfield was then laid out as a bomber base for the RAF, with three long runways in an offset-A pattern.

Construction carried on into the winter of 1943/44 and, when Squadron Leader R.G. Taylor of 38 Group arrived with the opening up party on 12 January 1944, the base was still incomplete. Work continued on the domestic sites, the technical areas and the operational buildings around the aerodrome. Two T2 hangars were eventually erected for essential aircraft repair work. The remaining structures were a mixture of permanent brick buildings, Nissen and Romney huts. As construction proceeded, the plans were modified and Fairford was eventually completed as an airborne forces transport and glider station.

A number of loop dispersals intended originally for bombers were built, mostly alongside the taxiways at the southern end of the airfield, for the storage of powered aircraft. Pierced Steel Planking (steel matting) was later laid by Royal Engineer teams at each end of the main runway, and at the western end of the secondary runway, for the storage of gliders.

The first unit to arrive at Fairford was 620 Squadron, equipped with the Short Stirling Mark IV. This squadron had been formed at Chedburgh on 17 June 1943, from C flight of 214 Squadron (a heavy bomber unit flying the Stirling Mk III). Like its progenitor, 620 Squadron also started as a heavy bomber squadron and carried out night bombing operations until 10 November 1943, when it moved to

Leicester East and was re-roled as an airborne force support unit, to tow gliders and drop paratroops. The squadron was then transferred to Fairford. It arrived in three parties on 18 March. The aircrew and ground servicing personnel came by aircraft and glider, the Mechanical Transport staff came by road with their vehicles, while the remainder travelled by train. Because of the bad weather, the squadron could not start flying immediately but when things started to improve on the 20th, twelve aircraft took part in Exercise Bizzi. Paratroops were dropped, then re-supplied by air. A USAAF Troop carrier wing also took part in the exercise to explore US/UK co-operation.

On 22 March, while the aircrew of 620 Squadron were practising glider-towing formation flying, the advance party of a second squadron arrived at Fairford. This was 190 Squadron, originally reformed as a Coastal Command squadron with Catalinas at Sullum Voe on 1 March 1943, where it flew anti-submarine patrols over the North Atlantic. Disbanded in December 1943, it was reformed on the 5th of the following month at Leicester East as an airborne squadron within 38 Group. Equipped with the Stirling Mk IV, the squadron then had 20 aircraft on charge and immediately began training in its new role of glider towing and paratroop dropping.

The Short Stirling was the first four-engine monoplane bomber to enter service with the RAF, and the first to see operational service. Its Air Ministry specification called for the design to fit a standard RAF

Short Stirling over a flooded area of the Netherlands in September 1944. (Aeroplane)

hangar of the day, and this resulted in the aircraft's 99 foot wingspan. Unfortunately this factor also contributed to limitations on the Stirling's operational capability as a bomber, and it could not fly as high as its later contemporaries with the same bomb-load, which made it vulnerable to flak. Nevertheless, the Stirling was the mainstay of Bomber Command until it was replaced in September 1944. By then the Mark IV version had been adopted for the airborne forces role of paratroop transport and glider tug. Powered by four 1,650 hp Bristol Hercules engines, the Stirling IV could carry 20 paratroops. Of the total of 2,368 built, 505 were of the Mark IV variety that flew with seven squadrons of Transport Command. A pure transport version, the Mark V, was later produced, and this carried on in service with the RAF until March 1946.

Transferred to Fairford, the main party of 190 Squadron arrived by road, rail and air on 26 March and started flying the following day. However, bad weather curtailed flying for the next few days, with limited short range cross-country navigation exercises taking place. Despite continued bad weather on 30 March the pressure to work up the squadrons to operational status was on, and an intensive training programme was flown that day. Formation flying, glider training and country navigation were practised, followed on return to base at nightfall by circuits, take-offs and landings. Some ground crews of 620 Squadron had been sent to Tarrant Rushton in Dorset and, on the evening of 30 March, one aircraft from 620 Squadron carried out the unit's first special operation. It was to fly to south-east France and drop 18 containers and two packages to the French Resistance. The weather was still unfavourable but, despite this, the crew found their way to the target area. However, because no signals were received from the ground, the Drop Zone (DZ) couldn't be identified and the aircraft brought its load back to base.

On 4 April 1944, 2706 Squadron RAF Regiment was established at Fairford to provide AA cover for the base with its 20mm Hispano cannons. They were later joined by 2886 Squadron. The following day, both Stirling squadrons sent aircraft to Tarrant Rushton for special operations in support of the Special Operations Executive (SOE). These continued over the next few days. Glider training and paratroop-dropping exercises carried on during this time and, on 9 April, Exercise Tour took place involving 20 aircraft on a cross-country navigation exercise. The SOE operations gradually increased in momentum and on 14 April five aircraft from 620 Squadron and four from 190 took part in operations over Occupied France. The first aircraft loss occurred on the following night, when Stirling LJ867 failed to return. The aircraft's New Zealander pilot, Flight Sergeant Brown and his five crew were posted as missing. Another New Zealander died that evening, when Flight Lieutenant Crindis and his crew of five were killed during a glider training exercise at Knighton Farm, Hampreston, Dorset. The following day a third aircraft was lost during training at Blandford Forum and only one member of the crew survived.

A spectacular accident occurred a few days later when, on 18 April, Horsa glider LJ263 crashed into Fairford's control tower. A member of the RAF Regiment was injured, but unfortunately the glider's pilot, Staff Sergeant Clark was killed in the crash. Nonetheless, exercises continued through April, such as Exercise Mash, which was a 38 Group effort, running from 21 to 25 April. The climax involved towing 30 Horsas to land troops of 1st Airlanding Brigade on Brize Norton airfield. Six aircraft aborted, but the remaining 24 aircraft successfully landed their jeeps, trailers, motorcycles, six-pounder anti-tank guns and troops onto the landing zone (LZ).

As well as participating in the war effort, it was decided that RAF Fairford should do its bit for the home front. On 24 April, the District Officer of the War Agricultural Committee, Mr Young, visited the station to view the gardens, as some 23 acres had been dug by hand in order to grow vegetables for the station kitchens. It was agreed that tractors and ploughs should be made available by the committee to assist in the work. Later that day, USAAF transport arrived at Fairford to deplane casualties from the campaign in North Africa.

Meanwhile exercises of various sizes and SOE operations continued throughout the rest of April and into May. By the very nature of their activities training airborne forces units was hazardous, and further accidents did occur. Another Horsa crashed on 29 April, killing both pilots and, on 7 May, a Stirling failed to return from operations over southern France. During Exercise Exeter, a large airborne forces exercise on 19 May 1944, the Stirlings released their gliders over the LZ at Netheravon, then returned to base. Unfortunately, while releasing their tow-cables over the rope dropping area at Kempsford to the south of Fairford, two Stirlings (EF244 and LJ880) collided and crashed, killing both crews.

The momentum of the squadrons' activities increased towards the end of May, as it was realised that the operation they were preparing for, the Invasion of Europe, couldn't be far away. On 22 May, Exercise Turnaround was intended to train the aircrews and ground crews in the speedy turnaround of the two Stirling squadrons. That morning, paratroops climbed aboard 44 Stirlings which took off in streams, then circled while making up their formations. The aircraft then flew cross-country to simulate the transit to the operational target, and dropped the paratroops onto a training DZ before returning to base. That afternoon, 44 aircraft were again flown and this time the crews practised hooking up the gliders and towing them off as quickly as possible. The exercise was viewed by Air Officer Commanding 38 Group Air Vice-Marshal Leslie Hollingshurst, CB, OBE, DFC, who considered it a great success.

Training in the time leading up to early June included Exercise Troop on 24 May, a ground exercise for operations and ground staff practising the logistics of the re-supply of aircraft at short notice. Exercise Kingo on 28 May was laid on to instruct aircrew in escape and evasion – 72 members of 620 Squadron were dropped in the countryside and had to return to base while avoiding search parties of Home Guard and local police. Thirty-four of the RAF personnel evaded capture in what was judged to be a very realistic exercise.

On 1 June 1944, guards were established on the glider and aircraft parks and senior staff attended briefings at 38 Group headquarters, on their part in Operation Overlord, the Allied landings on the Continent (later to be known as 'D-Day'). The following day at 14.00 hours the camp was closed and all personnel were forbidden to leave the site. A Gang Show was held in the open air to entertain the RAF personnel and the paratroops that were billeted at the station. All of the station's powered aircraft were air-tested during 3 June and on the morning of the 4th, to ensure that they were operational and that their systems were working. While the aircraft were grounded that afternoon for final check-ups, Air Chief Marshal Sir Trafford Leigh Mallory, KCB, DSO, Commander-in-Chief Allied Expeditionary Air Force (i.e. the commander of the Allied tactical air units), addressed the RAF aircrew and Army glider pilots. Later that day black and white identification strips were applied to the rear fuselage and outer wings of the station's aircraft, but due to bad weather the start of the operation was delayed by 24 hours.

The D-Day operations finally commenced with Operation Tonga, as the first of 45 Stirlings began to roll down Fairford's main runway at 23.33 hours on 5 June. The aircraft were carrying 887 paratroops of 5th Parachute Brigade, 6th Airborne Division, to DZ 'N', in order to secure and hold the bridges over the River Orne and to secure a base to the east of the river. Within 19 minutes, all 45 aircraft were off the ground and easing into formation overhead. Each of the two Fairford squadrons provided 23 Stirlings for the operation. Almost all of the 190 Squadron aircraft delivered their troops, with the exception of one which failed to locate its DZ and returned to base with its paratroops. There was heavy AA fire on the approach to the DZs and many aircraft were hit. Three Stirlings of 620 Squadron were brought down and crashed not far from the DZs. Of the aircraft that returned to base, it was found that 27 needed repairs before they could fly again. The engineers worked through the day and by 18.00 hours, 25 of the damaged aircraft were serviceable once more.

That evening, the next stage of the British airborne part of the D-Day operations was mounted. This was Operation Mallard, which was to land units of the 6th Airlanding Brigade by glider on LZs to the east of the beachhead, in order to reinforce the troops that had been landed in Operation Tonga that morning. Thirty-six Stirlings took off from Fairford between 19.10 and 20.01 hours, each towing a Horsa, the formation carrying in total 33 jeeps, 29 trailers, eleven motorcycles, eight 75mm howitzers and 254 troops. In mid-Channel one of the Horsas broke its tow-rope and had to ditch but all of the crew escaped from the sinking aircraft and were rescued.

The remaining 35 aircraft joined the main force of aircraft from the other airborne bases of 38 and 46 Groups and were an awe-inspiring sight and sound as they flew over the LZs at 21.00 hours. Troops on the ground heard the distant sound of engines increase to a roar as the sky filled with over 250 aircraft towing 220 Horsas and 30 Hamilcars. At a

Airspeed Horsa glider lifts off behind its tug. (Aeroplane)

height of some 800 feet, the gliders cast off and turned in over the LZs. The 35 Horsas from Fairford joined the throng and landed sucessfully. One aircraft was shot down after releasing its glider, but its pilot, Flight Lieutenant Turing, managed to crash-land the aircraft in a field one mile south of Lion-sur-Mer. The crew evacuated from the aircraft without injury and were able to contact friendly forces and later return to base. Although several other aircraft were damaged by flak, there were few casualties amongst the crews. However, one of the bomb-aimers, Sergeant Bevan, was killed by shrapnel.

On 8 June, 190 Squadron returned to the skies of Normandy when it sent six aircraft on Operation Rob Roy II, a re-supply sortie. All successfully found the designated DZ and dropped 144 containers and 22 panniers on target.

The D-Day re-supply missions continued on 10 June, when three aircraft from 190 Squadron participated in Operation Rob Roy V, dropping more supplies, ammunition and equipment to the troops in the beachhead. Back at Fairford, Sir Archibald Sinclair Bt, KT, GMG, MP, Secretary of State for Air visited the station to speak to the returning crews that had taken part in the D-Day missions. The final re-supply drop to the beachhead by the squadron took place on 14 June, in Operation Townhall IV, when its aircraft dropped 120 containers and 20 panniers.

No 620 Squadron had taken no further direct part in Operation Overlord after 6 June, but instead continued with SOE operations, making drops to the French Resistance. The first of these was on 7 June, when two aircraft flew out. Three aircraft from 620 Squadron took off on an SOE mission on 9 June, along with three from Keevil that had temporarily deployed to Fairford for the same mission. From 8 June until August, both 90 and 620 Squadrons flew on SOE re-supply missions. A number of aircraft (usually between two and five to start with, then between eight and 15 from mid-July) flew these sorties to drop ammunition, equipment and other supplies to the French Resistance. SOE agents were dropped on some of these flights deep within Occupied France and also troops of the SAS, who were then re-supplied in the same way. Generally, their missions went off successfully but occasionally aircraft failed to find the DZ, usually because the French were unable to mark the site due to the presence of enemy troops and in these cases no supplies would be dropped.

The survival rate on these operations was good, but the occasional aircraft did not get back to base. This happened on 17 June when the Stirling flown by Warrant Officer Crane of 620 Squadron was shot down. Further losses on 22 July were the aircraft of Flying Officer Kilgour of 190 Squadron and Flying Officer Coke of 620 Squadron. On 24 July five aircraft of No 620 dropped 120 containers on a DZ. Air Commodore F.N. Beadin, CBE, of 38 Group, flew on the operation as second pilot to Wing Commander Lee of 620 Squadron. The odd enemy aircraft, usually Focke-Wulf Fw 190s, were reported over this period in the vicinity of Fairford by crews returning from their missions, and during a couple of squadron exercises. It is possible that these aircraft were solo fighter-bomber intruders, or that they had shadowed the Stirlings on return from missions. However, no Stirlings were lost over southern England to enemy fighters, and no attacks on Fairford took place.

While some of the crews were mounting these SOE missions, the remainder of the squadron crews maintained their skills by flying navigation exercises, dropping paratroops onto training DZs and towing gliders to LZs on Salisbury Plain. The importance of this continued training was shown on 9 June, when two glider pilots, Staff Sergeant Fletcher and Sergeant Hebberd, were killed when their Horsa LJ562 was hit by Stirling LJ869. Another exercise on 24 June involved 16 aircraft, which homed-in onto a beacon set up in the Black Mountains and dropped sandbags on it. Aircraft also operated from Fairford on deployment from other bases during this time. On 28 July, for example, two Dakotas from Blakehill Farm took an SAS party of 22 men and 1,000 lbs of equipment to Airfield B14 (Amblie) in Normandy.

Many operational missions were flown by the Fairford squadrons over the following weeks. Those in August worthy of note included several on the 1st, when 19 aircraft flew from Fairford on Special Forces support missions, ten to the SOE and nine to the SAS. On 2 August, 23 aircraft (seven of 190 and 16 of 620) flew on SAS missions (Air Vice Marshal Hollingshurst flew as a passenger in aircraft 'K' of 620 Squadron on one of these). On 3 August, ten aircraft set out on SAS supply drops. One Stirling, of 190 Squadron, was attacked by a Ju 88 night fighter while heading for the DZ. The Stirling fired back and scored several hits on the enemy aircraft before it broke off its attack. On the following day, 4 August, 26 aircraft of both squadrons flew out to twelve different DZs. One aircraft flown by a New Zealander, Pilot Officer E.G. Robinson, with eight crew, failed to return; it was seen to be hit by flak near Lisieux.

Daily operations continued in this way through August into September. Occasional losses were sustained – such as the aircraft of Flying Officer Bell of 620 Squadron that was forced to ditch on the return from an SAS operation. The crew took to their dinghies and were picked up by an RAF Air/Sea Rescue launch. Aircraft 'O' of 190 Squadron failed to return on 25 August, one of twelve detailed to drop supplies to the SOE on six DZs. The pilot, Flying Officer N.H. Part, and his six crew were posted as missing. Air Vice Marshal Hollingshurst obviously enjoyed flying with his squadrons as he flew as a passenger from Fairford again on SAS operations on 10 August and again on 31 August! During that month the Fairford squadrons flew a total of 394 missions.

In a large operation on 1 September, 36 Fairford aircraft flew SAS support missions. The first two dropped 26 SAS troops, 22 containers and four panniers on their DZs, but the 34 that followed had limited success due to the deteriorating weather. Three of these found their DZs and dropped their loads (311 containers) but the remainder had to return to base. These missions continued for a while and included visiting aircraft. On 16 September, four Stirlings of 1665 Heavy Conversion Unit based at Tilstock in Shropshire used Fairford for a daylight SAS operation. They took 96 containers, eleven panniers and three bundles of tyres. After the aircraft left that morning, there was no further flying that day. The station was sealed at 14.00 hours and crews were briefed for their next operation, which was to be Market Garden, culminating in the airborne landings at Arnhem.

Fairford's squadrons were to have an important role in the operation, right from the start, as both 190 and 620 Squadrons were detailed to be the first over Arnhem. Six aircraft from each squadron were to carry paratroopers of 21st Independent Parachute Company, whose task was to mark out the DZs and LZs for the main landing. They took off on the evening of 17 September, found the target and dropped the troops successfully; once on the ground the paratroopers had just half an hour before the main formations were due overhead. Once the pathfinder aircraft had left, 19 aircraft from each squadron had hooked up a Horsa glider and taken off to follow them. Most of the gliders arrived successfully, but five were lost on the way due to broken tow ropes; three gliders landed in the UK and two on the Continent. As the last aircraft left, the ground crews could do no more, so they changed into their best uniforms and headed for the NAAFI, where a dance was held to the music of the Station Dance Band.

At daylight on the following day, 18 September 1944, preparations were made for the next lift to Arnhem – 21 aircraft of 190 Squadron and 22 of 620 Squadron took off with a Horsa glider apiece. On the flight over, three gliders were cast-off over the UK, two due to tow-rope

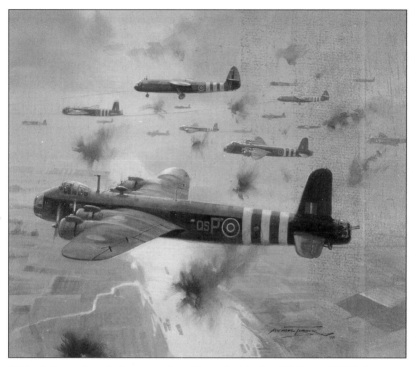

Michael Turner's painting reproduced here depicts the Stirlings of 620 Squadron towing Horsa gliders into action. (M.Turner)

failure and the third because the tug suffered engine problems. Although a further three gliders were released prematurely, some 25 miles from the LZ, the remaining 34 Horsas landed successfully.

A re-supply mission was mounted on 19 September, to drop supplies to the troops in the bridgehead. However, the day did not start well, as one Stirling swung on take-off and crashed, leaving 33 remaining aircraft heading for the Continent. Although no enemy aircraft attempted to interfere with the Stirling formations, flak from the ground on the run-in to the DZs was intense. Two aircraft of 190 Squadron were shot down before they could get close (all four aircrew and four despatchers aboard one aircraft were killed, but three aircrew and two despatchers escaped from the other). Despite this heavy opposition, 142 containers and 120 panniers were dropped by the remaining aircraft of the two squadrons, directly onto the DZ. Because of the three gliders that had cast off prematurely on the previous day,

111

Formation of 620 Squadron Stirlings return from Arnhem. (Aeroplane)

replacements were towed over by three Stirlings. Although two aircraft reached the LZ and successfully released their Horsas, one tug lost its glider over the North Sea, five miles from the Belgian coast.

Fairford aircraft returned to Arnhem on 20 September, when 34 aircraft (17 of 190 Squadron and 19 of 620) were detailed to re-supply the troops on the ground; 696 containers and 116 panniers were successfully dropped on the DZ, but heavy flak was met again in the area. Aircraft were hit on the run-in over the target and in the east once they had flown over the DZ and were turning for home. On this day many aircraft were damaged and five were brought down: 620 Squadron lost two over the DZ, with eleven crew killed (five crew survived but became prisoners of war), and 190 Squadron lost one aircraft over the DZ which crashed with the loss of ten crew. Two further aircraft were badly damaged and crash-landed while attempting to return to base.

The squadrons were sent to Arnhem once again on the 21st and it was then that they suffered their heaviest losses. The 21 available aircraft (ten of 190 and eleven of 620) left Fairford with panniers and containers of supplies, ammunition and food for the besieged paratroops. Although 240 containers and 34 panniers were delivered onto the DZ, this came at a heavy price. Nine aircraft (seven of 190 and two of 620) failed to return and one severely damaged aircraft landed at Manston. Once again intense flak was directed at the squadrons as they ran in to make their drops – one 620 Squadron aircraft was shot down right over the DZ (only two of the crew surviving) and another came down near Renkum while attempting to return to base (three crew were killed in the resulting crash but seven survived). Having left the Arnhem area, the RAF crews' troubles weren't over, as their aircraft were pounced on by enemy fighters. Having been peppered by flak, the Stirlings were now hit by machine-gun and cannon fire from Focke-Wulf Fw 190s. Seven aircraft were lost from 190 Squadron that day, with 24 aircrew and six RASC despatchers being killed, including the Squadron Commander, Wing Commander Harrison.

On 22 September, 18 aircraft were detailed to mount a re-supply mission, but this was cancelled because of the weather. Having learnt lessons from the massacre two days before, when the next operation was mounted on Saturday 23 September, fighter escorts were provided for the Stirlings. However, there were few serviceable aircraft left at Fairford. Seven aircraft from 190 Squadron and ten from 620 Squadron set out that day, and all successfully found the DZ, to drop their supplies in 429 containers and 58 panniers, along with 50 bundles of jeep tyres. Although many aircraft were again hit by flak, only one was lost, flown by the Officer Commanding 620 Squadron, Wing Commander Lee. Fortunately, he and his crew survived the crash-landing, evaded capture and returned to base shortly afterwards.

The final Market Garden sortie took place the following day, Sunday, 24 September when five aircraft of 620 Squadron took off for the DZ. Although one returned early because of trouble with its Gee navigation system, the others found their way to the Arnhem area, despite the bad weather. However, only one of the Stirlings located a DZ that gave the correct response to their signals, where it dropped its load of 24 containers and two packages. The other three aircraft received no response and returned to base. During the following night the remnants of the encircled British force escaped across the Rhine into Allied territory.

Operation Market Garden was mounted at great cost to the British forces, especially the Parachute Regiment and the RAF. The strength of 38 Group on 16 September 1944, just before the start of Operation Market Garden, was 112 Stirling Mark IVs in six squadrons. The entire force took part in the operation, and after the last re-supply mission was flown on 24 September, there were 43 aircraft left. The Group lost 69 of its aircraft, or 62% of its strength. Of the Fairford squadrons, 190 Squadron flew 98 sorties, and suffered the heaviest losses of any of the 38 or 46 Group squadrons that took part (twelve aircraft, and 39 aircrew and twelve RASC despatchers killed; in addition, 15 aircrew were captured, although 25 escaped). 620 Squadron lost five aircraft during 104 sorties (of their crews, eight aircrew and seven

RASC despatchers died, and seven aircrew were captured; 15 aircrew who survived being shot down over the DZs were later evacuated with 1 Airborne Division).

Despite the heavy mauling that they had received during the Arnhem operations, the Fairford squadrons continued with SOE and SAS re-supply missions, using the few serviceable aircraft that remained available. They often suffered from bad weather, for example on 26 September when seven aircraft of 190 Squadron had to return to base with their loads following the lack of a reception from the DZ, probably due to heavy rain and low cloud in the vicinity. An idea of just how busy Fairford was in the autumn of 1944 can be judged by the number of air movements (a take-off or landing) that took place during September – 1,438 by day and 323 by night, a total of 1,761 (an average of 59 per day).

In early October 1944, the two Stirling squadrons were detailed to mount Operation Molten, which was to ferry Horsa gliders to Italy. Sixteen crews from each squadron were nominated to take part and they duly took off in their Stirlings from Fairford, each Stirling towing a Horsa. The journey was long and arduous but by 10 October most had arrived at their destination, Ciampino airfield near Rome. The Stirlings then assembled at Pornigliano near Naples and returned to the UK in early November.

In the meantime it had been decided to move 190 and 620 Squadrons to a new base and on 18 October the remaining aircraft and crews went to Great Dunmow in Essex. The move included RAF Fairford's HQ element (as Great Dunmow was newly set up) and much of the heavy equipment, along with the units that supported the Stirling squadrons. These were 6190 Servicing Echelon and 3 Glider Support Echelon (with 190 Squadron) and 6620 SE and 4GSE (with 620 Squadron). From their new base both squadrons later (in March 1945) took part in Operation Varsity, the Rhine Crossing.

At this point Fairford became a satellite of Keevil, which was also part of 38 Group, and No 22 Heavy Glider Conversion Unit formed at the latter on 20th October 1944. This unit was issued with Armstrong Whitworth Albemarle glider tugs, along with Horsa and Waco Hadrian gliders. The Hadrian was a US glider design and although inferior to the Horsa, was in use with British units in the Far East. The unit's task was to rapidly train glider pilots in order to make up the losses suffered during the Arnhem operation. Three of No 22 HGCU's Flights (C, D and F) used Fairford for training with 29 Albemarles and 25 gliders. The unit got on with its training and flew intensively

Armstrong Whitworth Albemarle, as flown by 22 HGCU. (Aeroplane)

from Fairford during its stay. Many of the pilots that graduated joined units that took part in Operation Varsity in March 1945 and others went on to the Far East to fight the Japanese during the last months of the war. The three flights of 22 HGCU moved to Blakehill Farm in mid-June 1945, but kept Fairford as a satellite for training purposes. It finally gave up its presence at Fairford on 21 October 1945. As no other units remained at Fairford, the station was placed on Care and Maintenance.

Fairford was reactivated on 19 September 1945, when the station became part of 4 Group and No 1555 (Blind Approach Training) Flight (BAT) was formed there with Airspeed Oxfords. The flight's job was to train pilots in night flying techniques, particularly in how to use the airfield's electronic beam approach landing system. It was closely followed by 1556 (BAT) Flight in December, 1529 (BAT) Flight on 27 January 1946, and 1528 (BAT) Flight on 1 February. Fairford thus became a night flying training centre for a while, but this did not last for long, as the BAT flights were reorganised or disbanded during the spring of 1946. The remaining unit, No 1555 (BAT) Flight, moved to Blakehill Farm on 30 April 1946.

All remained quiet at Fairford for the summer of 1946, but in late September an airborne forces support squadron once again appeared at

Waco Hadrian, also flown by 22 HGCU from Fairford. (Aeroplane)

the station. This was No 47 Squadron, which flew Handley Page Halifax VIIs and IXs. No 113 Squadron, a second Halifax squadron, reformed at Fairford on 1 May 1947 and the two were joined by two more Halifax squadrons, Nos 295 and 297, on 10 September 1947. Employed on parachute dropping and glider towing, the squadrons took part in the final glider experiments that the British forces mounted. With the introduction of helicopters, however, gliders were falling out of favour and by October 1948, the squadrons had been wound down and disbanded. In December 1948 Fairford was once again put onto Care and Maintenance.

Fairford came to the attention of the USAF during the summer of 1950, when the Americans requested its use. In July, the 7507th Air Base Squadron arrived to redevelop the airfield as a USAF base. The runways were lengthened and strengthened, and aircraft hard standing areas enlarged. Three large hangars were erected and the airfield's buildings and accommodation upgraded. As a base within the Strategic Air Command, Fairford became the home of a succession of strategic bomber squadrons flying the ten-engine Convair B-36 and the eight-engine Boeing B-47 nuclear bombers.

Fairford returned to RAF use from 1964 to 1969, with a number of units passing through. These included C Flight, Central Flying School (and the school's newly-formed aerobatic team, the Red Arrows, both with Folland Gnats) from 1965 to 1966; No 53 Squadron which reformed with Belfasts at Fairford on 1 November 1965 (before moving to Brize Norton); and two Hercules units, 47 Squadron which formed at Fairford on 25 February 1968 and 30 Squadron which formed on 1 May 1968. Both of the latter moved to Lyneham in April 1971, but in the meantime a major highlight of Fairford's career came in 1969, when it was designated as the British Aircraft Corporation Concorde Flight Test Centre, and the home of the British Concorde prototype 002. This aircraft made its maiden flight from Fairford's main runway on 9 April 1969.

Following the end of the Concorde trials at Fairford in January 1977, the Americans appeared once again as the airfield had been identified as a base for strategic USAF aircraft on temporary deployments to Europe from the USA. Some Boeing KC-135 tankers and B-52 bombers then began to appear. Fairford's role as a forward operating location for the USAF continues today, with Lockheed U-2s, Boeing B-1s and B-2s also appearing. In this way, Fairford has returned to a war role, having been the base for strategic bombing missions to Libya and Iraq. Fairford is also of course today well known as the location for one of the world's largest air shows, the Royal International Air Tattoo. The airfield's use into the 21st century therefore seems secure.

9
FILTON

4 miles north of Bristol
ST 595802

The airfield at Filton is one of the earliest in Britain, dating back to February 1910 when the Bristol and Colonial Aeroplane Company was formed. The new company was financed by the millionaire Bristol industrialist Sir George White, and started off by leasing buildings from another of White's companies, the Bristol Tramways Company. Factory premises were established in two sheds that were part of the Tramways northern terminus, at Filton, four miles north from the city centre. (The two sheds were still in use 60 years later as part of the later aircraft factory's main machine shop.)

The company started licence-building Zodiac aeroplanes, which weren't very successful, then their famous Boxkite design, based on the Henri Farman biplane, which was. Within a year the company had set up flying schools at Brooklands in Surrey and Larkhill in Wiltshire, to produce customers for their products! Boxkites were to become the first British aeroplanes to be purchased for the Army Air Battalion, and equipped several flying schools set up over the following two years in Spain, Germany, Italy and Rumania. In February 1912 the Deutsche Bristol Werke was set up at Halbestadt to manufacture Boxkites. With the onset of war, the company's schools were taken over by the British Army (their importance was signified by the fact that at that point, almost half of Britain's military pilots had been trained at the Bristol schools). The company then turned to concentrate on manufacturing.

During the First World War the Bristol and Colonial Aeroplane Company expanded enormously, increasing its staff from under a hundred to over 3,000 at the time of the Armistice. Over that period the company built thousands of aeroplanes for the Royal Flying Corps, Royal Naval Air Service and Royal Air Force in their enlarged works at

Filton, and at the Bristol Tramways works in Brislington, which they also leased. These included initially the Royal Aircraft Factory BE2 under licence and later the Bristol Scout, the M1 Monoplane Scout and the famous F2 Bristol Fighter, the scourge of the German Albatross fighters and one of the most successful British aircraft designs of the First World War. The Brisfit, as it was known, went on to equip many squadrons in the post-war RAF. As the war ended, the company was constructing the Braemar, a four-engined triplane bomber with the range to bomb Berlin.

Between 1914 and 1918, the Royal Flying Corps had used Filton as a mobilisation and training station in order to work up new squadrons for France. Also at that time the South West Aircraft Acceptance Park was set up using 18 large hangars that were built on the airfield, to inspect and test aircraft manufactured by factories in the area before acceptance into service. At the height of its activity, the Acceptance Park was delivering over 80 aircraft per month to the front-line squadrons and training units.

After the Armistice, Filton was used as a demobilisation centre, with several squadrons being disbanded there on their return from the Continent. Despite the post-war cutbacks the Bristol and Colonial Aeroplane Company was determined to stay in the aviation business. The Air Board allowed the company to complete the 90 Brisfits in progress at the end of 1918, and this gave it the impetus that would see it through into the 1920s. Nonetheless, the company diversified into bus and coach bodies, motor cars and aero-engines. In March 1920 it became the Bristol Aeroplane Company (BAC), and as well as producing a number of small-quantity production types of its own design, also built others under contract, such as the Armstrong Whitworth Siskin fighter.

On 1 April 1923 the company became involved in flying training once more when it was awarded a Government contract to operate a flying school for pilots of the RAF Reserve. For this it initially operated a fleet of Bristol Fighters and Bristol PTM (Primary Training Machine) biplanes. A variety of Bristol types later followed in service with the Reserve School until 1933, when the Air Ministry decreed that DH Tiger Moths should be used in order to standardise training procedures.

The Bristol Bulldog single-engined biplane fighter was developed to meet an RAF requirement for a new fighter in 1927. It won the competition mounted by the Air Ministry, and orders for 312 were placed; 69 two-seat trainer versions were also made, and the aircraft

Filton airfield in July 1931. (Aeroplane)

remained in front-line service until 1937. Other Bristol products included a number of fighter, bomber and transport designs that never saw widespread service, including the Brandon (the first aircraft to be designed as an air ambulance) and the world famous Bristol 138 high altitude monoplane (which gained the altitude record for Britain twice in 1937, ultimately reaching a height of 53,937 feet).

A new RAF unit was formed at Filton on 14 June 1929 when 501 (County of Gloucester) Squadron was formed, as a Special Reserve bomber squadron. This was part of an initiative started by Marshal of the RAF, Sir Hugh Trenchard which called for the formation of Reserve and Auxiliary squadrons to back up the regular RAF (following the pattern of the Territorial Army). Initially equipped with the Avro 504N trainer, it later received de Havilland DH9A single-engined bombers. The squadron was based at the RAF site that had been established to the north of the airfield and the buildings there were extended in 1930 to accommodate more personnel. The Reserve Flying School continued with its training, many of its graduates then going to 501 Squadron. In 1935 the school was renamed No 2 Elementary and Reserve Flying Training School (E&RFTS), but it was still operated by the Bristol Aeroplane Company on contract to the Air Ministry. Among the school's pupils that year was a novice South African pilot who would later become famous as 'Sailor' Malan, the Spitfire pilot and fighter ace.

Guy Lawrence was another pupil; he joined the RAF Reserve and trained with the Bristol Flying School in July 1934. He went solo in a Tiger Moth after just six and a half hours' flying instruction. By September he had completed his *ab initio* course, having flown 50 hours, almost half of that solo. As a Reserve officer he had to attend an annual training camp at Filton for continuation flying of up to 20 hours. In 1938 he was selected for flying instructor training, and when war was declared was mobilised for active service. After a period as an instructor on bombers, he went on to fly Whitleys, and after promotion to Wing Commander took over 78 Squadron flying Halifaxes. He later converted to Lancasters and at the end of the war as Group Captain was station commander of RAF Warboys, a pathfinder station near Huntingdon.

Two important Bristol prototypes flew from Filton in 1935. The first of these, which flew on 12 April, was the type 142. This was a twin-engined cabin monoplane designed to the requirements of Lord Rothermere, proprieter of the *Daily Mail*, for his own personal use. When the aircraft went to Martlesham Heath for its Certification of Airworthiness tests, the Air Ministry pilots that assessed it were staggered by its performance – including a top speed of 307 mph, which was then 100 mph in excess of the fighters then in service. Lord Rothermere, realising the importance of the great stride in aeronautical engineering that the aircraft represented, gave the design to the nation, naming it 'Britain First'. The Air Ministry quickly placed an order for a bomber version of the aeroplane, which was later named the Blenheim.

The second prototype to fly in 1935, on 23 June, was the Type 130, later named the Bombay, a large twin-engined high wing monoplane, which could be used as a bomber or transport. It could carry 24 troops in addition to the crew of three, and was fitted with power-operated gun turrets of Bristol design. By the time that the Bombay was ordered into production for the RAF, the Filton production lines were busy on the Blenheim so manufacture was transferred to Short Brothers in Belfast, who made all 50 production aircraft. The type was used as a bomber by the RAF in the Mediterranean and later as a transport in the Middle East and North Africa.

Another important event for the company and for Filton was the award of several contracts by the Government, which had suddenly decided to respond to world events and re-arm its services by revitalising its industries. The first contracts for BAC were in fact not for Bristol types at all, but for the Hawker Audax, Hawker Fury and Gloster Gauntlet. This work did, however, give the company the

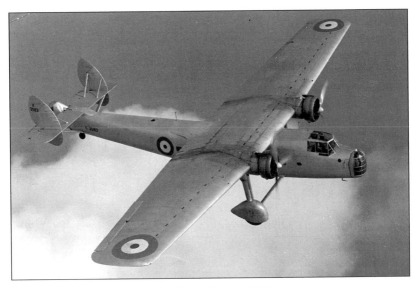

The Bristol Bombay, that first flew from Filton in 1935. (Aeroplane)

opportunity of expanding and training its work force, which doubled in size in six months, to 8,233 by Christmas 1935. The factory situated on the south side of the airfield was also extended to cater for both the new biplane orders and Blenheim production, an order for 150 of the latter having been received.

Extensions were necessary not only because of the size of the new bomber, but also because changes in manufacture were required for the new method of monocoque construction (where the outer skin carries the loading stresses as well as the internal structure). The erecting shop was doubled in floor area, the tool rooms and machine shops were extended and a new wing assembly shop built. New sheet metal stores and handling processes were needed, along with anodising and cadmium plating plant and a new spray shop for cellulose painting of components and whole aircraft. The aero-engine production facilities were also expanded and in addition a large new engine factory of 200,000 square feet was built in 1936 to produce the Bristol Mercury, Pegasus, Taurus and Hercules engines that were now required in quantity. A separate factory, named Rodney Works, was also built at this time to produce engine cowlings and exhaust systems. Administrative and drawing office extensions were made, along with recreational facilities that included a new works canteen and sports field. This development made the Bristol Aeroplane Company the largest single aircraft manufacturing unit in the world in September 1939, with 2,688,324 square feet of facilities covering 732 acres.

Even after the expansion of the British aircraft industry to meet the 1935 programme, it was apparent that more facilities would be needed to match the threat from Europe. The Government therefore decided to involve other industries to parallel or 'shadow' the aircraft companies. The first to be brought in was the automobile industry, initially for engines. In 1936 the Bristol Mercury was selected for the first of these schemes, and to accommodate the work No 2 Shadow Factory was erected next to the East Works at Patchway. Other shadow factories for Mercury manufacture were built in the Midlands. Later the Pegasus was included, and in 1937 complete aircraft were brought into the schemes, with the Blenheim to be produced at the Rootes factory in Speke, Liverpool.

The Bristol factory at Filton was working at full capacity in 1937 producing Blenheims, but more were needed. Orders were therefore also placed with other manufacturers which had spare capacity; for 250 Blenheims with AV Roe and Co Ltd at Chadderton, as well as with Short Brothers for the Bombay.

The Blenheim Mk I had made its first flight at Filton on 25 June 1936 and after successfully completing service trials was cleared for production six months later. The first deliveries to the RAF were made in March of the following year. The production rate increased from six per month in early 1937 to twenty-four in January 1938. A development of the design had also been requested by the Air Ministry to take on the roles of general reconnaissance and torpedo bomber. Because it meant a radical redesign, a new type was proposed, called the Beaufort. This aircraft was later accepted by the Air Ministry but until it became available to the squadrons, a lengthened version of the Blenheim with a navigator's station in the nose and increased fuel capacity was put into production. This was the Bolingbroke, later renamed the Blenheim Mk IV.

The Munich Crisis of 1938 provoked the aircraft industry into even greater activity, as it was realised that war wasn't far away. In October 1938, the Beaufort started to replace the Blenheim IV on the production lines at Filton. With the shortage of long-range RAF cannon-armed fighters, a fighter version of the Beaufort was proposed by Bristol to the Air Ministry. Retaining the Beaufort's wings, tail unit and landing gear but incorporating a smaller section fuselage armed with four cannon and powered by two Hercules engines instead of

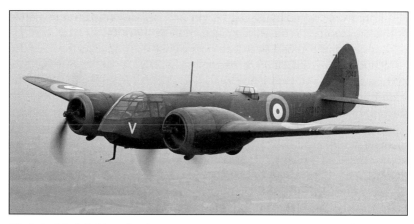

Blenheim Mark I. (Aeroplane)

Taurus engines (giving it 50% more power), the new project was named the Beaufort Fighter, later shortened to Beaufighter. Despite the lack of response from the Air Ministry, the company engineers were so confident of the new design that they went ahead and built the prototype of the Beaufighter anyway. It was almost ready to fly when, on 3 July 1939, the Ministry gave their official sanction to the aircraft and ordered the production of an initial batch of 300. The prototype flew on 17 July 1939 and was an immediate success, its performance exceeding expectations. The Beaufighter went into production at Filton and a shadow factory was later built to produce it at Old Mixon, Weston-super-Mare.

With the large numbers of Blenheims and Beauforts coming off the Bristol production line at the end of 1938, it was decided to form a ferry unit to deliver the new aircraft to the MUs. No 2 Ferry Pilots Pool was therefore formed at Filton on 16 January 1939. Air Transport Auxiliary staff joined the unit later in the year, and eventually ATA pilots were to take over all ferrying from Filton. The unit used a variety of aircraft including a Hawker Demon, Avro Anson, Westland Lysander and Lockheed Hudson.

With the increase in international tension during the summer of 1939, many airfields were taken under RAF control. This included Filton, and on 1 June 1939 RAF Filton was officially opened under the command of Wing Commander H.D. O'Neil, AFC. When war was declared on 3 September, Bristol aeroplanes were involved right from the start. Indeed, the first sortie by the RAF was flown by a Blenheim IV of

124

139 Squadron, piloted by Flying Officer McPherson on a reconnaissance of the German naval bases of Wilhelmshaven and Kiel.

No 501 Squadron had been part of the Auxiliary Air Force since May 1936 and at the end of 1938 became a fighter squadron, its Hawker Hart and Hind bombers being replaced with Hawker Hurricanes. The squadron had been on its summer camp at RAF Manston when the war started. It was immediately mobilised, put under the control of Fighter Command and returned to Filton to become part of Bristol's defences. There the unit's pilots started to fly patrols, and had quick response flights on standby alert. They were joined on 15 September by the Blenheim IF fighters of 25 Squadron which arrived at Filton under Squadron Leader J.R. Hallings Pott. The Blenheims were detached from their base at Northolt to boost the air defences of the Bristol and Avonmouth area.

No 2 EFTS had continued with its training activities throughout this period and had received Harts on which to give student pilots experience of service aircraft. In March 1939 the school had also received Ansons, for the training of navigators and wireless operators of the RAF Volunteer Reserve. When the war started, RAFVR training was stopped, the Ansons and Harts being reclaimed by the RAF. No 2 EFTS was to then continue in an elementary flying training role only.

On 2 October another fighter squadron appeared at Filton when No 263 Squadron was formed under the command of Squadron Leader J.W. Donaldson. They were initially equipped with Gloster Gladiator biplane fighters that were previously flown by 605 Squadron, another Auxiliary squadron that had converted to Hurricanes. The Gladiators carried the previous owners' pre-war squadron codes 'HE' and 263 Squadron retained these on their aircraft throughout the period of the Second World War.

No 25 Squadron's stay at Filton had been fairly uneventful and on 4 October they returned to Northolt. Ironically, later that day, 501 Squadron was scrambled. Flying Officer Rayner took off to intercept a potential intruder, but it proved to be a barrage balloon that had broken loose. He located the balloon drifting over the Severn and followed it over the Welsh mountains before shooting it down. It was some time before the Hurricanes were scrambled again. This was on 10 November, when enemy aircraft were reported in the area. Two Hurricanes went up, but their pilots saw nothing in the bad visibility. They scrambled again the following day, when six Hurricanes took off, but again made no contacts. On 28 November, 501 squadron was transferred to Tangmere in Sussex. From there it subsequently moved to France (in May 1940) to bolster Allied forces facing the German blitzkreig. The squadron's pilots acquitted themselves well against the Luftwaffe before withdrawing to the UK via the Channel Islands in June.

With the transfer of 501 Squadron, the air defence of the Filton area was taken over by 263 Squadron. On 4 December Enemy Raid 69 was identified east of Gloucester, and the unit's Blue section was scrambled. Twenty-five minutes later the Gladiators sighted their target five miles east of the city, but luckily identified the 'enemy' as an Avro Anson.

An unusual visitor appeared at Filton on 22 December. This was a Blackburn Botha from Gosport. Unfortunately the aircraft overshot in poor visibility, and crashed at the north end of the runway. It hit a house but the pilot and three passengers received only minor injuries. Another raid warning was received by Filton on 12 January 1940, when an aircraft was spotted at 20,000 feet north of Gloucester, and identified as Enemy Raid 51. Red section of 263 Squadron was already on patrol and went to investigate. When contact was made, it was found to be a Blenheim.

Bristol Bulldogs had been supplied to Finland in 1935 and these were to be the only ones to see active service (against the Russians – one of them is preserved today in Finland). These were followed by Blenheims, 18 of which were ordered in 1936. More were licence-built by the Finns and during January and February, 24 more Blenheim IVs from RAF stocks were delivered to assist the Finns in their struggle against the Russians (who at the time seemed to be allied to the Germans, having signed a non-aggression pact with them). The first twelve of these left Filton on 17 January for Perth on the initial leg of their journey. The aircraft were flown by Finnish crews, led by Captain Eskola, and for safety were escorted by four RAF Blenheims because the Finnish Air Force markings were large blue swastikas!

On 8 February, HM the King and Queen made an official visit to the Bristol Aeroplane factory, where personnel from RAF Filton provided a guard of honour. The Gladiators of 263 Squadron continued to mount patrols during this time and participate in exercises. On 1 March, for example, they took part in an air interception exercise and on 20 March were part of a night exercise with the searchlight batteries over Bristol, providing simulated targets. Accidents were few and far between, but unfortunately, on 29 March, Gladiators N5585 and N5690 flown by Pilot Officers D.E. Milsom and P.J. Nettleton collided in mid-air and crashed near Alveston, killing both men.

Blenheim IV in flight. (Aeroplane)

In mid April it was 263 Squadron's turn to move. They were given notice to travel to Norway under Plan X764 to reinforce local defences against the Germans. On 20 April the air party of the squadron, consisting of 18 Gladiators, led by Squadron Leader Donaldson, left Filton for Sealand on the first stage of their journey. The following day they embarked aboard HMS *Furious*. After a short campaign against overwhelming odds, British forces withdrew from Norway in early June. Tragically, the carrier on which 263 Squadron was returning to the UK, HMS *Glorious*, was sunk by German surface ships on 8 June, and virtually the whole squadron was lost.

No 263 squadron was not immediately replaced at Filton, although on 7 May 1940, the advance and main party of 145 Squadron's Hurricanes arrived from Croydon for air defence; within a few days they moved on to Tangmere following a signal from HQ 11 Group. Units flying from the station in the summer of 1940, apart from the home-based 2 EFTS, were the Ferry Pool and No 8 Anti-Aircraft Co-operation Unit (AACU), which had transferred from Ringway at the end of April in order to provide training for the anti-aircraft units in the Bristol area. Flying a variety of types, including Tiger Moths and Oxfords, No 8 AACU moved on after a few months.

On 23 May No 236 Squadron moved to Filton from Speke. This was a Coastal Command fighter unit flying the Blenheim IVF. The squadron had previously had serviceability problems, mainly because of lack of spares, but once at Filton these were sorted out and it was declared operational. The unit soon began flying convoy patrols over the Bristol and English Channels, protecting Allied shipping from enemy attack. It also started patrolling the French coast between Le Havre and Cherbourg looking for enemy shipping. On 14 June, 236 Squadron was moved to Middle Wallop.

Filton's defences were boosted on 1 June when No 935 (Balloon Barrage) Squadron arrived. Balloons and winch units were laid out around the airfield and it was arranged that the balloons would be flown from sunset to one hour after sunrise. They would also be flown on receipt of a Yellow Air Raid Warning (i.e. raids expected in the area) by day or night irrespective of any aircraft taking off or landing at the airfield. Other defences against enemy attack, (especially the landing of troop transports or gliders) included, with the assistance of the Bristol Aeroplane Company, arrangements to obstruct the aerodrome with old cars, from dusk to 8 am daily!

On 4 August, No 2 EFTS also departed, on transfer to Staverton near Cheltenham. This was due to the increasingly difficult flying conditions at Filton caused by the balloon barrage. Balloon sites had been set up over the Bristol area to deter raiders, but when the balloons were flown it made flying training extremely hazardous. On at least one occasion the balloons were raised while a student was flying his first solo. The pilot evaded the balloons and cables and returned safely – apparently not noticing that the balloons had gone up!

The Bristol Aeroplane Company was concerned over the vulnerability of the Filton works and had established its own fire, ambulance and ARP services. It had also set up a fully equipped underground hospital. The Luftwaffe were aware of the importance of Filton and its aircraft works, which appeared on German target maps. They raided Bristol for the first time at night on 24 June 1940. By then the Filton works were protected by the balloon barrages, along with light and heavy AA guns, and the area was left alone. However, a single German raider penetrated the balloon barrage in daylight on 4 July 1940, and dropped two bombs, which landed on a balloon site near Rodney Works. On 14 August three Junkers Ju 88s which attacked the factory were driven off by AA fire (two later being shot down by fighters) and the following night minor damage was sustained by the East Works at Patchway. Further night raids were made on 17, 18 and 22 August, causing a few casualties and some damage to the factory. Four bombs were dropped between the railway and the runway but did not explode, which stopped flying until they were defused by the Bomb Disposal Squads. A further raid on the night of 4 September resulted in a hit on No 3 factory and a resulting fire, with at least five bombs cratering the airfield.

Because of the airfield's location to the west of a large and distinctive railway junction, Filton was easy to find for the Luftwaffe pilots. In addition the single east-west main runway that had been built earlier in the year confirmed its position. On 25 September 1940, the Germans mounted a major raid on Filton. That morning, several Messerschmitt Bf 110 pathfinders appeared over the factory and dropped target markers. Then, escorted by Bf 110 fighters, 58 Heinkels of Kampfgeschwader 55 came in from the south-west and dropped their bombs right across the factory area. Over 100 bombs landed on the airfield and the works, causing much damage. Two air raid shelters were hit, killing 72 people inside. A further 166 were injured, some seriously, and 19 casualties later died. Production was halted, with eight Beaufighters completely destroyed and another twelve aircraft badly damaged. Three of the bombers were shot down by local AA defences, and four more were intercepted by fighters on their return leg, along with four of the enemy fighters.

The RAF response to the raid was to send another fighter squadron to be based at Filton. This was No 504 (County of Nottingham) Squadron, which was another Auxiliary Hurricane unit, previously based at Hendon. It was a member of this squadron, Sergeant Holmes, who two weeks before had rammed a He 111 over the West End of London after running out of ammunition. Sergeant Holmes escaped by parachute, and the Heinkel crashed into Victoria Station. Far from being too late, the move of 504 Squadron to Filton was opportune. Two days later, the Luftwaffe returned to finish off the Bristol works. Their main force of 30 He 111s of KG55 preceded by 17 Bf fighter bomber pathfinders and covered by a further 27 Bf 110 fighters was intercepted by RAF fighter squadrons on its run in over Dorset and Somerset. However, 19 of the Bf 110 fighter bombers managed to get through to Filton and dropped bombs on the airfield, damaging one hangar. They were intercepted by the Hurricanes of 504 Squadron and in a running battle three of the Bf 110s were shot down, including the one flown by their commanding officer, and the others were driven off.

On 30 September, 504 Squadron had patrols up at 0900 hours. Later that morning, three large formations of enemy aircraft, numbering 150 in all, crossed the coast between Portland and Bournemouth. No 504

Squadron was scrambled, but no contacts were made. That afternoon a formation of over 100 enemy aircraft crossed the coast heading north. Again, 504 Squadron's fighters were scrambled but this time the Hurricanes found their prey. They attacked the enemy bombers near Yeovil and, after a short engagement, the German formations turned for home. Over Portland the enemy aircraft were met by the Middle Wallop squadrons and several were brought down. One 504 Squadron Hurricane failed to return to Filton.

The unit was scrambled repeatedly during October 1940 to meet threatened enemy raids. Not all sorties resulted in contacts, but the presence of the Hurricanes helped keep the Luftwaffe at bay. For example, on 5 October the squadron took off to intercept a formation of 100 enemy bombers approaching from the south. When the Germans saw the Hurricanes in the distance, south of Bruton, they turned for home.

Immediately following the raid of 25 September, the company dispersed all departments whose presence at Filton was not essential. Houses were requisitioned for head office staff, while the drawing offices went to Clifton and Clevedon. This took place in stages and for some reason, the move of the production drawings to Lennard's Buildings in Bristol on 24 November was postponed. That night Lennards Buildings were destroyed in one of the first intensive night raids on Bristol. Only one further raid was in fact later made on the Bristol works, on 11 April 1942, when one bomb fell on the factory and destroyed a wind tunnel and the office building alongside it.

No 504 Squadron was transferred to Exeter on 17 December 1940

Messerschmitt Bf 110s of Erprobungsgruppe 210, the unit that led the raids on Filton in September 1940. (Aeroplane)

and they were replaced by 501 Squadron, returning to Filton from Kenley in Surrey. The County of Gloucester Squadron had been heavily involved in the Battle of Britain over South-East England, in the forefront of the attacks across Kent and making three or four scrambles daily throughout August and September. By the end of the battle the Squadron's score stood at a total of 149 enemy aircraft claimed destroyed since hostilities started, including 30 in France.

During their stay at Filton in 1941, 501 Squadron responded to several scrambles but managed few contacts. On 21 February, one of the Hurricanes hit a balloon cable near the airfield in poor visibility. The aircraft crashed and the pilot, Sergeant Grimmat, was killed. There was a good deal of enemy activity at night during this period, with several raids on Bristol, Gloucester and the surrounding area. Night fighters from Middle Wallop, Charmy Down and Colerne did their best to intercept the raiders and, on 15 April during a raid on Bristol, a Beaufighter night fighter of 604 Squadron based at Middle Wallop shot down a Heinkel He 111, north of Filton airfield. However, as a day fighter squadron, No 501 was not involved. Instead the unit's Hurricanes were sent on convoy escort duties, to protect shipping in the Bristol Channel from attack.

On 10 April 1941, No 263 Squadron returned to Filton. It had been reformed following the tragedy of 8 June 1940, to fly the new Whirlwind twin-engined fighter. Built by Westlands at Yeovil, the aircraft had formidable fire power, being armed with four 20 mm cannon. No 263 then joined 501 on convoy escort patrols. However, 501 mounted its last mission from Filton on 22 April, providing an escort for a bombing raid on France. It then moved to RAF Colerne, where it was to convert to Spitfires shortly afterwards. No 263 continued flying convoy escorts from Filton, interspersed with conventional fighter patrols. On 30 April the squadron lost its first aircraft while at Filton, when Pilot Officer Milligan crashed his Whirlwind at Aldermaston and was killed.

As well as convoy patrols the squadron mounted the occasional Rhubarb (or small-scale fighter attack on targets of opportunity). The first of these was on 14 June, when two pairs of aircraft went out to attack Luftwaffe fighter bases at Querqueville and Maupertus in Normandy. Convoy patrols followed over the next few weeks and during July the unit spent some time developing the use of the Whirlwind in anti-tank operations. In early August, a series of Rhubarbs were mounted by 263 Squadron against targets in Normandy, under the name of Operation Warehead. The first of these was on 2 August and involved attacks in the Querqueville area by two patrols each of two aircraft. One led by the squadron's CO, Squadron Leader A.H. Donaldson, attacked oil tanks and strafed troops and barrack blocks. The other led by Flight Lieutenant Pugh found an E-boat half a mile off the coast and left it on fire and listing badly. The next day the Maupertus area was attacked. The CO's pair raided the airfield, hitting vehicles and aircraft, setting a number of Junkers Ju 87s and Bf 109s on fire, while the second pair attacked a radio station nearby.

On 6 August a number of missions were flown, starting with attacks on E-boats and a radio station on Cap de la Hague. Then, enemy aircraft came under fire on Maupertus airfield, where one Bf 109 was hit as it was taking off and burst into flames; several other aircraft were strafed on the ground. Two 3,000 ton tankers were then attacked off the coast and both were set on fire amidships. During the last sortie of the afternoon the Whirlwinds were attacked by Bf 109s. In the ensuing melee, Pilot Officer Rudland and Flight Sergeant Brackley each shot down one of the German fighters, while Squadron Leader Donaldson damaged a third. The squadron returned to Filton having sustained no casualties. This was a fine note to end on, as on the following day, 7 August, 263 Squadron were moved to Charmy Down. They were the last operational squadron to be based at Filton during the wartime period.

On 5 May 1941 another unit formed at Filton. This was 10 Group Anti Aircraft Co-operation Flight, and it was issued with a varied fleet of aircraft, including the Westland Lysander, Bristol Blenheim and Hawker Hurricane. As with No 8 AACU, the flight's role was to provide training and practice for AA units in the area. Following the departure of 263 Squadron, 10 Group AAC Flight became the only RAF unit in residence at Filton. As part of its duties the flight travelled around to other RAF stations and to other AA units. In August this included a visit to Middle Wallop for an 8th Division course, then sorties to 46th Brigade and 8th AA Division units, including those along the coast between Portishead and Aust Ferry. The aircraft would fly at pre-arranged altitudes and courses to calibrate the gun-laying radar systems, then make low-diving simulated attacks on the gun-sites for them to practise tracking targets.

On 1 September 1941 Lysanders of 116 Squadron arrived at Filton on detachment from Roborough. This unit's role was to assist in the calibration of predictors and AA radar used by the various AA batteries in the UK. Although the squadron's HQ was at Hendon, due to the wide dispersal of the batteries, the unit had a number of flights that were based at convenient airfields around the country. The 116 Squadron detachment was to remain at Filton for almost twelve months.

The Lysanders and Blenheims of 10 Group AAC Flight spent much of September night flying, mostly to the east of Filton, over the 8th Division Searchlight School at Hambrook, north of Bristol. The school held a 'searchlight camp' for the month, training operators in their skills. It must have been one of those few occasions when pilots didn't mind being caught in the searchlights at night.

On 31 October Hurricane I P3031 of 52 Operational Training Unit (OTU) Aston Down crashed into Washing Pool Hill, Almondsbury. The pilot, Sergeant Cottman of the Royal Canadian Air Force, was unfortunately killed. His funeral was held at the RAF Filton station chapel. One of the 52 OTU representatives, Pilot Officer Weale, flew to Filton to attend, but hit a balloon cable on the way. The aircraft was damaged but the pilot was unhurt.

The task that 10 Group AAC Flight performed was a mundane but essential one. The importance of the unit was recognised when it was upgraded to squadron status on 17 November 1941, becoming No 286 Squadron. The unit was enlarged and issued with more aircraft, including Airspeed Oxfords and Boulton Paul Defiants. The addition to the inventory of the Defiant meant a change in the unit's duties, as the aircraft was fitted with a winch with which to tow sleeve targets. In addition to gunlaying training, the unit now had to provide actual target practice for the guns! This extension of role came with an enlargement in territory – No 286 Squadron was to provide training for all AA defences in the South-West. It was to do this by forming a HQ flight, along with several detached flights to be based at various convenient airfields throughout the region.

The author's father, Geoffrey Berryman, served with 286 Squadron, having previously been with No 18 (Blenheim) Squadron at Great Massingham during the Battle of Britain. Geoff was posted to the unit at Filton on 9 July 1941, when it was still 10 Group AACU, as a Corporal Fitter II (Airframes). Promoted to Sergeant he later moved with the squadron on detachments around its territory, including Colerne, Lulsgate, Zeals, Weston-super-Mare, Weston Zoyland and Culmhead. He stayed with the squadron until 5 December 1944, when he was posted overseas to join No 70 (Liberator) Squadron in Italy.

Towards the end of 1941 a secondary runway had been laid at Filton, as the single runway was a limitation in certain wind conditions. A new role for the airfield arose on 20 December 1941, when 3 and 4 Flights of the Overseas Aircraft Preparation Unit (OAPU) were formed (Nos 1 and 2 Flights of the unit were formed at Kemble a few weeks later). Responsibility for the preparation of Blenheims for ferrying overseas that had been previously undertaken by Bristol was transferred to the unit, as was also that for Beauforts and Beaufighters, which had previously been done at Kemble. This work was to continue at Filton for at least another two years. The actual preparation included the fitting of auxiliary fuel tanks inside the fuselage, to give the aircraft the range so that they could be ferried for the long distances necessary through unfriendly territory. On the Beaufighters the fuselage tanks were later replaced by additional tanks mounted in the outer wings instead of the Browning machine guns.

By early 1942 it was apparent that 286 Squadron needed more room for its operations, so it was decided to move the unit to Lulsgate Bottom on 24 January 1942. The squadron HQ Flight was later to move to other stations in Somerset and Wiltshire, while its detached flights led a nomadic existence around the South-West.

The security of the airfield was obviously a concern during the summer of 1942, for a number of ground defence exercises were held. The first of these was Exercise Thunder, held between 15 and 17 May. This involved the station being attacked by ground troops from New Zealand Army units by day, with the Somerset Light Infantry attacking the airfield at night. Another, Exercise Bogey, was a much bigger affair, with troops of the Home Guard, Somerset Light Infantry and the RAF Regiment, together with RAF 'Backers Up' Flights (airmen 'volunteered' to carry weapons and boost the defences) defending the airfield against three companies of the Home Guard. Five Hurricanes of 87 Squadron simulated air attacks on the defenders for 30 minutes, then on the attackers for another 30 minutes. Despite heavy fighting, the station defences held. A similar exercise the following month simulated attacks on the balloon units, but on that occasion the attackers won – probably, it was said at the debrief, because the Home Guard had local knowledge!

Many aircraft were now being despatched overseas by the OAPU, and on 6 August the unit was officially thanked by the Chief of the Air Staff, Sir Charles Portal, for the record total sent to the Middle East by the unit during July, which was a fine contribution to the battles being fought in Egypt. On 1 December 1942, the detachment at Filton was retitled No 2 OAPU.

During 1942 the Bristol Aeroplane Company reached its peak employment of 52,095 people at its factories, including Filton, Old Mixon and the Hercules engine shadow factory at Accrington in Lancashire which it also directly controlled. The company occupied over 100 dispersal premises, mainly in Somerset, including such places as Highbridge Cheese Stores and Wells Prison. There were drawing offices in hotels, turret manufacture in a chocolate factory and engine repair shops in a tobacco bonded store. Production of aircraft and engines was at its height, and the Bristol factories were an essential part of the war effort.

During 1943 aircraft and engine production went ahead at full steam, and the airfield was busy with flight testing, departures of aircraft on delivery, and visiting aircraft bringing officials for meetings or inspections. A new unit appeared during the year at the station. This was No 528 Squadron, which was formed at Filton on 28 June. Established as a radar calibration squadron to work with RAF radar units in the West Country, the unit was equipped with Bristol Blenheim IVs and DH Hornet Moth cabin biplanes. It was to stay at Filton for almost a year, moving to Digby in Lincolnshire on 15 May 1944.

To support the build-up of US forces in Britain, the USAAF needed a base in the vicinity of the port of Avonmouth for the establishment of a depot to receive aircraft being brought to the UK from the USA. In November 1943 they established the IX Base Aircraft Assembly Depot (BAAD) on the north-west side of Filton airfield, with technical and accommodation sites for 1,000 personnel near Charlton village, alongside the Patchway by-pass. The IX BAAD comprised an HQ and three Mobile Reclamation and Repair Squadrons (MR&RS). As their name implied, these units' normal task was to recover and repair crashed aircraft, but they were brought to Filton for the assembly and maintenance of aircraft arriving from the docks. The first MR&RS to arrive was the 21st, which came from Ramsbury in Wiltshire on 28 November. They were joined by the 22nd, also from Ramsbury, the next day, and by the 33rd, which transferred from Matching in Essex on 4 December. The US troops soon established their camp, and erected four Butler Combat Hangars in which to work.

The IX BAAD was established to assemble fighter aircraft such as the Republic P-47 Thunderbolt, North American P-51 Mustang, Lockheed P-38 Lightning and Douglas A-20 Havoc. These sometimes arrived in pieces in large crates, but were usually shipped in one piece as deck cargo (but with propeller(s), tail unit and wing tips removed). Cockpit canopies and engines were covered and the airframes were coated in a waxy substance called cosmolene. After being unloaded the aircraft were taken on low loaders to Filton, where they were degreased, and assembly began. On completion they were checked over and test-flown from Filton airfield, before being ferried to a 9th Air Force Tactical Air Depot, such as No 4 TAD at Charmy Down in Somerset.

The year of 1944 had started in much the same way as 1943, with production at the Filton factories proceeding apace and flight-testing and delivery being the main activities at the airfield. Arrivals at IX BAAD in March 1944 were 84 P-47s, 64 P-51s and 24 A-20s; a total of 172, which was exceeded the following month with the arrival of 220 aircraft. P-38s began to come in May, when 32 arrived from Avonmouth, along with 17 A-20s and four CG-4A gliders. The gliders, and other more fragile aircraft such as the North American Texan (the RAF's Harvard), Noorduyn UC-64 Norseman and the Cessna UC-78 Bobcat training and communications types were transported in crates and required more work to assemble them.

World events were to make themselves felt at Filton following the Allied invasion of Normandy in June 1944. On the day of the landings, 6 June, two North American P-51 Mustangs of the USAAF landed for refuelling on return from operations over the beachhead. No aircraft arrived at Filton from Avonmouth during June as, following the D-Day landings, it was decided to move the Mobile Reclamation and Repair Squadrons nearer to the Continent and to close the BAAD at Filton. The squadrons had all departed by 21 June, for Chilbolton in Hampshire and Membury in Berkshire.

On 23 June daily flights were started to take medical supplies from the Army Blood Plasma Depot at Southmead in Bristol to Redhill and Bognor Regis. An Anson aircraft of the Station Flight, RAF Watchfield, was employed for this purpose. On 25 June USAAF Douglas C-47s arrived from Normandy bringing 76 wounded personnel for onward flights to Prestwick. Filton was also used by the USAAF Courier Service and by US Navy liaison aircraft.

As an indication of the air traffic through Filton at this time, during the month of June, 794 visiting aircraft made inward and outward flights and 851 test flights were made along with six emergency landings (including a crash landing by a Bristol Buckingham). These figures increased in July, with 912 visiting aircraft, 1,027 test flights and 144 air experience flights for visiting Air Training Corps cadets. This resulted in an average of 67.2 air movements per day. During July, USAAF C-47 Dakotas were regular visitors, bringing wounded in from the front and taking personnel and supplies back to Normandy. US Army liaison aircraft also regularly used the airfield to maintain communications between the US Army HQ in Bristol and the front-line battle headquarters and units on the ground.

The Bristol Centaurus 18-cylinder, two-bank radial engine was of 53.6 litres capacity and first flew in its production form in the Hawker Tempest II in June 1943. This extremely powerful aero-engine was also fitted in the Hawker Fury (later the Sea Fury) and such types as the Blackburn Firebrand and the Bristol Brigand. A Centaurus Test Flight was therefore set up at Filton to assist in the development of the engine and its applications. Generally flight testing went well, but on 3 October 1944 Buckingham KV342 of the Centaurus Test Flight crashed. The aircraft, flown by Pilot Officer Porter, was just taking off on a flight test when it swung across the runway and struck the office block occupied by the Flight. Two rooms of the building were demolished and the aircraft was written off. Fortunately the pilot was only slightly injured. The Flight lost another aircraft eleven days later, when Warwick HG342 crashed on engine tests over South Wales. The aircraft came down at Capel Ifan, Newcastle Emlyn, killing the pilot, Flight Lieutenant L.A. Crozier, and his Flight Test Mechanic, Leading Aircraftsman McAllen.

Later in the month USAAF C-47s flew in from Northern Ireland to transport freight from the USN detachment at Avonmouth Docks to Normandy. Up to 30 aircraft came in at any one time. Some returned from Normandy with American casualties who were then taken on to Prestwick. In December aircraft movements included 432 visiting aircraft, 364 test flights and 207 delivery flights. One of the arrivals on 30 December was a US Army UC-64 whose pilot had mistaken the training camp at RAF Pucklechurch to the east of Bristol for an airfield and landed there. The Noorduyn C-64 Norseman was a tough Canadian-built high-wing aeroplane designed for rugged bush operations. The pilot managed to take off again from a field 200 yards long, and flew on to Filton, his intended destination.

New Year 1945 brought with it fog, gales and frost, which curtailed flying from Filton during the early part of January. C-47s managed to land despite the bad weather, bringing in more casualties. The weekly blood plasma flights continued, Dakotas having replaced the Anson. No 1 OADU carried on with its work. On 10 February Spitfire IX NH483 was on a ferry flight from Melton Mowbray when it crashed at Littleton on Severn. The pilot, Flight Lieutenant Waddell of 12 Ferry Unit, was unfortunately killed when the aircraft hit the ground. The weather improved in March, and 1,763 air movements took place that month from Filton, including 935 test flights by the Centaurus Flight and other BAC aircraft.

The following month 1,451 flights were made according to RAF Filton's Form 540 (the station's Operations Record Book), including 'two helicopters for the BAC'. Presumably these were Sikorsky Hoverflys, there for evaluation by the company (BAC later developed helicopter designs of its own). On 8 May 1945 the Station Commander announced that German forces had surrendered and everyone at Filton celebrated VE Day. However, with the war against the Japanese still in full swing, work at the BAC factories hardly faltered. Nonetheless air movements gradually reduced over the next couple of months to less than 1,000. Another flying accident occurred on 5 July 1944, to Beaufighter X NV246. It was returning to Filton after a test flight when the throttle linkage to the starboard engine broke and the aircraft crash-landed at Queens Charlton. No 2 OAPU was disbanded on 1 July 1945 and reformed with the Station Flight as No 15 Ferry Unit.

In September, movements rose again to 1,443 flights. That month two bad crashes occurred at Filton when Vengence '301' hit the ground, killing its pilot Warrant Officer Davies, and on the 10th, Tempest '825' also crashed on the airfield, badly injuring Pilot Officer J.M. Harris, who died later that day in hospital. On 15 September there came a sign that things were getting back to normal when a flying display was held at Filton. This was the RAF Station 'At Home Day', held to celebrate the anniversary of the Battle of Britain. Some 15,000 people attended the display.

In November 1945, Bristol University Air Squadron started flying from Filton, with DH Tiger Moth trainers. No 501 Squadron was reformed as a Royal Auxilliary Air Force Squadron on 10 May 1946 with Spitfire LF16s, and these were replaced by Vampire jet fighters two years later. The squadron continued to fly the Vampire until it was finally disbanded on 10 March 1957.

The Bristol Aeroplane Company had made a tremendous contribution to the war effort. In terms of production numbers alone, it had manufactured some 10,700 aircraft, but those aircraft filled important roles and performed magnificent feats in the hands of their crews. The legendary 'Bristol twins' (as in "twin-engined"), the Blenheim Beaufort and the Beaufighter won themselves an immortal place in Britain's history.

The first of the twins was the Blenheim. Powered by two Bristol

Mercury radial engines, the Blenheim I medium bomber had entered service in early 1937. Although it was state-of-the-art at the time, its reputation as Britain's fastest bomber was soon superceded, but the Blenheim continued in service in the Middle East and India. Fitted with Airborne Interception Radar, the Mk I became the first specialist night-fighter and achieved success against German night raiders, scoring its first triumph against an enemy aircraft on the night of 2/3 July 1940. Some 54 RAF Squadrons flew the Blenheim I, and several foreign countries. A total of 1,134 were built.

The Blenheim IV flew the RAF's first bombing mission of the Second World War, attacking German ships near Wilhelmshaven on 4 September 1939. The Mk IV, although originally an interim design, was the mainstay of the RAF's medium bomber squadrons between 1939 and 1942, and saw much operational use in all theatres during that time. Operating by day, the crews of 2 Group, Bomber Command, determinedly attacked their targets on the Continent time after time, despite appalling losses. The Blenheim V was similar, but with a different nose and gun turret. The Blenheim IV/V was flown by 52 RAF squadrons and several overseas air forces. A total of 3,296 Blenheim IVs were built in the UK, 676 in Canada and 55 in Finland, along with 950 Blenheim Vs.

During its period in service the Beaufort was the RAF's standard torpedo bomber. It entered service with 22 Squadron in November 1939 and remained on front line duties until 1943. Ten squadrons flew the type, mainly from the UK and in the Mediterranean. Production finished in April 1944 after 1,429 had been delivered. Another 700 were also built in Australia, including a transport version, the Beaufreighter.

The Beaufighter was probably the most successful Bristol aircraft.

Bristol Beaufort torpedo bomber. (Aeroplane)

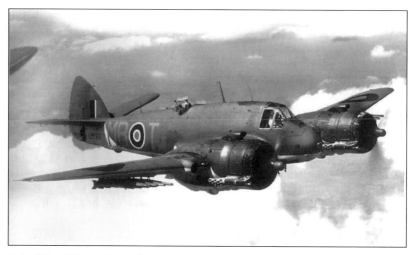

Bristol Beaufighter: this is the Mark X, one of the most powerful versions of the type, used on anti-shipping strikes. (BAe)

The first production aircraft fitted with two Bristol Hercules engines were issued to squadrons in September 1940 and took over from the Blenheim IF in the night-fighter role. Although the Blenheim pioneered the concept, the Beaufighter with its higher speed and increased firepower took the night-fighter into another dimension. The first enemy aircraft to be brought down by the type was a Junkers Ju 88 bomber, shot down on the night of 19 November 1940 by Squadron Leader John Cunningham of 604 Squadron based at Middle Wallop. They then went into service in North Africa, flying as long-range fighters over the Western Desert (the aircraft having been prepared for overseas operations at Filton), then from Malta.

Later, in 1942, the Beaufighter was used to great effect as a strike fighter with Coastal Command, and squadrons flying from St Eval had many successes against Ju 88s and E-Boats operating against Allied shipping in the Bay of Biscay. As well as cannon, the Beaufighter was fitted with torpedoes and rocket projectiles in this role. The Mark X with uprated engines and armament was the most potent version of the Beaufighter, and was used against U-boats to great effect. The Beaufighter also operated in the Far East, with the RAF and Royal Australian Air Force, as the aircraft was also manufactured in Australia. The RAF squadrons specialised in low level strikes against enemy targets, and the Japanese soon came to fear the aircraft, naming it 'whispering death'. The Beaufighter remained in service with the RAF until May 1960, having flown with 51 squadrons during its RAF career. The aircraft also flew with several overseas air forces including the Portuguese Air Force and the USAAF. A total of 5,557 Beaufighters were manufactured in the UK, with another 364 produced in Australia.

The Beaufighter's inbuilt versatility meant that it could perform most defensive and offensive roles without modification, but nonetheless, the RAF called for it to be used as a bomber. This led in 1941 to orders being placed for the Buckingham, a heavily-armed bomber version of the Beaufighter design. The aircraft appeared too late, however, to take part in hostilities. Production was cut back after VJ Day and incomplete aircraft were finished off as transports or Buckmaster trainers. A large-capacity transport version of the aircraft was proposed, but a simpler solution was found in a freighter transport version of the Bombay. This became the Bristol 170 Freighter and eased Bristol's transition from war to peace in 1945. However, a strike version of the basic Buckingham design was later produced as the Brigand, a light bomber that was used in the Far East. It was the last piston-engined light bomber to see service with the RAF, and a trainer version of the aircraft was also produced.

Four pilots were awarded the Victoria Cross while flying Bristol twins. Flight Lieutenant Kenneth Campbell of 22 Squadron, flying Beaufort Mk1 N1016, was awarded a posthumous VC after his attack on the German battle cruiser *Gneisenau* in Brest Harbour on the morning of 6 April 1941. He made the attack alone after the rest of his squadron failed to locate the target because of the bad weather, and flew into the harbour at mast height to deliver his torpedo. The flak ships shot the Beaufort down, with the loss of Campbell and his crew, but the Beaufort's torpedo hit the *Gneisenau* and caused considerable damage, putting it out of the war at a critical time for nine months.

Wing Commander Hughie Edwards, 105 Squadron, flying Blenheim IV V6028, was awarded the VC for his attack on the port of Bremen on 4 July 1941. He led a daylight low level mission to raid German factories, and despite heavy AA fire, Edwards pressed home his attack and did much damage. Of the twelve Blenheims, four were shot down. Hughie Edwards retired from the RAF in 1963 as an Air Commodore.

Squadron Leader Arthur Scarf, 62 Squadron, flew Blenheim L1134 from RAF Butterworth in Malaya on 9 December 1941, two days after the Japanese attack on Pearl Harbour. His was the first aircraft to take off on a bombing mission against a Japanese base at Singora in Thailand, when Japanese aircraft raided his base and destroyed all the other aircraft on the ground. Scarf evaded the Japanese, got through to the target and made his attack despite heavy AA fire. He attempted to return to Butterworth, but was caught by Japanese fighters and mortally wounded. Despite this he managed to crash-land his Blenheim without injury to the rest of his crew. He died later that day in hospital.

Wing Commander Hugh Malcolm was awarded the VC for his valour in leading a series of raids by the Blenheim Vs of 18 Squadron against enemy airfields in North Africa. This culminated in an attack on 4 December 1942 on an airfield near Chouigi. The squadron reached the target and attacked it successfully but was intercepted by a force of between 50 and 60 German fighters while trying to return to base. One by one the Blenheims were shot down until only Malcolm's (BA875) remained, then this too went down in flames and he was killed. Only one crew member survived the operation from the entire squadron.

With the end of the war, the Bristol Aeroplane Co was once more determined to continue in aviation, but had to diversify to stay in business. It manufactured high-quality motor cars, prefabricated buildings, plastics and marine craft. It also set up a Helicopter Division.

The company's major immediate post-war aircraft project originated in 1943, when the Brabazon Committee sat to look at possible post-war civil transport requirements. It identified five types of aircraft that

Bristol Brigand, the last in the line of the Bristol Twins. (Aeroplane)

would be needed, including a long-range transatlantic airliner. Bristol submitted a design for an eight-engined, 100-ton aeroplane and were awarded a contract to build a prototype in 1945. This became the Bristol Brabazon. To accommodate the Brabazon, new hangars were built at Filton and the main runway was extended, involving the closure of a new dual carriageway and demolishing part of Charlton village. The Brabazon prototype was completed in 1949. It had a 230-foot wingspan (the Boeing 747 Jumbo Jet's is 195 feet) with an all-up weight of 290,000 lbs. It could carry its 100 passengers over 5,000 miles. The aircraft first flew on 4 September 1949, and it made demonstration flights to Heathrow Airport and at the 1950 Farnborough Air Show. Its performance was above expectations and the future seemed assured. Unfortunately, the Government had lost interest in the project and the company received no financial backing. The Brabazon was an aeroplane ahead of its time, but that didn't save it from the cutter's torch in 1953.

Although it never went into service, the knowledge gained by the company in the research, development and construction of the Brabazon put it in an extremely advantageous technical position. It was able to put that experience to work in producing the smaller, but commercially successful, Britannia, of which 85 were built at Filton, with another 72 Britannia-derivatives being built in Canada under licence.

Although a number of other new projects were proposed and tenders submitted during the post-war period, very few were produced. However, the company built the Bloodhound air defence missile, and again the experience gained during its development and production process, together with that from building high speed research aircraft such as the Bristol 188, was an important factor in the development of the Concorde SST (SuperSonic Transport). Produced jointly with the French, the project was led on the British side by the British Aircraft Corporation, successor of the Bristol Aeroplane Company, using the factories and facilities at Filton. Further reorganisation of the British aircraft industry followed, but today the legacy of Bristols lives on, with the British element of Airbus Industries based at Filton.

10
KEMBLE

4 miles south-west of Cirencester
ST 960965

The RAF Expansion Scheme of the 1930s resulted in a series of phases of airfield building in Britain, and the production of modern aircraft to fly from them in order to counter the threat of the military build up in Europe. As part of this forward-looking scheme, Aircraft Storage Units (ASUs) were planned in which to store reserves of aircraft to back up the operational squadrons. Some of these ASUs were set up on established airfields, but others were to have airfields especially built for them.

The site at Kemble, four miles south-west of Cirencester, was selected for the building of an ASU airfield as it was situated on the Cotswold plateau, an area that is relatively flat, well-drained and of good weight-bearing capacity. It had the added advantage at the time of being out of bomber range from the Continent. Work started at Kemble under the Third Phase of the Expansion Scheme in August 1936. The fields were cleared of hedges and trees to enable a grass airfield to be laid out and the land was levelled, graded and reseeded where necessary. Around the airfield a series of hangars were built in groups (or 'sites'). At the main site (M site) to the south, a large C-type hangar was constructed for the assembly, maintenance and repair of aircraft, along with a number of technical and administration buildings. Two pairs of Lamella hangars were built on the east side of the airfield (on A and B Sites), with a paved taxiway connecting them. These hangars intended for storage were originally of German design, manufactured under licence in UK; the name came from *lamellendach* or 'segmented roof'. Then two sets of D-type hangars were built, one on M site and the other on the north-east side of the airfield, known as D site. Two more hangars were added, of the E-type, to the east at C site.

Where possible, undulations in the ground and other natural features were used to screen the hangars, and trees were planted to break up their outline and give the airfield a more natural setting. No 6 Aircraft Storage Unit was opened at Kemble on 22 June 1938. The task of the unit was to receive and store aircraft, either as new airframes on delivery from the manufacturers, or on transfer from other units. They were then to equip, maintain, modify, store and issue the aircraft as appropriate in response to requests from the ASU HQ at 41 Group, Maintenance Command, RAF Andover. However, as a security measure (its title giving away its important role!) the unit's name was changed to No 5 Maintenance Unit (MU). As such it was to be associated with RAF Kemble for all of its service life, until 1983, and was to become the RAF's longest serving MU.

The first aircraft to be received at 5 MU were Bristol Blenheims and Hawker Hurricanes direct from the manufacturers. These were to be made combat-ready by the installation of equipment that was held centrally by Maintenance Command and not issued to the manufacturer, ranging from gun-sights and machine-guns to first aid kits.

Following the declaration of war on Germany on 3 September 1939, air attacks were expected. As it was felt that the bomber bases of East Anglia were particularly vulnerable, many of the squadrons based there were withdrawn and redeployed to other areas. Therefore on 6 September, 14 Wellingtons of 37 Squadron based at Feltwell in Norfolk suddenly appeared at Kemble. The aircraft returned to their base a few days later, when it was realised that the Luftwaffe were not about to mount raids on East Anglia. There followed the 'Phoney War', when

Impressed DH Dragon Rapides in store at 5 MU. (Aeroplane)

nothing much happened until the following summer. This gave a well-needed respite for Britain, and full advantage was taken in building up reserves of munitions, weapons, vehicles, ships and aeroplanes.

As more fighters and bombers turned up from the manufacturers, they were joined by trainers. During September, 93 aircraft were received and 89 issued to units, with 376 on site at the end of the month. The large numbers of aircraft soon filled the storage hangars and were having to be stored outside. This situation was relieved somewhat in October when land for an additional four hangars was requisitioned. Two sets of 'L' hangars were constructed, one on E site to the south of the airfield and the other on F site to the south-east.

By the end of 1939 there were 488 aircraft in store at Kemble, with more arriving every week. More land was requisitioned from local farmers to allow dispersal in fields away from the main site and hard tracks were laid to give the aircraft and tractors access without getting bogged down. This outside dispersal caused problems of security over such large areas, and damage to aircraft resulted from the weather, such as rain getting into aircraft cockpits, and frost and high winds adversely affecting the airframes. By April 1940, however, 629 aircraft were on site including, as well as the Hurricanes and Blenheims, Fairey Battles, Bristol Beauforts, Vickers Wellingtons, Westland Lysanders, Handley Page Herefords, and Hawker Hectors.

Problems were also experienced with deliveries, so in May 1940 it was decided to move No 4 Ferry Pilots Pool from Cardiff. The unit arrived on 1 June, and set up its operations in the C site hangars. It flew a diverse set of aircraft, including Beauforts, Hurricanes, Avro Ansons and Handley Page Hampdens, in order to deploy and collect their pilots. With the arrival of the Pool, the despatch rate of outgoing aircraft soon increased, and on 3 July 1940 the 1,000th aircraft since the outbreak of war was despatched from 5 MU.

Enemy interest in Kemble was limited, but it was felt that the airfield was vulnerable so an air defence flight of Hurricanes was formed by the MU. A few weeks later, on 25 July, the flight received its first 'customer' in the form of a Ju 88 that was spotted heading for Kemble. The bomber was intercepted by a Hurricane and shot down, but celebrations of the victory were short-lived as the fighter went into a spin and dived into the ground, killing its pilot. The Luftwaffe returned on 14 August, when two of its bombers dropped 18 high explosive and four large incendiary bombs on the airfield. No one was hurt, but nine Armstrong Whitworth Whitleys on B site were damaged. During this period of the summer of 1940 the Battle of

The Curtiss Mohawk was but one of the many types stored and maintained at Kemble. *(Aeroplane)*

Britain was nearing its height and the German invasion fleet was assembling in the French Channel ports. The Air Defence Flight was kept on alert, and some aircraft such as the Hawker Hind biplane trainers in store were fitted with bomb racks so that they could be used to attack enemy troops should the need arise.

The work of No 4 Ferry Pool had expanded during the summer, and there now included ferrying aircraft further afield, to the Middle East and later the Far East, to reinforce Britain's defences abroad. On 9 September 1940 the Overseas Aircraft Despatch Flight (OADF) was formed at Kemble. It initially trained with Vickers Wellingtons, but also had Bristol Beauforts and Martin Marylands on strength, and later Bristol Beaufighters. Long distance ferrying was a hazardous affair at the best of times over vast areas of water such as the Bay of Biscay and the Mediterranean, let alone during wartime, when enemy forces are actively looking for you! The OADF was formed to ensure that suitable pilots, navigators and air engineers, having been selected and trained, maintained their skills as specialist long-distance aircrew. On 5 November 1940, No 7 (Service) Ferry Pilots Pool was formed at

Kemble, replacing No 4 Ferry Pilots Pool, which then became HQ Service Ferry Pools.

The total number of aircraft in store in November 1940 averaged 250, of about 35 different types. The MU had become a recognised Holding Unit for the Hurricane, Blenheim, Beaufort, Whitley, Hampden, Hawker Hind, Hart, Hector, Audax, D H Tiger Moth, Miles Magister, Westland Lysander, Blackburn Roc, Fairey Battle, Gloster Gladiator, Avro Tutor and Brewster Buffalo. There were 687 civilian employees working at the MU at this time along with 300 Service personnel. Flying incidents and accidents occurred from time to time. On 2 November 1940 for instance, a Curtiss Mohawk and a Hurricane being flown in by ferry pilots, collided in mid-air, but fortunately without too much damage and both pilots managed to retain control of their aircraft and land successfully. On 17 November a Blenheim came in to land, but over-ran and went through a wall at the end of the runway.

The Luftwaffe put in another appearance a couple of days later when at 0400 hours on 19 November, two German bombers dropped between 40 and 50 incendiary bombs on the airfield between C and D sites. The fires were quickly extinguished and no damage or injuries resulted. HE bombs were also dropped that night, at Rodmarton, half a mile away from the station. As a result of these attacks dispersal again became an issue, and aircraft were sent off to other airfields such as Stoke Orchard and Watchfield in Berkshire. However, these soon became full, and so in early 1941 specially camouflaged Satellite Landing Grounds were developed instead, with varying success. These included Barnsley Park in Gloucestershire, Bush Ban in Oxfordshire, Berrow in Worcestershire and Booker and Beechwood in Bedfordshire.

One of the few fatal accidents to occur at Kemble took place on 7 February 1941. Miles Magister P2448 of 7 (Service) Ferry Pilots Pool had just taken off with two Czech pilots, Sergeants F. Dolezal and O. Fiala aboard, when it stalled and crashed. Both pilots were killed.

On 20 February 1941 there became just one Ferry Pilots Unit at Kemble when No 7 (Service) Ferry Pilots Pool was absorbed into the HQ Service Ferry Pools. At this time the unit had 160 pilots on strength and included detached flights at Hullavington and Dumfries. Within the HQ, another unit was formed on 1 April 1941: the Service Ferry Training Squadron (SFTS), the role of which was to ensure that ferry pilots were adequately trained on type. With 35 different types of aircraft flying from Kemble alone, it was vital to ensure that pilots were

Light aircraft in store at 5 MU in this photograph include Austers and Miles Gull Sixes. (Aeroplane)

aware of their different characteristics. The RAF ferry pilots were supplemented by those of the civilian Air Transport Auxiliary organisation who became increasingly involved in ferrying Service aircraft from 1941 onwards. On 17 April HM Queen Mary paid an unofficial visit to RAF Kemble, hosted by the Station Commander, Wing Commander A.D. Adams.

Receipt, preparation and despatch of aircraft continued at 5 MU throughout 1941. By the end of the year 2,300 aircraft of 41 different types had been turned out by the unit. This included 1,300 Hurricanes and 200 Beauforts – an impressive average output of 191.6 aircraft per month.

A detachment of the Overseas Aircraft Despatch Flight (OADF) had been established at RAF Portreath on 28 June 1941, as the Cornish station had become one of the main departure points for aircraft crossing the Atlantic or heading south through the Bay of Biscay. The OADF itself was reorganised and renamed later in the year, when on 15 August it became the Overseas Aircraft Despatch Unit (OADU). However, as more emphasis was being put on the despatch of aircraft from their departure airfield, rather than the MU issuing the aircraft, the Portreath detachment of the OADU became the HQ for the unit, the element at Kemble disbanding on 5 November 1941 to become the

Overseas Aircraft Preparation Flight. This became the Overseas Aircraft Preparation Unit on 1 Jan 1942, with Nos 1 and 2 Flights at Kemble. It also formed another two flights, Nos 3 and 4 at Filton, to prepare Beauforts and Beaufighters.

Flying accidents at Kemble during 1941 included Hurricane P3263, which crashed on 17 April after an engine fire. The pilot (of the Service Ferry Pool) escaped with minor injuries. Spitfire P8199 was severely damaged on 3 September following a heavy landing which collapsed its undercarriage; the ATA pilot was unhurt. Hurricane L1956 flown by a pilot of HQ Service Ferry Pool force-landed west of Kemble on 16 September, and Magister T8681 of the Service Ferry Pool spun into the ground near Cirencester after taking off from Kemble on 13 October (casualties are not recorded).

Further changes to ferrying arrangements took place later in 1941. On 11 November, HQ Service Ferry Pools was disbanded, apart from the Service Ferry Training Squadron which was transferred to Honeybourne in Warwickshire and redesignated as the Ferry Training Unit. Ferrying from Kemble was then undertaken by the OAPU, other Service Pools, or the ATA.

More works were taking place at Kemble during the autumn of 1941 and spring of 1942, with metalled runways being constructed, along with more hangars. The Station Security Officer was visited by Special Branch on 16 February 1942. They wanted to discuss their concerns over security in view of the large number of casual Irish labourers employed by the Landing Grounds Corporation who were working on the runways. The Station Commander later commented that he wished he had labourers working on the station rather than the airfield. There were 1,000 personnel living and working at Kemble, but the accommodation was very poor, overcrowding was general and the sanitation was of a low level. He said, in a letter to Group, that the original planning of the station was all wrong and that it needed a re-think due to extensive waterlogging of the site.

During April 1942 there were several accidents at Kemble. The first of these was on the 10th, when Beaufort L4444 of 5 Operational Training Unit, based at Chivenor, stalled on the approach and spun in. The crew were killed and the aircraft was burnt out. On the 25th, Lockheed Hudson AM953 taxied into the excavations for a water main near the unfinished edge of the perimeter track and was substantially damaged, and on the same day Hudson V9059 swung on take-off and its port wheel collapsed. The aircraft caught fire, but the crew managed to escape unhurt.

Dornier Do 217s, similar to this captured example, attacked Kemble in 1942. (Aeroplane)

The main runway was finished in April 1942, and was then ready for use. Running roughly east-west, it was constructed of concrete and covered in tarmac. Also at this time another storage site was completed, G site consisting of two B1 hangars constructed side by side. Shortly after completion the hangars were used for the assembly of Hotspur, Horsa and Hamilcar gliders for the airborne forces squadrons.

HQ 44 Group congratulated 5 MU on the record clearance of Wellington reinforcement aircraft during April 1942 and in May the OAPU despatched a record 103 aircraft, an increase of 10% on the previous month. All personnel were addressed by the Station Commander and congratulated on their splendid effort. In appreciation of their work and as an incentive he authorised a day's holiday for all OAPU staff on the following Sunday! Output was maintained in June and increased to 122 in July. The main aircraft types being ferried at this time were Wellingtons and Hudsons. Of the former, 661 had been handled up to the end of 1942, and of the latter, 269. The Luftwaffe revisited Kemble on 27 July 1942 when two Dornier Do 217s attacked the airfield. They machine gunned the parked aircraft, but failed to hit anything.

As well as glider assembly, tasks for the rest of 5 MU in mid-1942 included the conversion of Hurricanes to fighter-bombers. The other main types of aircraft prepared during the year included Typhoons, Albemarles, Marylands, Beaufighters, Halifaxes and Wellingtons.

No 44 Group decided that the OAPU should be split between Kemble and Filton, so on 1 December 1942 it decided to retitle Nos 1 and 2 Flights at Kemble as No 1 OAPU, and Nos 3 and 4 Flights at Filton as No 2 OAPU. Tragically, shortly after this on 14 January, Halifax W7844 crashed into Oaksey Woods just after take-off from Kemble. The crew were preparing to take the aircraft overseas, but all eight aboard were killed. Also, Whitley EB283 crashed on take-off for a test flight on 24 February but no casualties are recorded.

Beauforts and Hurricanes continued to be processed through into 1943. Avro Lancasters began to arrive in February and Vickers Warwicks in August. One of the main concerns for the station commander in August, according to the station's RAF Form 540 (its Operation Record Book), was the number of bicycle accidents on the station, which 'remains at a high level'.

On 28 September 1943 the secondary runway was begun, running north-west/south-east. The main runway was also extended, and taxiways were built to connect the outlying dispersals with the airfield. Some of these almost reached the village of Culkerton, one and a half miles away. This construction work restricted movements around the airfield, but it was fully operational again by January 1944.

On 20 February 1944, 16 aircraft were despatched by 1 OAPU in one day, the highest since the unit was established. The unit continued despatching aircraft overseas through the summer. On 5 July it was retitled No 1 Aircraft Preparation Unit and was to carry on until 10 October 1944, when it was disbanded.

The priority for aircraft passing through 5 MU during the spring and early summer of 1944 lay with tactical support types such as the Typhoon and Tempest, assault gliders such as the Horsa and Hamilcar and glider tugs such as the Albemarle. These were of course in preparation for the invasion of Europe, but no one knew it at the time. In fact, the imminence of D-Day only began to be felt at Kemble in late May when, on the 27th, 24 US Douglas C-47s arrived to collect Horsa gliders for use by the USAAF in what was to be Operation Overlord. This was followed by a steady stream of replacements to the front-line squadrons. Because of the urgent need and high turnover of these aircraft, this work continued into the late summer. Aircraft types such as the Bristol Buckingham then began to appear, and work at 5 MU centred on upgrading Avro Lancaster bombers by installing the upgraded Rolls-Royce Merlin 45 engines.

Kemble became directly involved in the Allied offensive in the autumn of 1944. A critical shortage of fuel and ammunition had developed, so on 5 September 1944 C-47s of the USAAF began to arrive at Kemble to take supplies to Douai in France. Hundreds of trucks had earlier brought in several hundred tons of supplies, rations and equipment. During the day the C-47s of the 439th, 440th and 441st Troop Carrier Groups of the 50th Troop Carrier Wing flew in to be loaded up and return to France. There were 225 aircraft involved, some doing second trips, so that a total of 580 aircraft movements were recorded that day. The squadrons returned the following day for a repeat performance, flying 250 movements.

These re-supply flights from Kemble were obviously so successful that they carried on, virtually daily, until mid December. In September there were 2,769 C-47 flights from Kemble carrying 13,737,835 lbs of fuel and ammunition. Two aircraft took just maps, and others took currency. On 1 October, 200 C-47s of 52nd Troop Carrier Wing (previously based at Cottesmore) arrived, and later took off for Belgium. During October there were in total 2,718 C-47 flights to the Continent, mainly to Belgium. By November the need for combat supplies had eased, but still 688 C-47 flights were made out of Kemble and in December, 645. The last C-47 re-supply flights by the USAAF were made on 12 December, when 124 aircraft flew out.

In January 1945 Kemble was transferred to 47 Group, Transport Command. No 5 MU continued to operate, and became virtually fully engaged in dealing with transport aircraft such as Dakotas, Warwicks, Yorks, Lancastrians and Stirlings. A Transport Aircraft Modification Section was set up to undertake this specialised work. One of the aircraft produced during May 1945 was Dakota KN386, which had been refurbished for the use of the Chief of Air Staff. It had been taken back to a polished natural metal finish, and was fitted with a refridgerator, bunks, armchairs and washroom. VE Day was celebrated on 8 May 1945, and KN386 was delivered the following day, as if symbolising the end of hostilities in Europe.

As units returned to the UK to disband, their aircraft were brought to Kemble for storage. With the end of the war in the Far East, numbers increased, and at the end of November there were 925 powered aircraft and 85 gliders in stock. Numbers reached their peak in December 1945, when 1,030 aircraft were in storage. The vast majority of these would have to be disposed of. These included US aircraft which, under the terms of lend/lease, had to be returned to the USA or scrapped. However, the RAF had a shortage of transport aircraft, and were allowed to retain a number of Dakotas for an unlimited period. Some other US aircraft, such as Harvards, were similarly held on to. At the beginning of 1946 there were nearly 22,000 aircraft of 130 different types overspilling the storage areas of the RAF's various MUs. Some aircraft types were obsolete, and could be scrapped once the engines and other equipment were removed. Others were held back for sale to other Air Forces, or put to one side for possible civilianisation as freight, passenger or leisure aircraft.

A complication for the post-war disposals process was that aircraft were not all stored at the MUs by type. As operational aircraft in particular were seen as key targets they were spread around the MUs to minimise the effects of a successful raid. Non-operational types did, however, tend to be stored at particular locations. For example, in January 1946 there were 147 civil aircraft of 28 different types in storage, and the majority of these were held at 5 MU Kemble. (Kemble seems to have stored a number of unusual types during the war period such as two aircraft preserved from the First World War – Sopwith Triplane N5912 which later went to the RAF Museum and a German LVG CVI biplane). From December 1945 batches of these aircraft were placed on public view for sale, together with Tiger Moths, Magisters and Oxfords that had been declared surplus to requirements.

Once the surplus aircraft had been segregated and disposed of, the storage of the remainder should not have been a problem, as there was theoretically sufficient storage hangar space at Kemble. Some aircraft, however, such as the Avro Lincoln with its 120-foot wing span, could not be stored inside easily. A system of preservation was therefore used called cocooning, which involved spraying a liquid over the aircraft that would set like a hard plastic. This worked well for the Americans and was used at their storage bases. However, most of these were in the desert, and it was not appreciated until later that cocooning trapped moisture inside the airframes, which in the UK resulted in more corrosion, not less. Other aircraft, such as Lancasters (which were still in production in early 1946), Wellingtons, Ansons, Beaufighters, Harvards, Dakotas, Martinets, Mosquitos, Oxfords, Spitfires, Typhoons and Tempests were put into storage, in the hangars if at all possible.

Transport Command transferred Kemble back to the control of Maintenance Command in 1946, and the unit became one of the main MUs in the country. No 5 MU started to look after Meteors and other

Kemble's main entrance and headquarters site, seen from the air in 1997. (MoD)

jet fighters, and in 1952 the first of 550 Canadair Sabres arrived at Kemble, having been ferried over from Canada. These aircraft were modified to British requirements and painted in standard RAF camouflage at 5 MU before issue to the squadrons. The surface finish section at Kemble became justly famous for the high standard of its paint schemes and many prestigious tasks were carried out by them, on aircraft such as those of the Queen's Flight, the Battle of Britain Memorial Flight, and research aircraft.

Hunters arrived in the mid 1950s and were to remain in service with the RAF for another 40 years. No 5 MU became known as the 'Hunter MU' as the aircraft provided the mainstay of its work through to the 1980s. Hunters in the circuit at Kemble were therefore a familiar sight from the 1950s onwards, but some of these aircraft were actually based there, flying with a detachment of the Central Flying School at Little Rissington known as 4 Squadron. Gnats joined the Hunters at Kemble, and it was there in 1965 that the Red Arrows were formed. They became an official full time team in 1969. When 4 Squadron CFS left for

DH Tiger Moth seen during the Great Vintage Flying Weekend held at Kemble in May 2002. (DGB)

RAF Valley in April 1976 the Red Arrows remained, and re-equipped at Kemble with the Hawk for the 1980 season.

The Red Arrows moved in 1983 to Scampton when 5 MU was closed and Kemble was handed over to the USAF. The station then became a maintenance base for A-10 Thunderbolts and other aircraft flown by the US Air Force in the UK. Spares and stores were also held at Kemble, and these were distributed to USAF bases throughout Europe by Short C-23A Sherpa cargo aircraft specially purchased for the operation. The USAF eventually left in 1992, and Kemble was officially closed in March 1993 in a ceremony that brought the Red Arrows back to their former base. The airfield was then put onto a Care and Maintenance footing.

Interest in the use of the extensive facilities was expressed by several civilian companies and Defence Estates started to lease off some of the hangars for storage. A flying club was established, and Hunters reappeared at Kemble with the arrival of Delta Jets. The Bristol Aero Collection occupied another hangar. The airfield was sold by the MoD to its users under the name of the 'Kemble Heritage Group' in 2000 and with regular air displays now held there, Kemble's future as an active airfield looks secure.

11
LITTLE RISSINGTON

4 miles south of Stow-on-the-Wold
SP 215190

The airfield at Little Rissington came about as part of the RAF Expansion Scheme of the 1930s which called for the construction of a number of new permanent bases for an enlarged Royal Air Force. A site was selected four miles south of Stow-on-the-Wold, on a plateau in the Cotswold Hills, with deep valleys on three sides. Construction started in early 1937 and, at 750 feet above sea level, it would be one of the highest airfields in the country.

The plans for the new station were carefully drawn up in association with the Council for the Protection of Rural England, to ensure that its layout was as far as possible in sympathy with the local countryside, and its buildings in keeping with those of the surrounding villages. Cotswold stone was therefore used where possible to help the station blend in, and traditional Cotswold dry-stone walls erected instead of fencing. Hedges and trees were removed from the requisitioned farmland in order to provide a large grass airfield. Concrete runways were not laid at this time as it was felt that natural grass runways were robust enough and the ground compact enough to bear the weight of any aircraft then flying, or indeed foreseen in the future.

Four large C-type concrete hangars were built to the north-west side of the site, in front of which was added a curving apron upon which a control tower was built overlooking the airfield. Buildings constructed behind the hangars included a main store, workshops, barrack blocks around a parade ground, officers' and sergeants' messes and an airmen's dining hall. Midway through construction it was decided that the station was to be dual-roled, as an Aircraft Storage Unit as well as a flying training station, in order to rationalise resources.

RAF Little Rissington was opened as a Flying Training Command Station under the command of Group Captain A. Ellis, CBE, in August 1938. The first unit to move in was No 6 Flying Training School (FTS), which transferred from Netheravon on the 20th, with single-engined Hawker Harts, Audaxes and Furies, and twin-engined Avro Ansons. One of the school's pilots had already had the unenviable distinction of being the first to crash at Little Rissington, when Anson K6322 of 6 FTS went down on the approach during a visit to the new airfield on 25 February 1938.

A few months later, on 11 October, No 8 Aircraft Storage Unit (ASU) was opened for the storage of reserve aeroplanes, kept to back up and reinforce the operational squadrons. To accommodate the unit's stocks, a number of D-type hangars and Lamella hangars (later covered in turf) were constructed in the south-east corner of the airfield. Hard-standing dispersals were also laid out around the hangars for the outside storage of aircraft. For security reasons, in order to conceal the unit's role, No 8 ASU was renamed No 8 Maintenance Unit (MU) on 7 February 1939. Initially motor vehicles were stored, but shortly afterwards the first Bristol Blenheims, Supermarine Spitfires and Vickers Wellingtons began to arrive from the manufacturers. That autumn there were almost 270 aircraft in store within the MU's hangars.

On the day that war was declared on Germany, 3 September 1939, there were new arrivals at Little Rissington when the Wellingtons of 215 Squadron flew in from Bassingbourne in Cambridgeshire. It was feared that the Germans would immediately start bombing RAF stations, so all squadrons based in East Anglia were withdrawn to stations to the west. After a couple of weeks, when it was apparent that the Luftwaffe weren't coming, the East Anglian squadrons returned to their bases.

The role of 6 FTS was the advanced training of RAF pilots who had already learnt to fly in the DH Tiger Moth trainer, but were still novices. The unit, which was retitled No 6 Service Flying Training School (SFTS) on 3 September, consisted of two squadrons. The Intermediate Squadron flew biplane Hawker Audaxes, Harts and Furies which were supplemented and later replaced by the more modern North American Harvard all-metal monoplane from June 1939 onwards. They trained the novice pilots and took them up from elementary standard. The students then went to the Advanced Squadron, which flew the twin-engined Anson, on which they completed their 14-week training course before being posted to an Operational Training Unit.

Harvards had a long association with Little Rissington. They were in store at 8 MU, and flown by 6 FTS from June 1939 onwards. (Aeroplane)

Due to the nature of the airfield's role, accidents were inevitable at Little Rissington. During the three months of August to October 1939 for example, six aircraft crashed near the airfield. On 25 August Anson L7903 undershot while landing at Little Rissington and on 6 September Hawker Fury K3738 of 6 SFTS crashed on landing, while 11 October was an unfortunate day as Miles Magister P2404 visiting from 9 Air Observer School, Hawker Hart K5810 and Anson L7905, both of 6 SFTS, all crashed on or near the airfield in separate accidents. Injuries sustained by the aircrews involved were luckily fairly minor. The only fatal accident during the period occurred on 19 October 1939 when Gladiator K7950 flown by Sergeant K. Linton of 8 MU crashed into a field near Little Rissington following an engine fire shortly after take-off.

With the onset of war, the school's trainer aircraft holdings increased, as did the number of courses that it ran. Although training continued during the 'Phoney War' period it came to a sudden halt in January 1940 when Britain was hit by one of the worst winters ever recorded. No flying training was possible from Little Rissington for several weeks as snow drifts covered the airfield and surrounding area. When the weather improved, flying was restricted due to the waterlogging of the airfield by the thawing snow cover.

During the freeze, No 8 MU were able to get some aircraft off the ground however. These were Bristol Blenheims that were supplied to the Finnish Air Force in their fight against the Russians, who at the time were not exactly German allies, but also not their enemies. With the large number of 6 SFTS and 8 MU aeroplanes dispersed around the airfield in the spring of 1940, security was of great concern. Mobile patrols were mounted, pillboxes and local defence points constructed and poles were planted across likely glider-landing sites in fields nearby. In order to try to deter Luftwaffe raids on Little Rissington, the MU allocated a Spitfire for local air defence. By May 1940 8 MU had 350 aircraft in storage, although most of these were kept in tightly-packed hangars. Satellite Landing Grounds had also been opened up to increase storage capacity, at Windrush in Gloucestershire and Kidlington in Oxfordshire, to ease congestion on the main airfield.

Biplanes had gradually been phased out by 6 SFTS from late 1939 onwards, and by May 1940 the unit had an inventory of 45 Harvards and 63 Ansons. However, on 24 June 1940 6 SFTS became a twin-engined training school only, concentrating on advanced flying training. The unit's Harvards were returned to 8 MU and more Ansons were received in exchange. As well as the main airfield the SFTS used its satellites at Kidlington and Windrush for training. The

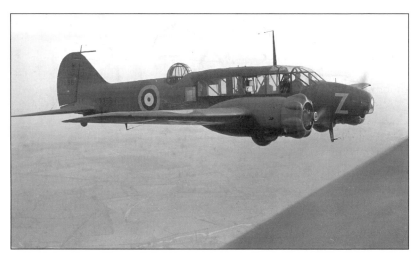

Avro Ansons were flown by 6 FTS. (Aeroplane)

latter was also used for night flying training, to avoid the need for Little Rissington to be lit at night.

As storage of aircraft at the satellites increased, so did the demand for more space. In June 1940 No 8 MU's complement included 58 Fairey Battles, 39 Handley Page Hampdens, 30 Supermarine Spitfires, 21 Miles Magisters, and 21 DH Tiger Moths, together with some 200 other aircraft of various types. These aircraft were also dispersed to additional temporary satellites that became available, such as Watchfield and Pembridge.

Incursions by enemy aircraft were common during the summer of 1940, the period of the Battle of Britain. The Luftwaffe had identified Little Rissington as a target, although it was one of many on the German charts, and the fact that no permanent runways had then been constructed on the airfield probably made it difficult to pinpoint. The first raider appeared in the area on 29 July, and dropped 17 bombs but these landed in fields over three miles away. Another raid occurred late at night on 18 August, when several bombs actually landed on the airfield. One Anson was destroyed, and an airman was wounded.

Training continued during the Battle of Britain, despite a series of alerts and air raid warnings. The need for front-line aircrew was just as important as ever, and 6 SFTS was doing what it could to maintain the number of trained pilots. Having been nominated as a twin-engine school earlier, 6 SFTS lost the last of its single-engined trainers and gained more Ansons; by the autumn of 1940 it had 108 on strength. However, in November the Ansons too started to leave, as they were needed for overseas training schools then being set up under the Empire Air Training Scheme. The Ansons were replaced at 6 SFTS by Airspeed Oxford twin-engine trainers. The unit's complement was increased to reflect the higher number of courses then being run, and there were eventually over 150 Oxfords at the school.

Another reason for the increased complement of Oxfords was unfortunately to allow for a high accident rate. There were the inevitable bumps and scrapes on the airfield, with the resulting damage being repairable but resulting in the aircraft being withdrawn from the flight line. Unfortunately there were also more serious accidents resulting in fatalities: on 29 September 1940 for example, Anson N9821 of 6 SFTS collided with Oxford P9039 of 2 SFTS (from Brize Norton) three miles south of Little Rissington, resulting in the deaths of all aboard both aircraft. A similar accident occurred ten miles north of Stow-on-the-Wold on 29 October when another 6 SFTS Anson, N5285, collided with Anson N9737 of 11 Air Observer Navigation

School (AONS), Watchfield. To ease the congestion at the main airfield a further RLG was opened on 16 November at Chipping Norton in Oxfordshire.

No 5 MU was very busy during the latter half of 1940. More aircraft arrived both from the manufacturers in the UK and from overseas. The latter included Curtiss Mohawks that had been ordered by the French Air Force and were diverted to Britain after the Fall of France, and five rather obsolescent Curtiss Cleveland biplane dive-bombers, the residue of a number that had been ordered by the French Navy. With limited facilities on site at Little Rissington and its few satellites, yet more aircraft had to be stored in the open. Concerns over the security of the parked aircraft on the airfield and dispersals led to more pillboxes and block houses being built, resulting in almost 30 defensive hard-points appearing around the site. They were manned by RAF personnel supplemented by a Home Guard battalion that had been formed towards the end of August by civilian staff working at the station.

The pressures on Little Rissington were eased towards the end of 1940 and early 1941 when more satellite airfields became available for storage, including Barton Abbey, Great Shefford, Worcester, and Middle Farm. Stoke Orchard was also used, shared with the Gloster Aircraft Company which had set up a sub-assembly factory there. Dispersal brought with it, of course, the problems of security on these scattered sites which stretched the ground defence teams even more. The records of 8 MU for mid 1941 show that in addition to those stored on the satellites, another 120 Oxfords, 39 Percival Proctors, 37 Spitfires, 27 Hampdens and 10 Curtiss Mohawks together with lower numbers of other miscellaneous types were held on the main 8 MU site at Little Rissington.

Flying accidents were unfortunately still an ever-present occurrence due to the volume of flying training taking place at Little Rissington. Few resulted in injuries being sustained by personnel, but occasionally more serious accidents did occur, such as on 23 May 1941 when two Oxfords collided over the airfield.

A new type of unit appeared at Little Rissington in October 1941 when No 23 Blind Approach Training Flight was formed at the station. The flight's role was to train pilots in night flying techniques, particularly on instrument flying in bad weather and at night-time. The large multi-engined aeroplanes of Bomber and Coastal Commands and many transport aircraft were fitted with Beam Approach equipment, later known as Instrument Landing Systems. These enabled the pilots to land the aircraft in poor visibility by following an electronic signal that was beamed out from the airfield. The British equipment was based on the Lorenz blind-landing system introduced by the Germans before the war, and later developed by them into a blind bombing system. No 23 BAT Flight used eight Airspeed Oxfords to train its pupils, and to fit in with a new standardised flight numbering system was soon retitled No 1523 (Beam Approach Training) Flight.

No 6 SFTS too was retitled some six months later, when on 1 April 1942 it became No 6 (Pilots) Advanced Flying Unit (although in official jargon, No 6 SFTS was disbanded, and no 6 (P)AFU was formed). This was to indicate that it had been given a new role, of providing advanced flying training for British and Commonwealth pilots arriving in the UK from overseas, having been trained under the Empire Air Training Scheme. It was important to get these newly-qualified pilots acclimatised to the conditions in which they would be conducting their operational flying – that is, not in the wide blue skies of Canada, Australia and South Africa, but in the congested grey skies of northern Europe! The unit took over 6 SFTS's complement of Oxfords and a few Ansons. It continued to use Little Rissington's satellites for flying training (mainly Windrush and Chipping Norton) and to these was added Akeman Street, a Relief Landing Ground, in July 1942.

At around this time the unit was allocated a few examples of the Blackburn Botha to evaluate in the advanced training role. The Botha had been designed as a maritime attack aircraft, but was underpowered and had restricted visibility for its operational role. The assessors of 6 (P)AFU declared the Botha to be unsuitable for their purposes, but the type was later used by other units on training duties.

The runways on Little Rissington's airfield were laid out on a grass surface for the early years of its existence, which was adequate for most of the time but left it prone to waterlogging during heavy rain, which restricted flying. With the increasing weight of the aircraft being flown from the airfield, it was decided to lay tarmac-covered concrete runways in 1942. The main runway was laid from north-east to south-west, the secondary one almost east/west and the third in a north-west/south-east direction.

Night flying had been taking place at Little Rissington's satellite airfields away from the main base, but with the reduced level of enemy night activity during 1942, night flying training was taking place at Little Rissington itself. This procedure was made easier following the building of the hard runways. The BAT flight had been using the main airfield anyway, as the SLGs did not have beam approach landing

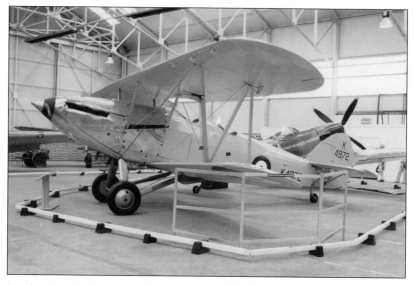

Hawker Hart Trainers were also flown by 6 FTS. This one is preserved in the RAF Museum, Cosford. (DGB)

systems. Unfortunately accidents still occurred. On 19 August 1942 Oxford AB700 flown by Sergeant Ed Francis, an Australian, crashed off the airfield and hit a tree when it lost power just after take-off, killing the pilot. During the night of 6 November 1942 another mid-air collision occurred involving two aircraft from 6 (P)AFU, AP473 flown by a New Zealander, Sergeant Farquharson, and BG551 flown by Sergeant Forrester. Both pilots were killed as the aircraft fell to the ground near the airfield and caught fire.

While flying training had been taking place on the airfield, 8 MU had been quietly working away supporting the flying squadrons. One of the tasks being undertaken during 1942 was the assembly of Hotspur training gliders. They also later received the operational Horsa gliders, which came in several large pieces that had to be checked over then assembled. Other work at this time included the repair and maintenance of the Hawker Hart series of biplanes still in service with training units. These included the Hart Trainer, the Hind Trainer and the Hector glider tug used to tow the Hotspurs at the Glider Training Schools. The MU was also dealing with Handley Page Hampdens (then being used as torpedo bombers), Spitfires of various marks, Oxfords and Wellingtons. By early 1943 these types were still

The Curtiss Kittyhawk was one of the many types stored and maintained by 8 MU. (Aeroplane)

being dealt with, although the Spitfires predominated, but also included were Halifaxes, Typhoons, and two US types, the Curtiss Tomahawk and Kittyhawk. In March No 8 MU took over a new SLG at Woburn Park.

The demand for trained aircrews continued through 1943, and the instructors of 6 (P)AFU worked hard to produce trained pilots who were able to attend the Operational Training Units and go on to join operational squadrons. By mid-1943 the unit's aircraft holdings had risen to 163 Oxfords, four Ansons and a single Tiger Moth, and it was training in the region of 350 pilots at Little Rissington and the three SLGs. Unfortunately accidents still occurred. On 11 September 1943 Oxford DF277 of 1525 BAT Flight collided with another Oxford, MP402 of 6 (P)AFU. Both aircraft crashed, but unfortunately the crew of DF277 were all killed – the pilot, Pilot Officer Barkworth, the co-pilot Warrant Officer Renault and Cadet 1st Class G. Store, a 16-year-old ATC cadet flying on air experience as a passenger.

As Little Rissington's aircraft visited other airfields so that trainees could gain experience, so aircraft from other bases flew to Little Rissington on training sorties. It was on one of these during the night of 7 October that Wellington R1028 of 21 OTU based at Moreton-in-

Handley Page Halifax, as supported at Little Rissington by 8 MU. (Aeroplane)

Marsh, crashed. The aircraft was on approach to Little Rissington but it came down in the garden of the Lamb Inn at Great Rissington. Only one member of the crew of six, the tailgunner, survived the crash, and he later arranged for a monument to be unveiled in the pub to commemorate his crew. Ten days later another Wellington, this time of 82 OTU flown by Sergeant Kirkland was making for Little Rissington after one of its engines failed. Unfortunately the second engine also failed, but the pilot was able to put the aircraft down at Windrush. The Wellington caught fire in the heavy landing, but luckily the crew managed to escape from the burning aircraft.

Little Rissington was a very busy station during 1944, with a high level of training by 6 (P)AFU predominantly by day, and by 1523 (BAT) Flight, mainly at night. BAT flying increased with detachments from 1516 (BAT) Flight from Pershore and 1517 Flight, Chipping Warden, being sent to Little Rissington to assist with the training of 6 (P)AFU's students.

There were also a lot of arrivals and departures at 8 MU by air, and flight testing of aircraft at the unit. More Wellingtons were being dealt with by the MU both for Flying Training and Coastal Commands. As the aircraft were being withdrawn from squadrons, either for modifications or storage, room had to be found for them. By the end of the year 757 aircraft were in storage, predominantly Wellingtons of the Marks III, X, XIII and XIV. The following year storage units were

The Hawker Typhoon was an important type dealt with 8 MU in 1944. (Aeroplane)

opened at Long Marston and Honeybourne to cater for extra volume, and at its zenith later in 1945, 8 MU held a massive 1,388 in store.

Flying training continued through the spring and early summer of 1945. After the end of the war in Europe training was scaled down somewhat, but pilots were still needed in the war against the Japanese. Training finally stopped towards the end of the year, with the completion of the last course on 26 November 1945. By that time it was calculated that No 6 (P)AFU had trained 5,444 pilots, of whom 705 had been awarded gallantry decorations, including four who received the Victoria Cross.

RAF Little Rissington remained open after the war, but without its SLGs which were no longer needed. Although 1523 (BAT) was disbanded in December 1945, No 6 (P)AFU remained, being retitled once more as 6 SFTS. The school received on its inventory a batch of new aircraft in the form of 54 North American Harvard Mk IIbs, two Ansons and a Magister. However, the school didn't stay at Little Rissington for much longer, for on 25 April 1946 it moved to Ternhill in order to make room for the Central Flying School (CFS). Having been disbanded at Upavon in 1942, the CFS was reformed at Little Rissington on 7 May 1946 from No 7 Flying Instructors School (Advanced) that had been moved from Upavon, having been the last remnant of the original CFS, and No 10 FIS (Elementary), that had been moved from Woodley in Berkshire.

Although 8 MU remained at Little Rissington, the end of the war meant that its stocks would have to be drastically reduced. The vast majority of the aircraft in store were sold off, scrapped, or in the case of US-supplied aircraft, returned.

The key role of the CFS was in the training of flying instructors, using South Cerney for basic instruction and Little Rissington for the more advanced training. The Harvards at Little Rissington were replaced by Percival Prentices in 1947 and they in turn were replaced by the Percival Provost in 1953, and the Jet Provost in 1960. Multi-engined training took place originally on the Mosquito T III and Avro Lancasters, then the Vickers Varsity.

No 8 MU remained at Little Rissington as an aircraft storage and maintenance unit until it closed in July 1957. The CFS operated throughout the 1950s and 1960s, constantly changing its organisation and methods to meet the requirements of the time, and updating its equipment as new aircraft came into service. Detachments were based at other stations, including Aston Down and Kemble. The CFS began to contract in the 1970s, the school then flying Jet Provost T4s and 5s, and Scottish Aviation Bulldogs. In 1976 the CFS moved to Cranwell, and Little Rissington closed as a station within Training Command. On 1 September 1976 Little Rissington was handed over to the Army, who renamed the station Imjin Barracks.

In November 1977 flying resumed at Little Rissington when No 637 Volunteer Gliding School moved in from RAF Gaydon. The Royal Irish Rangers arrived at the barracks shortly after this, and were to remain for a couple of years. In 1981 the station once again became RAF Little Rissington, a host base for the USAF. The Americans built a military contingency hospital in the hangars, and this eventually became the largest in Europe. The hospital was put on standby for the 1991 Gulf War, and when hostilities ended, the USAF moved out.

Most of the former RAF Little Rissington was sold off in the mid 1990s, and a housing estate has been built over the site of the barrack blocks and parade ground. The main technical site is now Upper Rissington Park Industrial Estate, the former station headquarters having been converted into commercial offices. At the time of writing the hangars and control tower still stand. The runways and taxiways are still in place on the airfield itself, which is in MoD hands. The airfield is in use by 637 VGS training Air Cadets to fly gliders, and so maintains a link with Little Rissington's long and eventful past.

12
MORETON-IN-MARSH

2 miles east of Moreton-in-Marsh
SP 230350

The site for an airfield needed by the expanding RAF was selected two miles east of the village of Moreton-in-Marsh in the late 1930s. Situated in a bowl in the Cotswolds, the area seemed ideal, being fairly flat and not far from a railway and main roads. However, it later transpired that the area was marshy and prone to fogs, mainly because of the boggy bowl it sat in! Nonetheless, because of its location away from major towns and cities, and being thought reasonably out of range of airfields on the Continent, plans went ahead to build an airfield here as a flying training station.

Just over 500 acres of land were requisitioned in late 1939 from Lord Dulveston, owner of the Batsford Estate in which the site lay, and construction was started by George Wimpey & Co early the following year. The airfield was in a standard bomber layout, as the station was to be the base for a bomber Operational Training Unit (OTU). Three runways were put down in an A-pattern, each of about 3,000 feet in length. However, these were judged to be too short and were later extended, the main runway to 4,200 feet, the other two to 3,300 feet each. Taxiways and dispersals were added, along with four T2 hangars, intended for servicing and maintenance of aircraft, and a single brick-built J-type, a larger hangar for maintenance and repair.

The first unit to fly from Moreton-in-Marsh was not intended to be a resident one but was to use the new airfield temporarily. This was 55 OTU, detached from its home of Aston Down on 27 November 1940 due to overcrowding there. The unit was a fighter OTU, training pilots for Spitfire and Hurricane day fighter, and Blenheim night-fighter, front-line squadrons. It flew mainly Hawker Hurricanes, but also a number of Miles Masters and de Havilland Dominies. Two days after its arrival 55 OTU had its first casualty when Pilot Officer Komenski was injured crash-landing his Hurricane at Moreton-in-Marsh. The new airfield was hardly complete at this time, the semi-finished runways apparently lying in a sea of mud! This may have affected the OTU's flying operations, as during its time at Moreton-in-Marsh its students crash-landed nine aircraft. The unit returned to Aston Down on 22 February 1941.

The opening-up party had arrived in January, as had a group from No 15 OTU at Harwell in Oxfordshire led by Pilot Officer Turner. They had been detached to Moreton-in-Marsh to form the station's first resident unit, No 21 OTU. This was officially formed on 21 January 1941. The first aircraft to arrive for the new unit were three Vickers Wellington Mk ICs and two Avro Anson Mk Is. More Wellingtons followed, and by the end of February 21 OTU had eight of the type on strength.

The Vickers Wellington was the mainstay of 21 OTU during the war years. (Aeroplane)

170

The Wellington twin-engined monoplane bomber was designed by Barnes Wallis, the chief designer of the Vickers Aeroplane Co. The aircraft's unusual geodetic lattice construction gave it great strength, capable of taking a lot of punishment and still surviving, whilst at the same time proving easy to repair. Powered by two Bristol Pegasus XVIII engines, the Wellington IC had a top speed of 235 mph at 15,500 feet and carried a bomb load of 4,500 pounds. It was armed with two .303 machines guns in the nose and tail turrets, and single guns in fuselage beam positions.

The aircraft formed the backbone of the RAF bomber force in the early years of the war and suffered heavy losses, especially early on until it was realised that unescorted bombers were vulnerable during daylight attacks. This resulted in most RAF bombing raids being flown at night. On the night of 25/26 August 1940, 17 Wellingtons joined 12 Hampdens and 14 Whitleys to make the first Bomber Command attack on Berlin. The Wellington was to be built in greater numbers than any other single bomber type in RAF history, achieving a total of 11,460 in a number of marks. The type was progressively upgraded and improved in service, the earlier versions being withdrawn for training as the more advanced versions replaced them. Finally withdrawn from front line service with Bomber Command in autumn 1943, the Wellington remained the mainstay of the Command's OTUs throughout the war. The aircraft was also used by Coastal Command, sinking 26 U-boats during the Second World War, and continued in service as a navigational trainer until 1953.

The role of 21 OTU was to prepare bomber crews for combat. The men who arrived at the unit had all been trained at separate specialist schools for a particular role – as pilot, navigator, air gunner, wireless operator and bomb aimer. At the OTU they would come together for the first time, and be formed into crews for the duration of their course, if not longer. The accent on their training was to work as a team, which was essential for the effective operation of the aircraft, the successful conclusion of its mission and for the crew's survival. The OTU was organised into four flights: A flight for initial conversion training, B flight for operational flying training, C flight for navigation and radio communications and D flight for aerial armament and fighter affiliation. This system worked well and produced a high standard of aircrews.

The intake of crews at the bomber OTUs was on a fortnightly basis, usually with between 10 to 15 crews joining. The course was planned to take ten weeks to include at least 40 day and 40 night flying hours but this depended on the weather. The syllabus included such exercises as synthetic training (including the link trainer for the pilots and the turret trainer and clay pigeon shooting for the gunners), gunnery (eg combat manoeuvres, air-to-air firing, fighter affiliation), bombing (eg from high level by day and night, pathfinder techniques), navigation (dead reckoning, cross-country, radar training), operational training (exercises with searchlights, AA batteries and night fighters, leaflet raids over enemy territory), drills (dinghies, parachutes, fire, oxygen, crash drills) and operational procedures (such as Darky (radio homing), searching homing, SOS).

The first course at 21 OTU started on 1 March 1941. The number of aircraft at the unit steadily increased over the next few weeks, which enabled more crews in the initial intakes (No 2 course started on 18 March) and by the end of the month it had 16 Wellingtons and four Ansons on strength. Bombing practice took place at Radway, a range approximately 13 miles north of Moreton-in-Marsh. It was fairly small, covering a radius of 750 yards from a concrete target. Small practice bombs were dropped by attacking aircraft, and their strikes on the target were marked by observers in two quadrant towers one on each side of the range's edge.

Although the Germans were aware of the airfield's existence, Moreton-in-Marsh was only attacked three times (twice in 1941 and again in 1942). The first raid was during the night of 3 April 1941, when two 500lb high explosive bombs were dropped on the north-west side of the airfield, without any significant damage, and a number of incendiaries were dropped on the main airfield. Some of these went under a taxiing Wellington, but without damage to the aircraft. The second attack occurred just over a month later on 8 May when incendiaries fell onto a dispersal area, but again without damage.

No 1 course completed on 14 April, and in accordance with the schedule, so did No 2 course on 28 April. That night several Wellingtons from the unit flew to Paris to drop propaganda leaflets, and it is possible that the crews included some from No 2 Course, to give them operational experience.

Operational training was to take a heavy toll of the trainees. With most of the crews having been trained in the sunny skies of Canada, South Africa or India, adjusting to different weather and terrain was a major challenge. Added to this were the difficulties of flying at night and the technicalities of flying heavier aircraft, in busier airspace; these factors contributed to a succession of accidents. During the course of the Second World over 8,000 Bomber Command aircrew were killed in training (in the region of 10% of all Bomber Command deaths) and well over 3,000 were injured.

Fortunately the accident rate at Moreton-in-Marsh was relatively low. The first aircraft loss for 21 OTU was an Anson, which crashed at Tredegar in Wales. Luckily only one member of the crew was injured, suffering a broken leg. The next was on 15 June when Wellington IC T2910 crashed while attempting to overshoot. The aircraft caught fire, but the crew managed to escape before it burnt out.

The unit's strength at the end of June was 37 Wellingtons, six Ansons and a Magister. Unfortunately more accidents would reduce this number. On 10 July a Wellington landed at high speed, having suffered a flap failure, swerved off the runway and hit a truck. On the 24th another Wellington crashed while on a bombing exercise over the Radway bombing ranges (presumably the crew escaped, as no casualties are recorded), but the first fatalities occurred on 28 July when Wellington X3198 crashed into a mountainside in North Wales killing all aboard. Tragically this was repeated on 17 August when Wellington R1098 flew into another mountain in the same area. On

Avro Ansons were also flown by 21 OTU. (Aeroplane)

9 September Wellington X9698, was lost when its pilot became disorientated in cloud. The aircraft went into a steep dive and the captain ordered the crew to bail out. This they did, apart from the tail gunner who was killed when the aircraft hit the ground.

The circuit at Moreton-in-Marsh was getting very busy by this time, and was relieved in mid September when Edgehill airfield was opened some ten miles away in Warwickshire as a satellite. The first official landing took place there on 20 September, and from then on Edgehill was in regular use for circuit flying by day and by night. Meanwhile, at Moreton-in-Marsh, a Wellington had run off the end of the runway and gone through a hedge, due to lack of supervision by an instructor on 13 September. More accidents came later in the month when on the 25th another Wellington hit treetops and crashed, killing four crew members and injuring two; on the 29th a Wellington burst a tyre on take-off from Edgehill and made a wheels up crash-landing on the grass back at Moreton-in-Marsh.

Accidents continued into October – on the 4th a Wellington hit treetops on approach to the airfield and crash-landed, fortunately without injury. The aircraft had been taking two ground crews to Edgehill, but couldn't find the airfield due to deteriorating weather and had to return to Moreton-in-Marsh. There had also been a number of taxiing incidents on the airfield. When, on the 16th, a Wellington collided with an Anson, it was decided that ground control measures ought to be introduced. Another flying accident occurred on 24 October when Wellington R1031 stalled at 400 feet just after take-off from Edgehill, and dived into the ground. Most of the crew were killed, only the tail gunner surviving.

Towards the end of October 1941, B flight was deployed to Edgehill along with its ground crews, to operate from there on a semi-permanent basis. A month later 21 OTU learned that they had been tasked with the training of crews specifically for Middle East Wellington squadrons. The first crews for these postings were due to graduate on 14 December.

More replacement aircraft for the OTU had arrived during November. Strength at the end of the month was 58 Wellingtons, nine Ansons, two Lysanders and a Magister. However, as more aircraft arrived, more were lost. On 7 December two Wellingtons crashed during night flying, one having hit a telegraph pole. Some members of each crew were killed, others seriously injured. Christmas celebrations at Moreton-in-Marsh were muted in 1941, as on 23 December Wellington DV422 spun into the ground, killing all aboard, including the Officer Commanding A Flight, Squadron Leader Willliams. Many members of the crew had arranged to return home on Christmas leave.

Having graduated on 14 December 1941, the first crews allocated to the Middle East returned to Moreton-in-Marsh after having taken some well-deserved leave, and readied themselves for their next undertaking. This was not only to deploy to their operational squadrons in the Middle East but to take an aircraft each with them! In this way both crews and aircraft arrived in theatre at the same time. The fact that the crews were inexperienced was obviously not seen as much of a problem by the planners, although the crews themselves probably didn't see it that way. Such a long-distance flight in wartime conditions was not to be taken lightly. Wellingtons assigned to the operational squadrons were ferried in by the Air Transport Auxiliary for the crews to take away, and the first left on 1 January 1942. They were routed across occupied France to Malta. Fortunately there were no mechanical problems, and the aircraft managed to maintain sufficient altitude in transit to be unmolested by enemy fighters. The Wellingtons all arrived in Malta safely, and were later flown on to Egypt or other destinations as needed.

The weather was good in early January and crew training carried on at Moreton-in-Marsh. Twelve more Wellingtons were received by 21 OTU during the month. Other activity on the airfield included the beefing up of ground and AA defences, and the camouflaging of the buildings, runways and defence installations. The second batch of crews for the Middle East left on 15 January, when seven Wellingtons took off for Malta. However, not much flying took place from Moreton-in-Marsh during the third week in January as the weather turned to ice and snow.

The first flying accident of the year was on 13 January, when Wellington T2911 crashed in bad visibility at dusk. The aircraft caught fire and burnt out, but the crew escaped without injury. A Wellington force-landed at Harwell on 26 January and was badly damaged, but again without injury to the crew. The next accident on 28 January involved two Wellingtons, R1165 and 21157, which collided over Radway bombing range during a night exercise. Both crews managed to bail out from their aircraft, with the exception of one crew member who was killed. Two more accidents occurred in February, on the 4th when a Wellington crashed on take-off, resulting in five deaths, and on the 8th when a low-flying Wellington hit a tree at Brize Norton, killing all aboard except for one survivor. On 13 February 1942 another

Wellington (R1082) crashed at Wellesbourne Mountford after an engine failure, killing four crew, and more died on 9 March when Wellington Z8774 crashed at Edgehill. Another aircraft, N2800, came down at Moreton-in-Marsh on 27 March, but no casualties are recorded.

The plan was to send 15 aircraft and crews per month to the Middle East in February, increasing to 18 in April, and 20 from May onwards. Due to losses over France, the route was later changed so that the first leg was to Portreath in Cornwall for refuelling and final preparations, then over the Bay of Biscay to Gibraltar, and eastwards through the Mediterranean to Malta. On 18 May No 1446 Ferry Training Flight arrived at Moreton-in-Marsh on transfer from Bassingbourn, also equipped with Wellingtons. This was effectively another training unit, specifically charged with giving the OTU's graduates suitable training for long distance ferry flying.

There were no accidents reported in April, but May brought another spate, when Wellington T2824 crashed near Edgehill killing the crew on 6 May, and two days later Z1161 force-landed at Beckenham in Lincolnshire, but with no recorded casualties. On the 19th Wellington DV811 taxied into the rear of Anson AX430, writing it off (with no casualties) and two days later the two types were involved again, this time in separate incidents, when Anson N5259 hit overhead power lines near Kingham in Oxfordshire resulting in two deaths and three injuries, and Wellington R1142 stalled while overshooting at Edgehill, killing four more crew. On the 26th there was a lucky escape for all involved when Wellington DV657 of 1446 Flight burst a tyre on take-off and swung off the runway. It collided with another Wellington, X9934 of 21 OTU, which was being bombed up in the dispersal area. Both aircraft were destroyed in the resulting explosion and fire, but the occupants managed to escape, three members of the ground crew being the only minor casualties.

The Wellington that was hit was being prepared for an operational mission by 21 OTU. The unit was to take part in the first of the Thousand Bomber Raids. This concept was devised by Air Marshal Arthur Harris soon after he took over as Air Officer Commanding Bomber Command in February 1942. The idea was to mount a spectacular demonstration of what his command could achieve in the war of attrition against Germany. His plan had the support of the Prime Minister, Sir Winston Churchill, and the Chief of the Air Staff, Air Chief Marshal Sir Charles Portal. However, to reach the magic figure of 1,000, aircraft had to be drawn in from the OTUs and conversion units, as well as every operational squadron. Of the 1,040 bombers eventually used in the first raid, 367 came from the training units. The bulk of the aircraft flown on the raid were twin-engined, mainly Wellingtons but also Avro Manchesters. Only 294 of them were the newer four-engined Short Stirlings, Handley Page Halifaxes and Avro Lancasters.

Many aircraft from 21 OTU took part in the raids, the crews consisting initially of a mix of experienced staff and students. Later, as their confidence grew, all-student crews took part. While the aircraft were being bombed up, Ansons from the unit were flown on simulated training sorties. They made all the usual radio transmissions that would be made by the trainee crews, so that German intelligence monitoring them would be under the impression that the Wellingtons were training as usual. Twenty-two Wellingtons took off from Moreton-in-Marsh on 30 May 1942 to take part in their first raid, on Cologne. One aircraft, DV598, hit a tree on take-off and crashed but without any recorded casualties, and two aircraft later abandoned the mission, but the remainder reached their target and returned to base safely.

Two days later, 23 aircraft took off for Essen (twelve from Moreton-in-Marsh and eleven from Edgehill). Three Wellingtons returned early due to technical faults, but the remaining crews reached the target. They returned safely to Moreton-in-Marsh, apart from W5618 which was lost on the return flight, presumably to enemy night-fighters, and another aircraft that was also attacked by a night-fighter but although damaged managed to evade it to land at Honington on return to the UK. Another raid was made by 21 OTU aircraft on the night of 25/26 June when eleven aircraft were sent from Moreton-in-Marsh and ten from Edgehill. They joined a force of 1,006 bombers attacking Germany that night. Of the force, 44 aircraft were lost, including one from 21 OTU. The other Moreton-in-Marsh aircraft returned safely, although six aircraft landed away from the station on their return. The three Thousand Bomber Raids were an enormous boost to the nation's morale, and to Bomber Command itself. However, the loss of over 100 aircraft in three raids was more than the Command could afford.

No 1446 Ferry Training Flight had become operational in June 1942, and despatched its first batch of Wellingtons later in the month. They got as far as Egypt, where one group of aircraft and crews went to 458 Squadron at Fayid, and the others flew on to Ambala in India, to join 99 Squadron. Despatches increased, and in July 36 Wellingtons were sent overseas.

Two aircraft were lost in accidents in July 1942; Wellington X9637 crashed into the sea off Fowey in Cornwall, killing all aboard, and T2962 went down at Llangrove in Wales, with three killed and four injured. Another was lost on 28 July, when the Luftwaffe made their third attack on Moreton-in-Marsh. They destroyed Anson N5022 and left five more Ansons severely damaged. Other losses included Wellington R1345 which crashed on a cross-country night flight, killing its crew, and R1232 which caught fire and burnt out after overshooting the runway (three of its crew were killed).

The OTU's crews took part in more operational missions over the next months, including Dusseldorf on the night of 31 July (eleven aircraft took off and all returned including seven all-student crews), and Bremen on 13 September (ten aircraft took off, one failed to return, one aircraft was badly flak damaged and another crash-landed at Laxford in Suffolk after being attacked by an enemy night fighter). The last conventional raid that the OTU's crews took part in was on the night of 16 September, when twelve aircraft (six each from Moreton-in-Marsh and Edgehill) took part in a 369 bomber raid on Essen. Of the 41 aircraft lost from the attacking force, one was from the OTU. With the increased number of aircraft and trained crews reaching the front-line Bomber Command squadrons during the sutumn of 1942, the need for the involvement of the OTUs on operations diminished, and they were generally no longer used from mid September 1942 onwards. However, the operational experience gained was felt to be useful for the student crews, and so they were subsequently used on leaflet-dropping sorties (codenamed 'Nickelling') over Occupied France.

The first Nickelling sorties were scheduled for the night of 21 November, but these were postponed due to bad weather and eventually took place on 24 November. All of the aircraft despatched by 21 OTU returned successfully, having flown to Paris and dropped leaflets explaining Allied attacks on French Colonial territory. More leaflets were dropped on 18 November over Nantes. Five aircraft took part, but not one returned to base – four landed away at other airfields on return to the UK but one Wellington, T2574, had turned back over the coast with engine trouble and crashed at Longmoor in Hampshire. Only one member of the crew survived.

During November 1942, 22 Wellingtons and crews left Moreton-in-Marsh for the Middle East, followed in December by another 13. No 1446 Flight then had twelve Wellingtons on its strength along with a number of Ansons and Oxfords with which to train the crews in ferrying techniques. More Nickelling missions took place towards the end of the year, with five Wellingtons flying to Nantes on 17 December, all returning to base without loss. However, a loss did occur on 22 December, when a Wellington crashed into Mount Snowdon in North Wales, leaving no survivors. Two days before, most of the occupants of R1344 had been lucky when a photoflash exploded in the aircraft flare chute on a training flight. The wireless operator/air gunner was killed in the blast, and the aircraft captain, Sergeant Muir, ordered the rest of the crew to bail out. This they successfully did, and Muir managed to put the burning aircraft down in a skillful crash-landing near Compton Wynates.

Crew training continued into the New Year. The first Nickelling operations of 1943 took place towards the end of January when, on the 29th, five Wellingtons departed for Nantes. One aircraft returned with technical problems, but the other four dropped their leaflets. Unfortunately one aircraft crashed on the return journey, coming down near Stroud, with no survivors. This was followed by a single aircraft mission on 1 February, which dropped its leaflets over Paris and returned safely. The next sortie on 25 February involved five Wellingtons flying to Nantes. They found the target, dropped their leaflets and returned safely despite solid cloud cover over France.

The satellite at Edgehill was transferred to No 12 OTU at Chipping Warden on 12 April. In its place Moreton-in-Marsh was allocated the newly completed airfield at Enstone, roughly twelve miles to the south-east of Moreton-in-Marsh in Oxfordshire. The 466-strong 21 OTU Edgehill detachment moved to its new location later that day. Unfortunately the first accident at Enstone occurred only a few days later when, on 15 April, Wellington Z1142 swung off the runway on take-off and hit the windsock; three of the crew died in the resulting crash. Other losses during the period included X3219, which crashed on a navigational exercise near Baltonsborough in Somerset on 8 March, all aboard being killed.

In the spring of 1943 No 21 OTU had 54 Wellingtons on strength, along with 17 Ansons and four newly-arrived Martinets. The latter were target-towing aircraft, and were delivered to the unit to provide targets for gunnery practice. Formed into X Flight of 21 OTU, the Martinets were moved to Enstone on 17 May. The Commander of X Flight at the time was Flight Lieutenant, later Wing Commander, W.H. Wallis, later to become famous as the designer and builder of autogyros/gyrocopters, and the pilot of the gyrocopter 'Little Nellie' in the James Bond film *You Only Live Twice*. On 1 May the other unit at

Miles Martinet, as flown by X Flight to provide practice for the trainee Wellington gunners. (Aeroplane)

the station, 1446 Ferry Training Flight, was re-designated 311 Ferry Training Unit, a title which more accurately reflected its role, which was one of ferry preparation and despatch as well as training.

Training carried on throughout May and into June 1943 without incident. However, on 2 July an Oxford on a solo training flight from Chedworth crashed near the guardroom at Moreton-in-Marsh, killing the pilot. Another accident followed on 7 July, when a Wellington of 21 OTU returning to Enstone was descending through cloud when it collided with an Oxford flying beneath it. Both aircraft crashed, killing both crews.

More Nickelling sorties were flown on 15 August; seven Wellingtons were despatched to the Tours area, and although all aircraft reached the UK safely, one was shot down by German aircraft that was raiding the English Coast. The crew bailed out, but the pilot and rear gunner were killed. A couple of weeks later, there was a change to the OTU's occasional operational sorties, as on 31 August, five Wellington crews were briefed to attack a target at Foret d'Eperlecques as part of a feint attack (or a 'Bullseye') to divert enemy attention from other missions that night. Two aircraft had to return early, but the remaining three found and attacked the target successfully and returned to base.

Another raid on the same area on 3 September by six OTU aircraft was similarly successful, with only one aircraft having to return early. The unit returned to Nickelling on 15 and 16 September to the Rennes/Le Mans area. By October the Wellingtons were flying a dozen of these operations per month; they were obviously seen as useful and worth the risk by someone in the command structure. The unit were also regularly flying Bullseyes at this time, and these were set at six per month.

More accidents occurred in November and December. Wellington Z9103 ditched off the west Devon coast near Mortehoe whilst on a Bullseye mission on 12 November, but with no loss or injury to the crew. The crew of R1293 also all escaped safely when their aircraft crashed at Enstone on 16 November. Unfortunately on 17 November, DV918 overshot the runway at Enstone and crashed, killing four of the crew, and on 18 December Wellington Mk III BK132 dived into the ground at Atcham in Shropshire, all aboard being killed in the impact. The year ended on a sad note, when Wellington IC X9666 crashed on a hillside near Aberdovey in north Wales while on a bombing exercise. Three members of the crew were killed and two badly injured.

New Year 1944 started with the usual mix of training, Bullseyes and Nickelling, with the residents of Amiens, Abbeville, Cambrai, Orleans, Arnas and Cherbourg being selected to receive reading matter courtesy of His Majesty's Air Force! The sortie of 14 January was made by newly-received Wellington Mk Xs, and that of 5 February to Compiegne and Beauvais was the last by Wellington Mk ICs which were then withdrawn from use. The Mark ICs used at 21 OTU were among the earliest to be flown by the RAF, and had been in service since 1938. Many of these aircraft were veterans, having flown with several front-line bomber squadrons before being transferred to the OTUs for training. One, R1523, even survived the war, not being scrapped until March 1946.

A new type of assignment was given to 21 OTU on 20 February, in the form of a 'Special Bullseye' mission. The purpose of this diversion was not to make a feint on a specific target, but to assemble off the coast of Denmark as if to threaten a raid in a general area. The 21 OTU Wellingtons rendezvoused with aircraft from other OTUs, and German fighters were duly scrambled to meet them. The decoy bomber force flew around over the North Sea, and while the German fighters waited for them over the Netherlands the main bomber force raided Stuttgart to the south. Having already been committed to the north, the German fighters did not have the time or fuel to get to the main raid, with the result that only nine British bombers were lost over Stuttgart (this was a much reduced casualty figure for such a mission at the time).

X Flight returned to Moreton-in-Marsh from Enstone on 24 February. They made room for 1682 Bomber Defence Training Flight which had transferred from Stanton Harcourt, with five Curtiss Tomahawks, later replaced by Hurricanes. Sorties by 21 OTU continued into the spring of 1944, with the mix of flying consisting of scheduled training, Bullseyes and Nickelling. The routine was occasionally varied, such as on 27 March when (by prior arrangement with their 'victims') the Wellingtons made a simulated raid on Portsmouth. Local air defence fighters intercepted the bombers, and made dummy attacks on them.

With the call for the ferrying of bombers decreasing, the need for 311 Ferry Training Unit had diminished in early 1944. It was decided to disband the unit on 1 May 1944, its Wellingtons being handed over to 21 OTU. There was an influx of personnel to Moreton-in-Marsh in early June when various units used the station as a transit camp while waiting to proceed south to the Channel ports as part of the D-Day invasion force. Numbers at the station rose from 2,970 at the end of May to 4,096 in June. Once the landings had taken place there was a steady movement through the station as more follow up support units moved through, but by the end of June personnel numbers were back to normal.

Flying incidents continued during the first half of 1944 but the accident rate had generally improved, even though 21 OTU was then operating 54 aircraft. Some losses did occur, however, and these included Wellington Mk X LN878 which disappeared on 24 April 1944 with its crew on a navigation exercise over the North Sea east of Hull, and Mk X HE870, which suffered engine failure while visiting Barton-on-the-Heath (the aircraft overshot and crashed, killing several members of the crew). Another Wellington X, LN635, crashed after a mid-air fire over the Radway range on 12 June. Fortunately all the crew managed to bail out successfully. Wellington X LN696 was a total loss on 16 May when the fuel bowser that was refuelling it caught fire.

Visiting aircraft were also involved in accidents. On 30 July a Halifax returning from an operation crashed on approach to the airfield. Although the survivors were rushed to the station sick quarters, they died of their injuries shortly afterwards. The twelve Halifaxes from 10 Squadron that were diverted to Moreton-in-Marsh on 27 August however, landed without incident. They had returned from a 'Gardening' operation (laying mines) to Kiel Bay, to constrain German naval forces. Most aircraft returned to base at Melbourne, Yorkshire, the next day, leaving behind two aircraft for repairs.

Operations by 21 OTU crews continued into the autumn of 1944. Most of these were successfully completed without loss, but on the raid of 30 August three of the eight aircraft that took part did not return to base. One aircraft, LN895, crash-landed at East Kirby in Lincolnshire after being fired on by an Allied convoy off Cromer, the crew managing to escape without injury. The other two, Mk IIIs BJ 790 and HE444, were probably intercepted by enemy fighters.

Steady losses continued during training. On 31 August Mk III BK135 was hit by lightning and crashed into the ground near Odstone Farm, Berkshire. There were no survivors. Two aircraft collided at Enstone on 16 September, when LN771 was given permission to take off but was hit by LN429 coming in to land. The wireless operator/air gunner from LN771 was the sole survivor of the crash. Two more Wellingtons were lost in October when Mk X LN693 crashed into the ground on the 12th during a cross country navigation exercise, and on the 31st NC649 hit the ground in low cloud near Stow on the Wold. There were no survivors from either aircraft.

Christmas was celebrated with particular gusto in 1944, with the news that the Allied armies were doing well and approaching the borders of Germany. Training carried on almost uninterrupted into the New Year, and a number of Bullseyes were flown. A milestone was reached by 21 OTU on 7 February 1945 when course No 100 started at Moreton-in-Marsh. The crews coming through the unit during this time were predominantly Australian. With the war in Europe still going at full swing, and the Japanese fighting fiercely in the Far East, the demand for crews to man the operational squadrons continued throughout the spring of 1945. Accidents inevitably occurred, and on 8 April Wellington Mk III BK133 crashed during night flying on Rollright Heath not far from the airfield. Its crew of six were all killed.

Pressure on Germany continued, as there were no signs of the enemy giving up and Allied bombing missions continued. Some of the aircraft involved were diverted to Moreton-in-Marsh during April – on the 9th, 17 Lancasters arrived, on the 14th, nine Halifaxes and on the 19th, nine Lancasters and two USAAF B-24 Liberators.

Eventually, the Third Reich did capitulate, and VE Day was celebrated at Moreton-in-Marsh on 8 May with a church service, followed by a 48-hours leave pass for all non-essential personnel (and no doubt a party or two for those left to man the station!). Following everyone's return two days later, flying training resumed, as trained crews were still required for the Far East.

In June some of the long-distance navigational training flights took the form of 'Cook's Tours' for the ground crews to view the damage sustained by German towns. Three routes were taken – to Emden and Wilhelmshaven, to the Ruhr, and to Aachen, Bonn and Cologne. With the end of the war on 15 August, VJ Day was celebrated at Moreton-in-Marsh with parties and dances at the station. Once again personnel were given time off.

Unlike many front line units, 21 OTU continued to operate after VJ Day, and although numbers of students dropped, courses continued. It was decided that Enstone was no longer needed as a satellite and on 24 November it was closed for flying. At the end of 1945, personnel numbers at Moreton-in-Marsh had more than halved, from over 4,000 in June to 1,959 in December. Numbers reduced even further in 1946 and the resulting shortage of labour on the station was such that German prisoners of war were brought in to undertake cleaning and routine maintenance around the camp. RAF Moreton-in-Marsh achieved a kind of fame after the war, as it inspired the title of a BBC radio series, *Much Binding in the Marsh*, a comedy set on an RAF station. One of the show's writers and presenters, Kenneth Home, had, in fact, an intimate knowledge of Moreton-in-Marsh, having been an Intelligence Officer at the station during the war.

Eventually, after five years at Moreton-in-Marsh, on 18 November 21 OTU left the station, on transfer to Finningley in Yorkshire. They were replaced by No 21 (Pilots) Advanced Flying Unit which arrived with a fleet of Oxfords from Wheaton Aston towards the end of November. They were joined by No 1 Refresher School, formed in mid-December, also with Oxfords – over 85 of the aircraft were then based at Moreton-in-Marsh. The two units were combined into No 1 (Pilot) Refresher Flying Unit in August 1947, with Wellingtons, Harvards and Spitfire 16s, in addition to Oxfords. In January 1948 they too were transferred to Finningley.

A couple of months later the Technical Training Command Medical Training Establishment was opened at Moreton-in-Marsh. They were joined by No 2 Refresher Squadron of the Central Flying School in

North American Harvards flew from Moreton-in-Marsh with several training units post-war. (Aeroplane)

November, and both units remained until October 1951 when they left. They were replaced by the last RAF unit to be based at Moreton-in-Marsh, No 1 Flying Training School (FTS), which transferred from Oakington with over 100 Harvards. The airfield was soon so congested that new aprons had to be constructed. Percival Prentices were introduced at the FTS in December 1951, and the unit flew from Moreton-in-Marsh for another four years. On 20 April 1955 No 1 FTS was disbanded, and RAF Moreton-in-Marsh was put under Care and Maintenance.

Handed over to the Home Office, the station became a training school for RAF Reserve fire-fighters for which a fleet of Green Goddess fire engines was used. In 1959 the Fire Service College at Dorking took over the airfield to train civilian firemen, and this gradually expanded over the ensuing years. Eventually, after much redevelopment of the site, in May 1974 the Fire Service Technical College was opened at Moreton-in-Marsh. Although few wartime buildings now remain, much of the former RAF airfield does. Over 65 years after its original construction, the station still fulfils the function for which it was built, that of training the nation's guardians.

13
MORETON VALENCE
(Haresfield)

1 mile west of Haresfield village
SO 796104

Opened as an Emergency Landing Ground in November 1939, this airfield was originally known as Haresfield after the village one mile to the east. It was used occasionally by various units, mainly for training. These included No 6 Air Observers Navigation School (AONS) which would bring its Ansons over for flying training away from its base at Staverton. Albemarles on test from Brockworth would also drop in.

It was decided that Haresfield could perform a useful role for such training on a more permanent basis, and during 1941 the airfield was upgraded. Three tarmac-covered concrete runways were built and buildings erected, including two Blister hangars. The airfield was reopened as Moreton Valence, and in August 1941 a permanent detachment was set up there by 6 AONS.

The Avro Anson aircraft used by the school detachment (initially B and C Flights) were kept in the hangars at Moreton Valence. For everyday maintenance the aircraft were looked after by the ground crews on site, but for servicing and more major work, they were returned to Staverton. The detachment resumed its role of training observers and navigators for multi-engined aircraft, preparing them for their move to the Operational Training Units, such as No 21 OTU at Moreton-in-Marsh, not far away. There they would join a crew and train together before being posted to the front-line bomber squadrons. During the autumn of 1941 bomber crews were sorely needed and training units like 6 AONS were busy trying to satisfy that need. On

Avro Tutors were flown from Moreton Valence by the PRTU and 6 AOS. This one, preserved by the Shuttleworth Trust, is painted in pre-war training markings. (Aeroplane)

17 January 1942 the unit became No 6 Air Observers School (AOS), but its purpose remained unchanged.

In the spring of 1942 the Pilot Refresher Training Unit was formed at Moreton Valence, with Miles Master II single-engined trainers. It later also acquired Avro Tutor single-engined and Airspeed Oxford twin-engined trainers. The unit was established to provide refresher training for pilots who had not been engaged in flying duties for some time. Its students were given courses of instruction in single-engined aircraft, and conversion courses to twin-engined aircraft. The unit was retitled as the Refresher Flying Training School on 1 May 1942, then moved to Kirknewton in Scotland.

No 6 AOS continued to fly from Moreton Valence during the summer of 1942 and into 1943. During this time it received other aircraft types in addition to the Ansons and Rapides, including Avro Tutors, DH Tiger Moths, Miles Magisters and later Blackburn Botha twin-engined crew trainers. On 11 June 1943, 6 AOS was once again retitled, this time as No 6 (Observers) Advanced Flying Unit ((O)AFU).

One of the students to pass through the school during 1942 was Guy Fazan, who had trained as a radio observer. Re-categorised as a 'navigator/radio', he completed his flying training on the Ansons at Moreton Valence before moving on to 62 OTU at Usworth,

The Blackburn Botha also equipped 6 AOS. (Aeroplane)

Northumberland. There, in more Ansons, he learnt to operate the Air Interception radar and was posted to 291 Squadron, a night-fighter unit flying Beaufighters in North Africa. The squadron later returned to the UK, re-equipped with Mosquitos and after D-Day moved to the Continent where Guy Fazan and his fellow pilots shot down four enemy aircraft (a Ju 88, He 177 and two Bf 110s).

During the summer of 1943 the Ministry of Aircraft Production arranged for the construction of hangars at Moreton Valence for use by the Gloster Aircraft Company. The main runway was also lengthened, to allow for the operation of the Gloster F-9/40, later known as the Meteor, the first British production jet fighter. The first jet to appear at Moreton Valence however, was not the F-9/40 but a Bell YP-59A Airacomet. This aircraft had been exchanged by the Americans for a prototype Meteor in the interests of 'Allied co-operation'. The Meteor was technically a much better aircraft than the Airacomet, so the Americans definitely got the better deal! The YP-59A was assembled by Gloster personnel in the hangar at Moreton Valence and flown on 28 September 1943. It remained based at the airfield on test until

Bell YP-59 Airacomet, flying in the USA, with P-63 Kingcobra chase-plane. (USAF)

November when it was transferred to the Royal Aircraft Establishment at Farnborough for further evaluation.

From October all F-9/40 and Meteor test and development flying took place from Moreton Valence. This was a careful and conditioned process, particularly as it involved the development of a step-change in aircraft and powerplant technology. The implications of flying jet aircraft were not then fully understood, and test flying the jets was a risky business. Given the circumstances, there were not that many accidents. The first F-9/40 to be lost from Moreton Valence was DG205 on 27 April 1944. The aircraft was being flown by test pilot Mr J.A. Crosby-Warren on trials to reduce aileron instability at high altitude. Following the loss of aileron control, the aircraft rolled and crashed inverted into the ground three miles south-east of Stroud, the pilot being killed in the impact.

Gliders were added to the variety of aircraft types flying from Moreton Valence with the formation of No 83 Gliding School in May 1944. They flew such types as Dagling Primary and Kirby Cadet gliders to train Air Training Corps cadets to fly to solo standard.

With the need for bomber aircrews much reduced, the work for training units such as 6 (O) AFU had diminished by late 1944, and on 12 December the unit was disbanded. Its place at Moreton Valence was

Air Cadet Gliders, similar to this Slingsby Falcon, flew from Moreton Valence with 83 Gliding School. (Aeroplane)

taken in January 1945 by 3 (Pilots) Advanced Flying Unit ((P)AFU) based at South Cerney, as they needed another satellite airfield for training in place of Southrop, which had closed. Ansons and Dragon Rapides that No 6 (O)AFU had used for navigator training at Moreton Valence were replaced by 3 (P)AFU's Airspeed Oxfords for advanced pilot training.

The end of the war in Europe meant that flying training was generally slowing down, and by VE Day major contractions in the RAF's training organisation had begun. No 3 (P)AFU's Moreton Valence detachment was withdrawn in July and the airfield was transferred to Little Rissington as its parent station. It was used by No 6 (P)AFU for flying training until December 1945, when the unit was disbanded. When the Harvards, Tiger Moths and Oxfords of No 6 (P)AFU were withdrawn, the last RAF aircraft to use Moreton Valence were the gliders of 83 Gliding School. They too departed on 13 October 1946 when the school was transferred to Aston Down, leaving the airfield to the Gloster Aircraft Company.

After the war, Glosters used Moreton Valence as its main flight test centre, particularly for Meteor development and test flying. In September 1945, with the co-operation of the Air Ministry, Ministry of Aircraft Production and Rolls-Royce, Glosters prepared Meteors at Moreton Valence for the establishment of a new World Air Speed record, which they claimed on 7 November at a speed of 606 mph. A year later two Meteor F4s increased this by 10 mph. They were joined by aircraft of the Rotol Flight Test Department in June 1947, who used Moreton Valence as well as Staverton. From then until the Department was closed in 1954, they flew the Spitfire, Sea Fury and Wyvern on propeller unit flight test and development from the airfield.

In 1943 Gloster had designed single-engined alternatives to the Meteor, in case of engine shortages. Although engine supply problems were remedied, they continued with development of this promising concept and three airframes were constructed. One was later improved and eventually completed as the Gloster GA2 (and known unofficially as the Ace). Prototypes were built and test flown from Moreton Valence in 1948 but the project was abandoned as it was not a sufficient advance on the Meteor design and had limited development potential. The two prototypes joined the RAE Farnborough test fleet, and were flown by the Establishment for several years on flight trials.

The ten years after the war were a period of stability for the Gloster Aircraft Company, with steady production to meet orders from the RAF and 14 overseas customers. The Meteor became the first type of jet aircraft to see service in two conflicts when on 29 July 1951, in service with the Royal Australian Air Force, Meteor F8s started fighter sweeps together with USAF F86 Sabres over North Korea. After a production run of 1,036, the last Meteor (FMK8, WL191) left the production line at Hucclecote on 9 April 1954 and was flown to Moreton Valence for flight testing before delivery to the RAF.

Meteors were replaced on the production lines by the Javelin two-seat, twin-engined all-weather fighter, the first examples of which were tested at Moreton Valence and delivered to the RAF in December 1955. The last Javelin to be manufactured was flown from Hucclecote to Moreton Valence on 8 April 1960. The aircraft were later updated by being modified to FAW8 and 9 standards in the Gloster Works at Moreton Valence. Work also subsequently took place there on the conversion of Meteor NF11s to TT20s (ie from night-fighter to target-tug).

Work eventually wound down at Moreton Valence and the last aircraft movement from there was a Javelin that left the runway on 25 July 1962. Shortly afterwards the airfield was closed. It was subsequently sold off for industrial development, and the M5 motorway was built through the centre of the site. A few buildings remain as a reminder of the importance of Moreton Valence's past.

14
SOUTH CERNEY

3 miles south-east of Cirencester
SP 045985

The site for an airfield was selected in the 1930s on a plateau in the Cotswold Hills near to the village of South Cerney, to the south-east of Cirencester. When construction was started by Chivers and Sons of Devizes in 1936, the airfield was laid out as a flying training station. It was to have three C type hangars constructed by Kier and Co of London and a distinctive three-storey chief flying instructors' block type watch office fronting onto the airfield. There was also to be an aircraft repair shed, and later two Bellman and eleven Blister hangars were added. Operations buildings, maintenance, technical and instructional buildings were designed as a set, of neo-Georgian design and fronted in Cotswold stone to blend in with the local environment as far as possible (a principle that the Air Ministry had agreed with the Council for the Protection of Rural England).

When RAF South Cerney was opened on 16 August 1937 construction work was still in progress. Nonetheless the station had been allocated to No 3 Flying Training School (FTS), which moved from Grantham during mid-August, between training courses. The main reason for the school's relocation was that Grantham's location in Lincolnshire was then fast becoming a busy flying area due to the presence of an increasing number of military airfields, and not conducive to the training of student pilots. The Cotswolds was altogether a far quieter area for this activity! No 3 FTS flew mainly Hawker biplanes in the form of the Audax, Hart trainer, Hind, Demon and Fury, but also had the Westland Wallace, Avro Tutor and DH Tiger Moth. Students and instructors found the accommodation at South Cerney fairly basic to start with, but as the building work progressed, facilities improved. Eventually the

Hawker Hind Trainers were flown by 3 FTS at South Cerney following the unit's arrival in August 1937. (Aeroplane)

main hangars were complete, and the school's aircraft could then be stored under cover.

The re-equipping of No 3 FTS started during the summer of 1938, when in June, Airspeed Oxford twin-engined trainers began arriving to replace the Audaxes. A few of the biplanes were kept on, but within a few months the school went over almost entirely to the Oxford. Although other aircraft were later to supplement them, and enable other varieties of tuition, the Oxfords were to be the mainstay of No 3 FTS over the next few years, with at one time over 150 of the type on strength.

When war was declared on 3 September 1939, No 3 FTS became No 3 Service FTS in a reorganisation of the RAF Flying Training organisation. All of the RAF's flying training schools were retitled, some taking on other types of training, while others were closed and their aircraft and instructors reallocated. No 3 SFTS remained at South Cerney, and received more Oxfords and staff. The outbreak of war also sparked off other events for the station. It was decided to move Headquarters No 23 Group, (which was the part of Training Command that controlled advanced pilot training at eleven of its airfields and was then also located at Grantham), to South Cerney. It brought its newly established Communications Flight, which flew such aircraft as Percival Proctors and DH Dominies.

Other aircraft appearing during this time were the Vickers

Percival Proctors were used by the South Cerney Station Flight. (Aeroplane)

Wellington bombers of No 37 Squadron, that flew into South Cerney on 8 September from their base at Feltwell in Norfolk. It was thought that attacks would be made by the Luftwaffe on the RAF airfields of East Anglia as their opening gambit once war had been declared, and under 3 Group's Scatter Plan for such a situation, 37 Squadron were dispersed to South Cerney. Once it was apparent that the German bombers weren't coming just yet, the Wellingtons returned to Feltwell.

During the Phoney War period of late 1939 into the early summer of 1940, No 3 SFTS was busily mounting its training courses to produce pilots that could fly multi-engined aeroplanes, as bomber, coastal and reconnaissance pilots were sorely needed.

The role of the SFTS was to train pupil pilots who had passed out from an Elementary Flying Training School (EFTS). A course at 3 SFTS would normally be 30-strong of Leading Aircraftsman rank. At the EFTS there would have been a series of assessments, so that the less able students were weeded out and did not progress to the next stage. The successful students went on to take their first solos, and were then taught basic aerobatics (spins, loops, rolls and inverted flight), cross-country navigation and basic instrument flying (under a blind-flying hood that was pulled over the student's cockpit).

As most of the students had been taught on the Tiger Moth, the transition to the twin-engined monoplane Oxford, with its complicated instruments and controls for retractable undercarriage, flaps and boost control, was quite a culture shock. Nonetheless, some students went solo on the new type within a couple of hours, whereas others took up to six. Three-quarters of the way through the course the students began night-flying. To light the airfield at night, goose-neck flares (oil lamps, each with a long spout) were laid out and lit manually by the ground crews. On a fine moonlit evening, this wasn't too much of a challenge, but when the night was overcast it was a different matter. With the wartime blackout so rigorously enforced (particularly at RAF stations), the darkness was total. This was particularly pronounced on take-off. Once the aircraft passed the final flare, the inky blackness enveloped the aircraft, and without the blind flying instrument panel the pilot would have become disorientated and spun into the ground.

With no radios fitted to his Oxford, the student pilot had to fly visually and keep the lights of the flare-path, albeit a faint glimmer, in view so that he could plan his circuit and return to the airfield. Apart from the flare-path, which was laid to guide him in, the pilot's other main aid was the Angle of Approach Light. This was positioned near the downwind end of the flare-path, and its beam shone through a multi-coloured lens. It was adjusted to the correct approach angle for a landing aircraft, so that when viewed by a pilot coming in to land the light appeared red if he was too high, white if too low, and green if on the correct line of approach. The students would be continually assessed by the instructors during their night flying, and when it was felt that they were ready, were sent off solo. After at least five night hours solo, the student pilot qualified for his wings, and would be ready for posting to an operational training unit.

Accidents were an inevitable consequence of flying training, with mistakes being an important process of the learning process. Although most of these mistakes would result in minor damage and slight injuries, unfortunately they could also cause catastrophic damage and fatalities. During the first half of 1940, at least 15 aircraft of 3 SFTS were involved in flying accidents, the majority at South Cerney. Of these seven (four Oxfords, three Audaxes and two Harts) crashed, mainly on take-off or undershoots on landing. Some of these accidents were fatal. The others involved heavy landings (the undercarriage of three Hart Trainers collapsed as a result and another overturned on landing, as did an Oxford – not an easy thing to do!) and in the case of one Hart trainer a collision on the ground, its student pilot taxiing it into an Oxford.

This period was eventful one at South Cerney. The station was visited by their Majesties King George VI and Queen Elizabeth on

A formation of Airspeed Oxfords of 3 FTS accompanied by a lone Audax fly near South Cerney in July 1939. (Aeroplane)

10 February 1940, who came on an official visit and showed great interest in its activities, including the work of 3 SFTS. At the end of May several hundred British and Allied troops passed through the station on return from the Dunkirk evacuation. More visitors arrived a few days later in the form of the Oxfords and Harvards of 15 SFTS, which had been flown out of Middle Wallop in an emergency move to make room for fighter squadrons. No 15 SFTS stayed at South Cerney for a short period while awaiting the allocation of another base. Its aircraft were flying with the Oxfords of No 3 SFTS one evening when the next visitor to South Cerney arrived, but it was not so welcome. Just before midnight on 4 June a German bomber flew overhead and dropped one 100 kg and five 50 kg bombs, along with some incendiaries. The ordnance landed on the airfield, but well away from any buildings or aircraft, and no casualties resulted.

No air raid warning had been received for this first raid, but over the next three nights warnings were put out. No further bombs were dropped on South Cerney at this time, probably because the enemy bombers were passing overhead on their way to blitz the Midlands and Merseyside. On the night of 29/30 June however, more bombs were dropped in the South Cerney area but away from the airfield to the east, when 22 bombs fell near the main Cirencester-Cricklade road. Night flying training was severely disrupted during this period, as the approach lighting was extinguished whenever enemy aircraft were thought to be in the area. This meant that the students had to orbit in their Oxfords until the all clear was given, with hopefully none having engine problems or fuel shortages in the meantime! South Cerney was raided again on 25 July, this time in a daylight attack by two Heinkel He 111s. They appeared in the early afternoon, dropping their bombs across the airfield. Once again, although the landing ground was cratered, there were no casualties, or damage to buildings or aircraft.

During the late summer of 1940 German landings were seen as a real threat, and anti-invasion measures were widespread. These included the planting of poles in open fields to prevent glider and paratroop landings, and the arming of training aircraft. At No 3 SFTS the Oxfords were fitted with bomb racks and in August 1940 the school's instructors stood by ready to fly operational sorties. They could have been tasked to fly ground-attack missions against German army formations under co-ordinated operations that had been prepared by HQ 23 Group entitled 'Plan Banquet'. Fortunately they were never called into action.

Although enemy air activity diminished in the local area during the autumn of 1940, the Luftwaffe (which had switched to mainly night operations), did make the occasional appearance. On the night of 24 November a Junkers Ju 88 bomber was shot down in the grounds of Coates Manor near Cirencester after it had been intercepted by Hurricane night-fighters. The crew of four were killed in the impact, and were brought to South Cerney's station mortuary before being buried at Coates church.

Flying training at South Cerney went through a period of change during that autumn. At the end of August the aircraft of No 15 SFTS moved out, on transfer to Kidlington in Oxfordshire. Shortly after this there were changes for 3 SFTS too, as following another reorganisation of RAF flying training, the syllabus being run by the unit was changed from that of advanced training to one of intermediate training, ie that of taking pilots who had trained on single-engine aircraft and converting them to fly twin-engined ones. A Relief Landing Ground had been opened at Bibury under South Cerney's control, and the RLG was used for landing, take-off and circuit flying training away from the main airfield.

However, the flying accident rate of the South Cerney-based units hardly improved during the second half of 1940, with eleven aircraft being involved in accidents. Of these at least four were fatal, the first on 3 August, when two Oxfords of 3 SFTS collided during formation flying practice. P1821 crashed into the ground near the airfield, killing its crew, while the other aircraft, P1955, lost a large piece of wing, but its pilot, who was an instructor, managed to land it safely. Nine days later Oxford II N4803 of 3 SFTS broke up in the air near Hankerton, and just under a month later, on 9 September, Harvard I P5885 of 15 SFTS spun into the ground at Brockworth. On 18 November Oxford I P1078 of 3 SFTS flew into a hillside near Woodchester. Other accidents involved four Oxfords of 3 SFTS and two of 15 SFTS, mainly on landing or take-off from South Cerney or Bibury. Training continued through the winter into 1941 and throughout that year, as the demand for aircrew was ever increasing, with more and more squadrons being formed as the RAF went over to the offensive.

The Airspeed Oxford flew from South Cerney throughout the wartime period, as it was the RAF's standard multi-engined trainer of the day. The first deliveries of the type were made to the RAF in November 1937, just five months after the prototype's first flight! Constructed almost entirely of wood, the Oxford was produced in two main versions, distinguished by their armament, or lack of it. The Mark I, a general purpose, bombing and gunnery trainer, was fitted with an Armstrong Whitworth turret with a single .303 inch machine gun for the training of air gunners. It was powered by two 375 hp Armstrong Siddeley Cheetah X radial engines. These engines were also fitted into the Mark II, which had no turret and was a pilot, radio operator and navigator trainer. (The Mark V was similar to the Mark II, but had two 450 hp Pratt and Witney R-985-AN6 radial engines).

There was an enormous demand for the rugged and adaptable Oxford, which became a standard type for the Empire Air Training Scheme (which utilised 1,610 of them in Australia, Canada, New Zealand, Rhodesia and South Africa). However, the supply of aircraft from Airspeed's factory in Portsmouth could not meet this demand, and so the Oxford was also manufactured by de Havilland at Hatfield, Percival Aircraft at Luton and Standard Motors in Coventry. Total production was 8,586 aircraft, and the type remained in service with the RAF until 1954.

The South Cerney flight safety record improved during 1941, with twelve aircraft (now mainly of 3 SFTS) being involved in accidents during the year (ie half the number of the previous year). No fatalities are recorded for the period (although there may have been some serious injuries). Eleven Oxfords and one Audax were damaged. One of the Oxfords suffered an undercarriage collapse, while the Audax turned over on landing while visiting Kemble. Another Oxford crashed after colliding with an aircraft in formation, two crashed while on low-

Hawker Audaxes were used by 3 SFTS until it became 3 (P)AFU in 1942. (Aeroplane)

flying practice, while the remaining seven crashed on take-off or landing practice, mainly at Bibury.

The spring of 1942 brought about another change for No 3 SFTS. It was to be re-titled as No 3 (Pilots) Advanced Flying Unit ((P)AFU) with effect from 1 March 1942 and its role was to be revised. The unit was in future to teach pilots to an advanced standard once more, but this time the pilots were coming from abroad. Their new students were those taught to fly under the Empire Air Training Scheme, and had got used to flying in the wide open sunny skies of Canada, South Africa, India and Australia. They were to come to No 3 (P)AFU to be taught to fly in the congested skies of the UK, in British weather! As well as this acclimatisation training, the unit also undertook beam approach training. This involved flying at night or in bad weather conditions, using an electronic beam guidance system for approach and landing. Southrop was used as a Relief Landing Ground (RLG) by 3 (P)AFU from 13 July and this proved to be a useful addition to the unit's facilities. Oxfords remained the mainstay of the unit, but they were supplemented by other types such as the Avro Anson, Blackburn Botha and the DH Tiger Moth.

The year had got off to a bad start on the flight safety front, with Oxford I L9699 of 3 SFTS diving into the ground near Shorncote on 3 January, killing all aboard. Another Oxford crashed on the approach to Bibury on 21 March. Once the (P)AFU had formed, a further five Oxfords were badly damaged or destroyed in accidents. The first of these, Oxford II V3869, crashed near Lechlade on 5 April, and another went down near Bathurst Park, Cirencester on 24 May. Oxford I AT603 crashed on take-off from Southrop on 21 July, while AT738 similarly crashed at South Cerney on 12 August. The final accident of 1942 was on 28 October, when an Oxford came down near the airfield.

A new unit formed at South Cerney on 15 April 1943. This was No 1539 Beam Approach Training (BAT) Flight, which was formed to take on the specialist beam approach training role for No 3 (P)AFU. Also flying Oxfords, but with special markings of large yellow triangles on their camouflaged upper surfaces and fuselage sides, the Flight moved to Bibury on 13 July. It was replaced at South Cerney by another BAT Flight, No 1532 which had formed at Hullavington on 15 October 1942, also on Oxfords. This unit continued to work with 3 (P)AFU, although it was later moved to Babdown Farm.

The first accident to a South Cerney based aircraft in 1943 was suffered by an Oxford I of 3 (P)AFU, which crashed at Whiteway near Cirencester on 8 January. There were no more recorded accidents until 11 July when an Oxford II came down near Long Newnton. September proved to be a bad month for the unit's flight safety, as three Oxfords crashed, one near Bibury on the 24th, another at Brimpsfield on the 26th and the third at Windrush on the 30th. Another Oxford crashed on approach to Bibury on 26 November, and the final accident of 1943 was on 17 December, when an Oxford of 3 (P)AFU crashed near Little Rissington. Casualties for the year are not recorded, but some serious injuries at the very least must have been sustained.

The work of No 3 (P)AFU and its BAT Flights continued into 1944 as the demand for trained crews continued. The period was uneventful at South Cerney, despite the fact that momentous world events were taking place. During the summer of 1944, while preparations were being made for the invasion of Europe, South Cerney's units carried on with their training tasks, uninterrupted apart from the occasional visiting aircraft passing through or landing due to an in-flight emergency. Only two serious accidents are recorded for the year at South Cerney; Oxford II AB719 crashed near Somerton Keynes on a cross-country navigation exercise on 14 July and Oxford I HM729 came down near the airfield a few weeks later on 31 July.

Training continued into 1945, but the demand for crews was then slowing down. Southrop was closed as a RLG on 22 January, but the need for similar facilities remained and Moreton Valence was then used until July 1945. Fewer courses were mounted during the summer. Aircraft losses continued, with three Oxfords of 3 (P)AFU destroyed in crashes while flying in the local area, two in April and one in June.

With the end of the war in Europe training at South Cerney started winding down. On 1 June 1945, No 1539 BAT Flight disbanded at South Cerney (it had returned from Bibury on 5 November 1944), and a fortnight later No 1532 BAT Flight closed at Babdown Farm. Strangely, a new BAT Flight formed at Watchfield in Oxfordshire (ten miles to the north of Swindon) on 1 June 1945. This unit, No 1547 BAT Flight, also on Oxfords, flew in support of 3 (P) AFU on attachment to South Cerney, but this arrangement ceased on 4 December.

With the initial post-war reorganisation of the RAF flying training organisation, No 3 (P)AFU was disbanded on 17 December 1945 to become No 3 Service Flying Training School (SFTS) once again. The school was then equipped with DH Tiger Moths, Miles Magisters and North American Harvards. The school moved to Feltwell in April 1946, leaving South Cerney to No 23 Group Communications Flight. They were joined by the Flying Training Command Instructors School (FTCIS) on 24 May.

HQ 23 Group moved on 1 October, followed by the FTCIS in February 1947. In March 1948 No 2 FTS arrived at South Cerney from Church Lawford with Tiger Moths and Harvards. They were replaced by the Central Flying School (Basic) Squadron in May 1952 with Harvards, Percival Prentices and Percival Provosts. The CFS remained in control of the station until August 1961. They were replaced by the Primary Flying School which flew Chipmunks from the airfield until January 1967 when they too were moved. South Cerney then supported a number of ground units and was a dormitory station for Brize Norton, until it was closed as an RAF station.

On 1 July 1971, South Cerney was transferred to the Army, who are still in residence. Today it is the Duke of Gloucester Barracks, home of 29 Regiment, Royal Logistic Corps. It is also the Air Mounting Centre, used to co-ordinate major deployments of military units via the nearby RAF stations at Brize Norton and Lyneham. The airfield at South Cerney and most of its buildings remain in well-kept condition, largely unchanged from their Second World War appearance.

15
STAVERTON

3 miles north-east of Gloucester
SO 887218

Private flying was popular in Britain during the 1930s, promoted by people such as Sir Alan Cobham who made a flying tour of the UK during the summer of 1929, visiting over 100 towns and cities. If there was no aerodrome at a particular place on his itinerary, Cobham would often land his aircraft, DH61 Giant Moth *Youth of Britain* in a field and suggest to the local council that they build an airport for their town. What is now Gloucestershire Airport (Staverton) originated during this period.

The Cotswold Aero Club started using a field at Down Hatherley near Gloucester in September 1932. The airfield became popular, and when it was suggested that an airport be built there to provide public services, the councils of Gloucester and Cheltenham became interested. However, Down Hatherley was too small for the planned facilities and instead a site not far away, across the main Cheltenham to Gloucester road which ran nearby, was selected. This lay between the road and the LMS/GWR main railway line, three miles north-east of Gloucester. The two councils agreed to purchase 160 acres of land, and in November 1934 work started on the construction of the airport.

The airfield surface was levelled and compacted, then runways were laid out on the grassed surface. Hangars and a passenger terminal were built on the north-west side of the site. The project was completed in July 1936 and licenced for public use on 18 November of that year. The first scheduled air service started on 25 May 1936, when Railway Air Services started calling in, as a request stop on its Birmingham to Bristol route. Aircraft used by the company included a brand-new DH 84 Dragon G-ADDI, the aircraft in which the author made his first flight, from Squires Gate, Blackpool some 25 years later (it still flies today in the USA). Railway Air Services continued to use the airport until September 1938.

The RAF needed more flying training facilities to support its expansion during the 1930s, and one of the airfields that it wanted to use was Staverton. In return for funding improvements to the airport, the councils agreed to this and on 29 September 1938, No 31 Elementary and Reserve Flying Training School (E&RFTS) was formed at Staverton. Operated by the contractor Surrey Flying Services, the school flew Tiger Moths in order to give initial flying training to student RAF and RAF Reserve (RAFR) pilots. It also gave continuous flying training to RAFR pilots so that they remained proficient, and for this latter task the school operated military aircraft in the form of the Hawker Hart Trainer, Hawker Audax and Hawker Hind.

Rotol Airscrews was formed in 1936 jointly by the Rolls-Royce and Bristol Engine companies. They specialised in aircraft propellers, particularly of the variable-pitch variety, an idea that had been developed originally by the Gloster Aircraft Company. Rotol built a factory at Staverton, across a road on the north-west side of the airfield. They set up a Flight Test Department on the airfield in the spring of 1939, and one of the first aircraft to be flown on trial from Staverton was a Vickers Wellesley single-engined long-range bomber that arrived in April, closely followed by a Gloster Gauntlet single-engined biplane fighter.

A second flying school appeared at Staverton in May 1939. This was

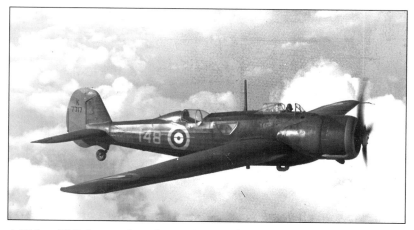

A Vickers Wellesley was flown by Rotol on flight trials from Staverton during 1939. (Aeroplane)

the Airwork Civil School of Air Navigation. Operated by civilian contractors, Airwork Ltd., the school provided training for RAF Observers, using DH 89 Dragon Rapide twin-engine biplane cabin trainers. The school was redesignated as No 6 Civil Air Navigation School (CANS) on 6 August 1939, although it was still operated by Airwork. By then it was also flying Avro Ansons. On 3 September 1939, Britain declared war on Germany and on that day, as part of a previously prepared plan, there was a change in the RAF flying training organisation. The E&RFT schools were redesignated or closed down. No 31 E&RFTS was one of the latter, and was disbanded, its aircraft being reallocated to other training units. The airport came under Government control and was renamed RAF Staverton.

However, No 6 CANS remained in business and acquired additional aeroplanes, which included Hawker Demons along with civil aircraft that had been impressed from their owners, such as the Miles Whitney Straight and Percival Q-6 single-engine cabin monoplanes. On 1 November the unit was redesignated again, this time as No 6 Air Observers Navigation School (AONS). Training included long-distance navigational exercises in the Rapides and Ansons, with three students usually being carried, each one taking it in turns to navigate the aircraft on a leg of the flight. The pilot would be a member of the school's staff and a radio operator would also be aboard, so that if all else failed and they did get lost (or temporarily displaced!) they could request headings that would get them back to base.

As with many other grass airfields operated by the RAF, due to the steady increase in the all-up weight of aeroplanes and the resulting wear and damage to the runway surface it was decided to lay tarmac-covered concrete runways at Staverton. This started during the autumn of 1940 and eventually three runways were constructed, each of 3,000 foot length.

It was during this period that another unit appeared at Staverton, in the form of No 2 Elementary Flying Training School (EFTS) which transferred from Filton on 4 August 1940. Flying Tiger Moths, the school's role was to teach novice pilots to fly. The successful students would fly solo, then be taught at the school to an elementary standard before they moved on to an advanced flying school. Unfortunately because of the works taking place to the runways not much flying could be done as the airfield was unsuitable for the operation of such flimsy aircraft as the Tiger Moth. The school therefore looked for a Relief Landing Ground from which to do its intense flying training, such as circuit work, and landing practices. Eventually they found such an airfield near Worcester. Until buildings or installations could be erected, the ground staff and some of the students travelled by coach to Worcester every morning, while the remainder of the students flew up with the instructors in the aircraft. All of the ground instruction and a limited amount of flying instruction, along with the aircraft maintenance and overhaul still took place at Staverton during this time.

H.P. Folland, the former chief designer of the Gloster Aircraft Company, set up his own company at Hamble in 1937. The first product of Folland Aircraft Ltd was the Fo 108, a large single-engined flying test-bed which was specifically designed for the testing and development of high-powered aero engines. Twelve of these aircraft were manufactured during 1940, each accommodating a pilot and two flight-test observers. Towards the end of 1940 Folland's Flight Test Department was instructed to leave Hamble because it was vulnerable to enemy air attack. It therefore moved to Staverton, to share a hangar with 6 AONS. There ten more of the Fo 108s were assembled. The whole fleet of twelve then operated from Staverton, and continued to do so for the rest of the war period. Based and maintained at the airfield, they were flown to the engine manufacturers such as Napier at Luton, Bristol at Filton and Rolls-Royce at Hucknall for the installation of the relevant engines for flight trials. They therefore flew with a variety of engines, including the Napier Sabre I, II, V, and VII, Bristol Hercules VIII and XI, Centaurus IV and various Rolls-Royce Griffons.

The Folland Flight Test Department was joined by Gloster in early 1941, who also set up a flight test centre. This was for the production testing of aircraft manufactured at Brockworth, which were flown from Staverton to ease the congestion at Gloster's airfield.

The Rotol factory was operating at full capacity at this time. Their Flight Test Department fleet included a Whitley, Wellington and Spitfire, later to be joined by Typhoons and Tempests. It worked to flight test and to develop modifications and designs for new propellers and components before they were put into production. The Rotol factory was an important part of Britain's aircraft industry and produced over 100,000 propeller units during the Second World War, that were fitted to more than 60 different types of aircraft.

No 6 AONS too was operating to capacity during the summer of 1941 and had grown in size to reflect the need for more aircrew, flying 63 Ansons in June. It was training 240 pupils at any one time, just starting, finishing or part-way through their course. Although the main part of its training activities took place at and from Staverton, the school needed additional capacity and so set up detached flights in

August at Moreton Valence, which it had been using for off-base flying training, and at Llanbedr in Wales. With the increased need for flying instructors, on 1 November No 2 EFTS became No 6 (Supplementary) Flying Instructors School. The school continued to operate from both Staverton and Cirencester, using Masters and Magisters along with its Tiger Moths. Another name change came a couple of months later, when one word was dropped and the unit became simply No 6 FIS.

Flying from both locations continued into 1942, but as Staverton became busier, instructing students there became more difficult. The work of 6 AONS (retitled No 6 Air Observers School on 17 January 1942) continued at an intense level, and the three flight test departments were busier than ever. As facilities at Worcester were improved during the spring of 1942, it was decided to relocate No 6 FIS there. The school therefore gradually moved its operation to Worcester during April 1942.

Flight testing by the other Staverton-based companies continued through 1942. This went without incident in the main part but accidents did occur from time to time. The first loss to the Folland flight test fleet occurred on 19 May when Folland Fo 108 P1777 crashed. The aircraft was being flown by Gloster test pilot N.M. Daunt, and undertaking a diving trial to take it up to 400 mph, or the Bristol Centaurus CE-1M engine to 2,800 rpm. Unfortunately, on the fourth

Folland Fo 108 at Staverton, fitted with a Napier Sabre II engine. (Aeroplane)

dive the port tailplane rear spar failed, which put the aircraft into a violent manoeuvre resulting in the break up of the airframe. The pilot was thrown from the aircraft, but remained conscious and was able to deploy his parachute. Although badly injured, he landed safely, while the Fo 108 crashed west of Tewkesbury, leaving a trail of wreckage five miles long. This was the only Fo108 accident that resulted from structural failure. Although two others crashed later (in 1944), their accidents both resulted from engine failure and not a problem with the aircraft.

Flight Refuelling Ltd had been established by Sir Alan Cobham at Ford in Sussex in 1934, to develop methods of extending the range of transport and bomber aircraft. The company pioneered the techniques of air-to-air refuelling using Handley Page Harrow aircraft as tankers. With Ford being vulnerable to enemy air attack it was decided to move the company's operation. They relocated to the requisitioned Morgan Motor Works at Malvern Link during May 1940, while deciding where to move the flying department. Unfortunately the company's three aircraft (an Armstrong Whitworth AW23 and two Harrows) were still stored in the hangars at Ford when the Luftwaffe struck on 18 August. Twenty-eight Ju 87 Stukas bombed the airfield, destroying buildings and installations. The hangars were hit and 17 aircraft were wrecked, including the three belonging to Flight Refuelling. The company's Flight Test Department was eventually re-equipped and re-established at Staverton, initially sharing a hangar with Folland.

In June 1942 trials took place into the feasibility of saving fuel by air-towing fighter aircraft to overseas squadrons, or for positioning them on long-range patrols. Flight Refuelling modified a Whitley for use as a tug by installing towing bridles in each wing. The bridles were connected to a tow-line fitted with a grapnel hook at the end, that was streamed behind the bomber. The fighter flew under the tug, where the pilot manoeuvred to pick up a line with a hook and reel it in to a locking device ahead of the cockpit, then stopped his engine and propeller. Originally a Hurricane was used for the trial, but it proved unsuitable because of its fabric covering and a Spitfire Mk V was used instead. Although the flight trials were then successful, the idea was not proceeded with, presumably on the basis that it was too risky to try operationally! Indeed, on one occasion a Spitfire being towed nearly came to grief when the tow-rope broke, whipped back and wrapped itself around the aircraft's propeller and fuselage. Fortunately the test pilot, Charles Barnard, managed to land the whole tangled mess in one piece.

The Handley Page Halifax was flown by Dowty on undercarriage trials work. (Aeroplane)

Other proposals along these lines (but which were not flight-tested) included towing three fighters behind a Wellington, and also mounting a Spitfire on the back of a Whitley (rather like the 'Mistel' combination later flown by the Germans). However, Flight Refuelling also did work on projects that did see service, such as de-icing equipment, flame-dampening exhaust systems, heated windscreens and self-sealing fuel tanks. The company also undertook flight trials of aircraft with various bits of equipment produced by the Telecommunications Research Establishment (TRE) at Malvern. These included the H2S scanning radar that was later fitted into the aircraft of Bomber Command. In 1943 the company moved to a purpose-built Bellman hangar at Staverton, which meant that they could undertake installation work on large aircraft under cover.

Flight trials also took place at Staverton during this period on behalf of the Dowty Company. They manufactured undercarriage systems, and their equipment was fitted to virtually every British aircraft built during the Second World War. Aircraft flown by Dowty included the Handley Page Halifax for undercarriage development trials. By the end of the war Dowty had manufactured some 87,000 landing gear units at their factory in Cheltenham.

Despite all this flight-testing activity, 6 AOS continued to operate from Staverton, as well as Moreton Valence and Llanbedr. By the early part of 1943 the unit had also acquired other aircraft types that it flew along with the Ansons and Rapides. These included Avro Tutors, DH Tiger Moths and Miles Magister two-seat trainers. On 11 June 1943, it was re-titled once again, this time to No.6 (Observers) Advanced Flying Unit ((O)AFU). Shortly after this the unit also received Blackburn Botha twin-engined crew trainers.

Training and flight-testing carried on quietly (and not so quietly!) at Staverton throughout the rest of 1943 and 1944. Despite the high level of activity and large number of aircraft movements, the accident rate at the airfield does appear to have been very low. One of the exceptions was the unfortunate Spitfire Mk IX JL349 operated by the Rotol Flight Test Department. It was being flown by company test pilot Mr J. Hall on 29 July 1944, employed on endurance testing of a contra-rotating propeller. Having completed the trial, the pilot manoeuvered the Spitfire into a low-level circuit in preparation to land at Staverton, when the propeller broke up. Large parts of it hit the tailplane, which caused him to lose control of the aircraft. The Spitfire dived into the ground beside the main road running alongside the airfield, killing Mr Hall.

As the war moved on, Flight Refuelling's engineers were involved in more projects as part of the ceaseless drive for weapon development. They undertook trials of a Vickers Wellington fitted with a radar array to detonate magnetic mines, with qualified success (it worked, but only under ideal conditions). The company was also tasked with the preparation of demolition charges that were to be dropped in tubes by aircraft onto the Normandy invasion beaches to demolish anti-landing craft obstacles and minefields. Although a practical method of deploying the charges was perfected by the company, officialdom decided that there was insufficient time to prepare the ordnance, so flail tanks were relied upon for mine-clearance instead. Other projects later in 1944 included a radio-fit for the Airspeed Oxford trainer and trials into leaded fuel in aero-engines, as well as ongoing work concerning wing and tailplane de-icing systems, heated windscreens and fire-extinguishing systems.

However, Flight Refuelling's main priority was refocused following a meeting in Downing Street to which Sir Alan Cobham was called in February 1944. The company had spent years developing and refining air-to-air refuelling techniques (i.e. using a tanker aircraft to refuel others in mid-air to extend their range or endurance) using a loop-line system with no interest from the Air Ministry or the RAF whatsoever. At the February meeting the company were called upon to develop and manufacture air-to-air refuelling equipment for the Lancaster four-engined bomber. This was urgently required for long-range operations in the Far East, and was for 600 tanker aircraft and 600 receiver aircraft of the RAF's Tiger Force that was being formed to attack Japan from bases in Burma and China. The company's efforts were therefore largely concentrated on this project during the rest of 1944.

A new unit formed at Staverton on 16 August 1944. No 44 Group Communications Flight was equipped with the Proctor III, Tiger Moth II, Dominie (the military version of the Dragon Rapide) and Anson, and the flight also had at least one Douglas Boston II twin-engined bomber on strength. The unit flew personnel of 44 Group HQ, which was located in Gloucester and was part of Transport Command.

By late 1944 it was apparent that more than sufficient aircrew were available to maintain Bomber Command's level of operations, due to the fortunate situation that the Command's losses were decreasing. Crews were still needed, but not in the numbers provided by the training schools. It was therefore decided to reduce the flying training organisation, and on 12 December 1944 No 6 (O)AFU was disbanded at Staverton.

The closure of the AFU dramatically reduced RAF flying from Staverton, with just No 44 Group Communications Flight operating from the airfield in early 1945. Flight testing continued, by the aircraft of the Flight Refuelling, Rotol, Folland and Gloster Flight Test Departments. Aircraft flown by Rotol in 1945 included the Martin Baker MB5, which was fitted with a contra-rotating Rotol propeller unit. Powered by a Rolls-Royce Griffon 83, it was one of the fastest piston-engined aircraft of World War II, but its requirement was overtaken by the advent of jet-powered fighters.

Meanwhile, the staff of Flight Refuelling were busy in their part of Staverton, working away on producing modification kits for the Tiger Force Lancasters. One day in the spring of 1945 Sir Alan Cobham was called to another high-level meeting, this time at the Tiger Force HQ at Bushey. There he was informed that the Americans had captured an island that was only 400 miles away from Japan, and that his in-flight refuelling equipment would no longer be required! Sir Alan returned to Staverton that afternoon, to convey the disappointing news to his workforce. Production work, that had been in full flow, was stopped immediately, and the vast mountain of materials that had been urgently manufactured and stockpiled was put up for disposal. The flight trials that had been performed under the programme had, however, provided useful data that was to prove invaluable when the RAF decided that air-to-air refuelling was once more required during the post-war years.

Due to the relatively short runways at Staverton, there was little

Several Avro Lancasters were used by Flight Refuelling for trials from Staverton. (Aeroplane)

room for error, particularly where the large four-engined bombers were concerned. On 27 August 1945 Lancaster B III LM681 had made a test flight from the Royal Aircraft Establishment, Farnborough, when it suffered a hydraulic failure while landing at Staverton. This meant that the flaps wouldn't work, and the aircraft ran off the end of the runway through the boundary fence and into Bamburlong Road. The aircraft was seriously damaged, but no one was hurt. A similar incident occurred on 11 October 1945 when another Lancaster B III, this time ND623, returned to Staverton from an in-flight refuelling trial. The aircraft landed at too high a speed, and it overshot across a stream and into trees. Although the aircraft was a write-off, none of the crew was hurt.

The end of the war saw a general run-down in the armed services and the aircraft industry, and this was felt at Staverton just as elsewhere. The Folland and Gloster Flight Test Departments closed and early in 1946 Flight Refuelling returned to their previous base at Ford. On 29 July 1946, No 44 Group Communications Flight was disbanded (the Group itself disbanded just over two weeks later). This left the only service presence at RAF Staverton to be provided by the RAF Police

Dog School, which had opened at the station in the early 1940s. On the actual airfield, Rotol remained as the sole operator.

Staverton returned to civilian control on 29 September 1950. Apart from Rotol there were no other operators at the airfield for a few years, but in March 1953 Cambrian Airways took over its management, and shortly afterwards Smiths Industries Aviation Division moved in. Although Rotol closed its Flight Test Department in 1954, the company amalgamated with Dowty Equipment Ltd on April 1960 and this secured an aviation-related manufacturing industry on the site, which continues at Staverton today.

Wartime aircraft reappeared at Staverton in 1963, when the Skyfame Museum was opened by aviation preservation pioneer Peter Thomas, in the old Flight Refuelling hangar. An Oxford, Anson, Mosquito and several other aircraft were preserved by the museum, which was the first in the UK to be devoted exclusively to aviation. Most of the museum's exhibits were flown regularly, and when in 1978 it had to close due to financial pressures, the exhibits went on to become important parts of other collections, such as the Royal Air Force Museum, Hendon, and the Imperial War Museum at Duxford. Airline services continued from Staverton in the 1960s and 1970s, by such concerns as Derby Airways, British Midland Airways and Intra, operating mainly to the Channel Islands.

Today Staverton remains operational, in the role for which it was originally built, as Gloucestershire Airport. Scheduled services are still flown to the Channel Islands, and a number of flying schools, air taxi, charter, air freight, maintenance and repair companies operate from this busy and thriving airfield. The historical connection is maintained by the Gloucestershire Aviation Collection, which is based at the airport. Its 22 aircraft all have local connections, and are visual reminders of the important place that Staverton and Gloucestershire have in aviation history.

16
STOKE ORCHARD

2 miles west of Bishops Cleve
SO 925275

Stoke Orchard seems to have been identified as a potential site for flying training in 1939. Although an airfield was laid out there the following year, the RAF did not take up residence until 1941.

In the meantime the Gloster Aircraft Company had also realised the potential of Stoke Orchard as a site for aircraft production, strategically dispersed away from the company's main factory at Hucclecote. Accordingly, two Dispersal Factory Units (numbered 39 and 40 by the company) were erected at the airfield during 1940, to parallel and support the work being undertaken at Hucclecote. Unit No 39 at Stoke Orchard was the assembly building and No 40 was the Flight Shed. Various aircraft were in production at Glosters from 1940 onwards, including Hawker Hurricanes and Typhoons that were manufactured by the company under sub-contract arrangements. The large components and sub-assemblies of these aircraft were sent from other Gloster factories to Stoke Orchard, where they were put together. Once erected, the aircraft were test flown from the airfield before delivery.

The first RAF unit to use Stoke Orchard was No 10 Elementary Flying Training School (EFTS), based at Weston-super-Mare. It was in fact decided to move the whole school from Weston to Stoke Orchard, rather than just a detachment. Therefore between 23 and 27 September 1941, as training courses were completed, the training and support staff, pupils and the 54 Tiger Moths of 10 EFTS moved in to their new base.

Stoke Orchard had been well prepared for its tenants. Runways of steel tracking had been supplemented by a perimeter track. There was

Students receiving instruction on the Airspeed Hotspur glider. (Aeroplane)

a technical site in the south-east corner of the airfield, which consisted of four large Bellman hangars and other facilities in assorted huts and small buildings. Undercover storage for aircraft was provided by 13 Blister hangars of various types erected around the airfield. These included a Triple Extra Over Blister, six Double Extra Overs, one single Extra Over, two Standard Doubles and three Standard Blisters. There were workshops, stores, lecture rooms, MT section and station HQ, an officers' mess, sergeants' mess and accommodation for WAAFs and other ranks in Laing and Seco huts.

No 10 EFTS got down to work, and was soon filling the circuit with its Tiger Moths. Mishaps were few and accidents minor until 23 May

1942, when Tiger Moth R4894 spun into the ground near the airfield, killing both occupants. The school was not in fact to remain at Stoke Orchard for much longer after this, as it had been decided to reorganise the flying training organisation and disband some of the Elementary Flying Schools, including 10 EFTS.

Meanwhile Stoke Orchard had been considered for glider training, and in March 1942 operating trials had taken place with a Hotspur glider and tug. These had been successful, and so a glider training organisation was gradually built up at Stoke Orchard. It officially opened on 21 July 1942 as No 3 Glider Training School (GTS), the day that 10 EFTS was disbanded. Initially equipped with Miles Master IIs that had been modified to tow gliders, and Hotspur two-seat training gliders (which could also carry eight troops or a simulated load), the school also flew the Tiger Moth, Miles Magister and Airspeed Oxford.

However, before flying at 3 GTS got off to a start, the airfield was given an upgrade, and while this was taking place received an unscheduled visitor in the form of a Douglas Havoc. This aircraft, the AW410, was a Turbinlite aircraft of 1456 (Fighter) Flight based at Honiley in Warwickshire. The constant speed unit had failed on one engine, and so its propeller was feathered. The aircraft made an emergency landing at Stoke Orchard, but unfortunately had no hydraulic pressure and therefore no brakes. To avoid running into a group of workman on the runway, Pilot Officer R.J. Armstrong retracted the Havoc's undercarriage to bring it to a halt, somewhat dented.

Course No 1 of 3 GTS started on 4 August 1942 and with the urgent need for glider pilots, the school was kept busy at Stoke Orchard over the ensuing few years. Flying training often involves mistakes being made, which should result in lessons being learnt but often also results in accidents occurring. The first gliding accident at Stoke Orchard came on 10 August, when a Hotspur crashed on the airfield. The pilot, Corporal Masson, was injured. Unfortunately the school's first fatal accident took place only a week later, when Hotspur HH519 being flown by Corporal McQueen of the Glider Pilot Regiment was caught in the slipstream of the tug aircraft just after take-off. The pilot lost control and the glider crashed into a tree, killing him instantly.

The tugs also had their share of accidents, starting with Master DL368, flown by Sergeant J.F. Alexander. After releasing his glider on the morning of 25 August, he flew low over the village of Bishops Cleeve not far from the airfield, forgetting that his tow-rope was still attached. The rope struck the roof of the vicarage and carried away its chimney! Five days later Master DL526 stalled during a landing attempt, its wing struck the ground and the aircraft crash-landed, injuring its pilot. During the rest of the year three Masters were involved in serious accidents, none fatal, and four Hotspurs. The glider accidents usually involved undershooting (ie coming down short of the runway, and not flaring in to land at the right angle). Two pilots were killed in such an accident on 2 October. In another fatal accident the tow-rope of one glider got entangled with that of another and it crashed on take-off.

On 2 November 1942, 3 GTS took over Northleach airfield as a Relief Landing Ground (RLG) in order to ease the congestion at Stoke Orchard, which was becoming very busy. However, with repeated use

Final checks on a Hotspur before night flying. (Aeroplane)

by glider and tugs the airfield surface at Northleach soon started to suffer and became muddy and waterlogged. Flying was concentrated at Stoke Orchard once more, and training continued throughout the winter of 1942/43. The routine of take-off by tug and glider, cast-off by the tug and return to base with the glider carrying out a flying training exercise or practice before coming into land itself, was followed repeatedly throughout the period. There were quite a few accidents during the first half of 1943, some serious. A Hotspur undershot the runway on 23 February and went into the trees, while another landed short almost a month later, on 20 March. On 3 April another Hotspur crashed onto the north-east corner of the airfield. Accidents with Masters included DL448 which taxied into a fuel bowser on 17 March, two undercarriage collapses while landing on 14 May and 15 June, and a fourth aircraft which collided with a fence after its brakes failed after landing.

During the second half of 1943 there were nine serious accidents at Stoke Orchard. Two Hotspurs undershot the runway during July, another in August and a fourth on 19 November after the aircraft lost its canopy. The other five accidents involved Masters. Two Masters crashed at Stoke Orchard on 19 July, the first being DL373 which struck

217

the airfield boundary wall, injuring its pilot, Sergeant Jones. The second, DL491, hit a telegraph pole at night and crashed to the ground, killing its pilot, Sergeant Thoroughgood. On 26 July the undercarriage of Master DL467 collapsed on landing. Sergeant C.E. Petre was practising aerobatics in Master DM404 near the airfield on 31 August when the aircraft caught fire and crashed, killing him. Master T8740 was visiting Stoke Orchard from 5 (P)AFU at Ternhill on 5 October, when it developed engine trouble and crash-landed short of the airfield. The fifth Master accident at Stoke Orchard during 1943 involved DL518, which overshot the runway and crashed into the boundary hedge.

No 3 GTS had used Northleach during the summer of 1943, but wet ground conditions made the airfield unusable in the winter of 1943/44. By then the pressure was on to train more glider pilots for the airborne operations that were being planned for the summer of 1944. Although few people were aware of the actual plans for the D-Day operations, there was a general feeling that preparations were being made for 'something big' during that spring. The aircraft and instructors of 3 GTS were kept busy, turning out as many qualified pilots as possible for the Glider Pilot Regiment. Most of the flying accidents recorded at Stoke Orchard during 1944 occurred during the early part of the year, when this intense pressure was on. The only gliding accident was to Hotspur HH605 on 14 February, when the aircraft crashed on landing. The remaining four involved the Master glider

Hotspur on the approach. (Aeroplane)

tugs. One aircraft crash-landed in a field nearby when it developed engine trouble on 6 March, while another crashed onto the airfield while landing two days later. On 15 March Master DL433 crashed on take-off after having collided with a stationary Hotspur and on 24 March, DL476 struck another Master while landing.

Northleach was used again during the summer of 1944, and a detachment of 3 GTS was based there. Several accidents were recorded at the RLG during the period, probably indicating the shift in the training emphasis there. It was undoubtedly with great pride and satisfaction that the instructors of 3 GTS learnt of the D-Day landings on 6 June, and the significant contribution made by glider pilots (many of whom were trained at the school) to the operation's successful outcome. The training continued of course, as the demand was still there for glider pilots, many of whom were later to take part in the Arnhem operations.

The most serious and tragic flying accident to occur in the vicinity of Stoke Orchard airfield was on 26 August 1944 when Halifax III MZ311 of 78 Squadron crashed on nearby Cleeve Common. The aircraft based at Breighton in Yorkshire, was returning from a raid on La Rochelle. All seven crew members aboard the aircraft were killed.

With the onset of the autumn, the weather started to deteriorate and this had its effects on the flying programme. The airfield at Northleach became waterlogged and was finally abandoned by the 3 GTS detachment there on 21 October. Rather than return to Stoke Orchard, the surface of which by then was not much of an improvement on Northleach, the detachment moved to Zeals in Wiltshire, where they had a large airfield all to themselves.

Because of the poor surface condition at Stoke Orchard, little use was being made of it by 3 GTS during the winter of 1944/45 and it was decided to move the unit to another airfield. Therefore in mid-January 1945, along with the Zeals detachment, the school was moved to Exeter. From that time no further flying took place from Stoke Orchard. The airfield was taken over by 7 MU Quedgeley, and the hangars used for storage for some months, but it was closed at the end of 1945, sold off shortly afterwards and returned to agriculture. A few buildings remain today to signify the vital role that Stoke Orchard played during the Second World War.

17
WINDRUSH

4 miles west of Burford
SP 180120

RAF Windrush came into use in the early summer of 1940 as a Relief Landing Ground (RLG) for No 15 Service Flying Training School (SFTS) based at RAF Kidlington in Oxfordshire. The airfield, to the west of Burford, was then basically a field with several Nissen huts provided for the ground crews. North American Harvards and Airspeed Oxfords of 15 SFTS used Windrush for routine flying training, which included practising circuits, landings and take-offs.

Some day flying took place, but the airfield's main use was at night, the runway approach being marked with goose-neck flares, which were oil lamps laid out by the ground party. The first flying accident at Windrush in fact occurred at night, when Harvard P5901 of 15 SFTS crashed during a take-off attempt on 25 July 1940. A similar accident, this time to an Oxford, occurred a few nights later, on 30 July. Although other units used Windrush for training, the only accidents during the summer of 1940 appear to have happened to the aircraft of 15 SFTS. The unit's Oxford N6323 hit trees on its approach on 1 August and crashed, killing its crew of two. Another fatality followed on 6 August, when Oxford P1869 dived into the ground shortly after take-off at night.

The other major user of Windrush was No 6 SFTS, based at South Cerney. The Ansons and Oxfords of the unit's Initial and Advanced Training Squadrons increasingly used the facilities at Windrush both by day and by night to the extent that it was decided to transfer the control of the RLG to 6 SFTS. This took place officially on 19 August 1940.

As if to mark the occasion the Luftwaffe visited Windrush on the night before the handover. Earlier that day, 18 August, several RAF

The North American Harvards of 15 SFTS were the first aircraft to use Windrush. (Aeroplane)

airfields had been bombed including Biggin Hill, Kenley and Manston, and that evening some 50 German bombers crossed the Channel coast and were individually prowling over southern England. At the time, Sergeant Bruce Hancock of 6 SFTS was making his last solo night flight before qualifying and was circling over Windrush in Anson L9164. As the Anson turned and flew across the airfield at about 1,000 feet a Heinkel He 111 bomber appeared behind it. The German crew had been attracted by the Windrush flarepath, and dropped ten 50 kg bombs. As the bombs exploded near the airfield, the Heinkel followed the Anson ahead and its nose gunner opened fire. Alerted by tracer fire passing his unarmed aircraft, Sergeant Hancock seemed to realise the predicament that he was in. Observers on the ground watched in horror as the German aircraft closed on its helpless prey. Then the Anson slowed, and when the Heinkel was on the point of overshooting it, the trainer pulled up and crashed into the German bomber. Both aircraft broke up and fell to the ground at Blackpits Farm, some two miles from the airfield. The four crew-members of the He 111 were killed in the impact, as was Sergeant Hancock who is buried in Windrush churchyard.

The Luftwaffe visited Windrush again on 2 and 11 September, dropping bombs, but again missing the airfield on both occasions. Other visitors to the airfield, friendlier this time, included the Hurricane night-fighters of 87 Squadron based at RAF Colerne. Unfortunately one of their aircraft, P3755, crashed in circuit on the evening of 19 December 1940.

Training by 6 SFTS continued at Windrush into 1941 and they were joined early in the year by the Harvards and Oxfords of 2 SFTS from Brize Norton. The majority of the aircraft to be seen flying from Windrush, however, remained those from 6 SFTS. As with all other flying training stations, Windrush was being worked at full capacity

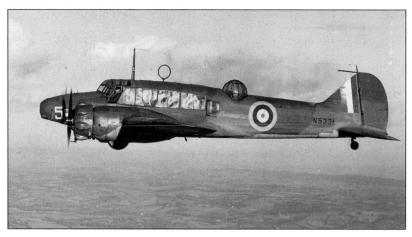

The airfield was also used by the Avro Ansons of 6 SFTS. (Aeroplane)

during this time as it eased congestion on the main stations at Little Rissington and Brize Norton. Accidents often resulted because of this and during 1941 seven Oxfords were involved in serious accidents at Windrush, (one from 2 SFTS, the remainder from 6 SFTS). Take-offs and landings were the most critical times, with two Oxfords crashing on take-off, one on the approach and three on overshooting the runway. The other Oxford caught fire while on the ground.

In 1942 Windrush was upgraded, with the construction of a concrete perimeter track and the laying of two runways of steel Sommerfield tracking. Nine Blister hangars were erected on the western side of the airfield to house aircraft and equipment. Other installations put up at the time included pre-cast concrete and brick buildings for an instructional site in the north-east corner of the site, and permanent brick and concrete-built accommodation for personnel in a living site on the north-west of the site. A standard RLG control-tower was built on the northern side of the airfield.

No 6 SFTS became No 6 (Pilots) Advance Flying Unit ((P)AFU) on 1 April 1942, its role changing to that of advanced flying training only. The new unit retained an interest in Windrush and flying training at the airfield continued unabated. An unusual visitor on 12 September was a Whitley, which crashed-landed at Windrush following an engine failure. A fire in the port wing was extinguished by the station's fire crew and only one slight injury was sustained, by the rear gunner. The only other accident recorded that year was on 30 November 1942, when Oxford W6624 crashed on the airfield, killing its pilot Sergeant Crossley.

Unfortunately the flying accident record for 1943 was not quite so good, with six accidents occurring at Windrush, five involving Oxfords. The most serious was on 4 April, when an Oxford crashed into the flight offices at night, resulting in two crew being killed. Two further fatalities occurred later in the year – on 30 September, an Oxford caught fire on landing, and on 20 October, another crashed on the airfield, killing their pilots.

On 17 October 1943, Sergeant Kirkland of 82 Operational Training Unit (OTU) was flying his Wellington in the area when one engine failed. As he prepared to make an emergency landing at Little Rissington, the second engine packed up and so, having spotted Windrush, he made a last-minute diversion and came in to land there. The aircraft crash-landed and caught fire, but the pilot and his crew escaped without injury.

Flying continued at Windrush throughout 1944. Only two aircraft are recorded as having accidents that year. One, an Oxford, crashed on 25 April, unfortunately killing its pilot Flight Sergeant Cormack. The other was an Armstrong Whitworth Albemarle, V1612 of 297 Squadron based at Brize Norton, which overshot while landing on 12 May from a pre D-Day training flight. The last flying accident at the RLG was on 19 January 1945, when Oxford MP403 struck another Oxford, L4584, which was damaged beyond repair. There were no recorded aircrew injuries.

With the end of hostilities in Europe, flying training at Little Rissington started to ease back, with the result that a RLG was no longer needed at Windrush. By June 1945 No 6 (P)AFU had moved its equipment, personnel and aircraft back to its main base. Windrush was closed as a flying station on 12 July 1945, and later sold off and restored to agriculture.

Aeroplanes can still be seen at Windush today, as flying takes place there by members of the resident flying club. Some wartime buildings remain, including the control tower which has been carefully restored and is a fitting monument to the airfield's past.

18
YATE

9 miles north-east of Bristol
ST 706830

No 3 (Western) Aircraft Repair Depot was established at Yate in 1916, in four large sheds along the southern edge of a large grass airfield. The depot, situated to the north-east of Bristol, repaired a large number of aircraft for the Royal Flying Corps during the Great War, ranging from the early BE2 to the later Bristol Fighter and Sopwith Camel. It also rebuilt at least 260 aircraft, from spares and salvaged parts and assemblies. When the war finished in 1918, the airfield was abandoned.

Yate remained empty until 1925, when George Parnall and Co Ltd of Park Row, Bristol, began to use it. The company had its origins in Parnall and Sons Ltd, a Bristol cabinet making and shopfitting company that was awarded a contract to manufacture a few aircraft for the Admiralty. They went on to build over 750 aircraft to the designs of Sopwith, Avro and Short, and even produced several designs of their own, including the Parnall Panther two-seat naval biplane that achieved production status. The company had been taken over by W & T Avery Ltd, the weighing machine manufacturers, and when George Geach Parnall, the Managing Director of Parnall and Sons, fell out with Averys over the scale of future aviation work, he resigned and set up his own concern, George Parnall and Co Ltd.

At its Park Row factory the new company produced its first design, the Puffin naval amphibian. This was assembled in the cabinet works and test flown from the Isle of Grain Naval Air Station. The next design, the Plover single-seat naval fighter, was flown from Filton. The company needed to expand and found Yate, with its works, office block and design office, along with a reasonably sized airfield, to be ideal. Under the leadership of its Chief Designer, Harold Bolas, George Parnall & Co built a series of aircraft designs at Yate, including the

Pixie, Peto, Prawn and Parasol. None was particularly successful, although they flew well enough, and most were one-off prototypes or experimental machines. After Bolas left for the USA in 1929, the company ran on for a few more years licence-building other designs, including the Percival Gull. In 1935 George Parnall sold the Yate site and retired.

The Yate site was then bought by Nash and Thompson Ltd, manufacturers of power-operated gun turrets, as fitted to the Hawker Demon two-seater fighter. In conjunction with the Hendy Aircraft Company a new concern was set up to run the Yate site, known as Parnall Aircraft Ltd. Aircraft production continued at Yate on a small scale, their most successful design being the Heck touring monoplane, the development of a Hendy design. However, the company's main interest became more focused on power-operated gun turrets.

With the onset of the RAF's Expansion Scheme, aircraft production increased in Britain and so did the demand for the company's Fraser-Nash turrets. Initially fitted to the Armstrong Whitworth Whitley bomber, this was soon followed by the Vickers Wellington bomber, the Blackburn Botha torpedo bomber and the Short Sunderland flying boat. A large new factory was built to produce these in the south-west corner of the airfield, and this was in full production by the time that war was declared. The airfield remained in use for visiting aircraft, including prototypes and test aircraft on turret development work.

Nash and Thompson gun turrets, manufactured at Yate, were fitted to the RAF's Hawker Demon two-seat fighters of the 1930s; the prototype Demon, J9933, is shown here. (Aeroplane)

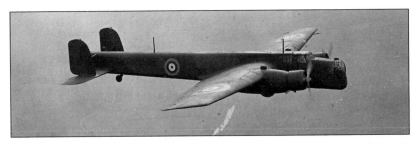

Yate-built Fraser-Nash gun turrets were initially fitted into the Armstrong Whitworth Whitley. (Aeroplane)

Based at Yate were three Parnall Heck IIc aircraft which were used by the company for communications work to other factories and RAF units.

The Luftwaffe were obviously aware of the importance of the Parnall Aircraft factory, as Yate appeared as an objective on German target maps. Their unwelcome interest materialised on 27 September 1940 when ten Messerschmitt Bf 110 fighter bombers were tasked to attack the factory. The aircraft took off from Cherbourg escorted by a further 42 Bf 110 fighters. Over the English coast some of the escort split off to disguise the force's target, but the fighter controllers of 10 Group Headquarters had predicted their intentions and scrambled the Hurricanes of 504 Squadron from their base at Filton. As the main formation appeared over Yate and the bombers began their dive, they were set upon by 504's Hurricanes. The Bf 110s abandoned their attack, and in trying to evade the British fighters, jettisoned their bombs. During their frantic withdrawal they were attacked by the Spitfires of 152 Squadron from Warmwell and 609 Squadron from Middle Wallop, then the Hurricanes of 56 Squadron, Boscombe Down and of 238 Squadron, also from Middle Wallop. Ten of the Bf 110s were shot down, including that of the bombing group's commander. One of the Spitfires was shot down and one Hurricane damaged during the melee.

However, this event was not to deter the Germans, as they realised the importance of Yate. A few stray bombs were dropped near the factory on 7 December 1940, but this was followed by a much more serious attack a few months later. At lunchtime on 27 February 1941, a lone He 111 followed the railway line at low level southwards to Yate. As it neared the airfield it lowered its undercarriage (presumably to deceive the defenders into thinking that it was a friendly aircraft

The Vickers Wellington also had Fraser-Nash turrets. (Aeroplane)

coming in to land) and dropped six high explosive bombs into the factory. There were over 4,000 people working there at the time, and no one had time to get to the shelters. Three bombs exploded, wrecking the drawing office and part of the shop floor. Many people were injured and 22 draughtsmen died. A delayed-action bomb then went off, destroying more of the production area and killing more workers. Two bombs failed to go off, including one that fell through the roof and rolled across the shop floor to land at the feet of a group of workers, who were mesmerised with fear. In only a few seconds tremendous damage was done to life and property by just one raider. Over half of the factory was damaged, and 52 people had been killed, with a further 150 injured.

This attack led to dispersal plans, but as these were being carried out another Heinkell He 111 attacked the factory on 7 March. It appeared out of the clouds at two o'clock in the afternoon and dropped a number of bombs, machine-gunning the factory before flying away. Three people were killed in this attack, and 20 more injured. This accelerated the removal work, with heavy machinery and equipment being moved in fleets of lorries to dispersed sites including Boulton Mills, Dursley. Within just over a week the main factory was empty, and production of gun turrets had resumed in the dispersed factory units.

Several other sites in Gloucestershire and the Bristol area were used by Parnall Aircraft during the remainder of the war, as well as at Yate, where the bombed-out factory was largely rebuilt as a modern works. Gun turrets for Lancaster bombers were built, along with airframe assemblies for Lancasters, Spitfires and then later Lincoln bombers and Meteor jet fighters.

After the war gun turret manufacture continued for a period, until Parnall moved into the field of domestic appliances. The Yate factory is still in existence today, although it was subsequently enlarged to take in most of the airfield. The remainder has been sold for housing.

It is interesting to note that, despite the reluctance of W & T Avery to allow Parnall & Sons Ltd to get more involved in aviation in the 1920s, it did just that over a decade later. On the outbreak of war in 1939, Parnall & Sons once more began wooden aircraft manufacture. They started building DH Tiger Moth fuselages at their works at Brislington and Fishponds, followed by Airspeed Oxford wings, Short Stirling fins, Handley Page Halifax flaps, Bristol Beaufighter tailplanes, Fairey Barracuda components, DH Mosquito assemblies and Airspeed Horsa fuselages. They therefore made a significant contribution to the output of the British aircraft industry during the period. After the war, they continued to be involved with aircraft manufacturing, moving onto fabricating metal components including sections of the CH Venom jet fighter, and tailplanes for DH Herons. Other parts were made for the Bristol Freighter, Bristol Britannia, DH Comet, HS125 and later Concorde.

Parnall Aircraft also built gun turrets and main airframe assemblies for the Avro Lancaster. (Aeroplane)

19

THE SMALLER AIRFIELDS

Barnsley Park

4 miles north-east of Cirencester (SP 075075)

Barnsley Park was opened on 23 June 1941 as No 22 Satellite Landing Ground (SLG) and allocated to No 6 Maintenance Unit (MU) at Brize Norton. The site consisted of some open fields on a heavily wooded estate north-east of Cirencester, and was intended merely as a temporary landing ground while a more permanent satellite was developed at Woburn Abbey. Facilities at Barnsley Park were fairly basic, consisting of wooden administrative offices, guard buildings and rudimentary AA defences. Although the fields were used for landing and taking off, the aircraft were actually stored in clearings in the park, the trees providing useful natural camouflage cover.

However, the SLG proved difficult to use, due to the unsuitability of its surface, and in November 1941 it was closed to enable regrading to take place. Contractors W.G. Chivers and Son Ltd were brought in to undertake the work, but due to the bad weather during the winter of 1941/42, this was not started until the following spring. The task was to prove difficult however, and when it was felt that the work had been completed, a Gladiator was landed to test the surface. The test proved unsatisfactory, and 6 MU then looked to other SLGs for storage.

More remedial work then took place, including the laying of steel mesh to reinforce the airfield's surface; altogether some 120,000 square yards of mesh were laid at Barnsley Park. Other work included the construction of a brick building to house the guards and administrative staff. To blend in with the local area, it was designed to look like a domestic bungalow, and other buildings were constructed to resemble farm machinery sheds. When the airfield was reopened on 28 September 1943, it was allocated to 5 MU Kemble for dispersed aircraft storage.

Hawker Hurricanes were stored at Barnsley Park. This Mark IIC is from 1 Squadron. (Aeroplane)

The SLG was not immediately needed by 5 MU, and few aircraft were initially moved there. In November, only three Hurricanes were on site. This changed the following year, as Kemble became very busy and a large number of aircraft were transferred from there to Barnsley Park. The end of the war in Europe changed the storage situation just as rapidly, and aircraft were soon returned to Kemble or transferred to other sites for inspection, then disposal or further storage. By the late summer of 1945 Barnsley Park had been emptied and in September it was closed.

Today nothing remains of the SLG at Barnsley Park, apart from the security and administration building, which has been converted into the type of building that it was designed to resemble – a bungalow!

Down Farm
3 miles south-west of Tetbury (ST 855906)

Down Farm was used for the open-air storage of aircraft from 10 Maintenance Unit (MU), Hullavington. The site, not far from Tetbury, had been selected in 1940, when a suitable field had been found alongside the woods in Westonbirt Park. Clearings provided adequate storage areas where the aircraft would be naturally camouflaged by the overhanging trees.

After preparation of the site and the provision of basic facilities Down Farm airfield was opened on 15 April 1941 as No 23 Satellite Landing Ground (SLG). Initially, four Boulton Paul Defiants were flown in from Hullavington and picketed out in the woods. They were joined shortly afterwards by three Handley Page Hampdens, then more aircraft followed, as Hullavington got busier.

As with all of the dispersed aircraft storage areas used by the MUs, Down Farm's isolated location meant that security was a problem. Intruders were seen in the area, who were probably only aircraft spotters or souvenir hunters. Nonetheless saboteurs were feared and airmen from 10 MU were put on guard at the SLG, until they were replaced by an Army detachment and guard dogs.

More aircraft arrived for storage during 1942, and the provision of additional dispersals in Westonbirt Park was in progress when the MU were informed that the site had been selected for development as an aerodrome for the USAAF. These plans were dropped later in the year, possibly following protests from the Ministry of Aircraft Production, which urgently required storage sites for the stream of aircraft then coming off the production lines and being received from the USA.

When Down Farm was cleared for the handing and storage of four-engined bombers, Sommerfield Tracking was laid to help the grass surface bear their weight. Eventually a total of 147 tons of the tracking was laid at the SLG, on the runways and dispersals.

In the autumn of 1943, 110 aircraft were in store at the site, including Short Stirlings. More aircraft were received in the spring of the following year, as the build up to the invasion progressed. Most of the aircraft for storage at the SLG were brought in by air and following

Short Stirlings were stored in the open at Down Farm. (Aeroplane)

231

issue were flown out again, though some aircraft types, particularly obsolescent ones, tended to be in store for longer periods than others. Activity increased during March 1945, when the Oxfords of 15 (Pilots) Advanced Flying Unit ((P) AFU), based at South Cerney, started using Down Farm for flying practice. Most of this took place at night, and resulted from problems with waterlogging at the unit's RLG at Babdown Farm. A flarepath of sodium lights was laid by a detachment of ground staff whenever night flying practice took place. After a month or so, Babdown Farm was back in use, so the Oxfords resumed flying from there.

The end of the war in Europe came the following month and this resulted in the disbandment of squadrons and the withdrawal of aircraft. There was an increase in the use of Down Farm, and during July over 180 aircraft were in store under the trees. This peak in numbers was of course only temporary, and over the ensuing few months the aircraft were gradually returned to Hullavington. There being no further requirement for Down Farm, the SLG was closed and returned to its owners in February 1946. Little sign of the airfield's wartime use remains on the site, which nowadays is well known as housing the Westonbirt Arboretum.

Long Newton
1 mile east of Long Newnton village (ST 929920)

Long Newnton was one of the very few airfields that were developed from dummy ones. Located along the Gloucestershire/Wiltshire border from Kemble, Long Newnton was selected as a decoy site for the RAF station in July 1940. It occupied a similar topographical position, but was some four miles to the south-west.

Long Newnton was laid out as a Q site, which meant that it was a night decoy lit with electric lamps to simulate the full lighting of a real airfield. These would include a set of yellow lights to imitate the T-shaped wind direction indicator, red lamps to mark buildings, an airfield recognition light (usually flashing green and yellow), and sets of car headlamps to mimic taxiing aircraft. This equipment would all be controlled from a concrete bunker. Q sites could be built anywhere as they would only be seen at night, but Long Newnton was unusual in that it was laid out across flat fields, which would later prove suitable for an airfield in its own right.

Indeed it was not long before the decoy airfield's potential was spotted by pilots of passing aircraft, and by November it was being used by the Harvards of 15 Service Flying Training School (SFTS) from Kidlington as a Relief Landing Ground (RLG) for night flying practice. Other aircraft using the airfield at the time included the Harvards of 14 SFTS, Lyneham, and the Oxfords of 3 SFTS, South Cerney. It was 3 SFTS that recognised the long-term value of Long Newnton as a training asset, and they took over the airfield in February 1941 as one of their satellites. The site was closed for a period, while the school arranged for two runways to be laid, from Sommerfield tracking, as well as a perimeter track. A control tower was put up and at the same time a technical site was built, consisting of several buildings including four Blister hangars for the storage of aircraft and equipment undercover. The first flying accident at Long Newnton occurred during this period, when Oxford V3234 of 14 FTS, visiting from Ossington in Nottinghamshire, crash-landed on the overshoot.

The airfield was reopened for flying in February 1942 for the use of 3 SFTS, which the following month became an advanced flying school and was retitled No 3 (Pilots) Advanced Flying Unit ((P)AFU). Battles, Hurricanes and Bothas were regular visitors to Long Newnton, as well as the unit's Oxfords, which undertook most of the night flying. During the summer of 1942 accommodation sites were built and more Blister hangars were added around the airfield to house the increased numbers of aircraft then being deployed there. A T1 hangar was added to those on the technical site, and the whole area was camouflaged. Another visiting aircraft crash-landed at Long Newnton on 19 September. This time it was a Master, W8723 from the ECFS at Hullavington, which landed with its undercarriage retracted. Its South African pilot was uninjured.

The aircraft of 3 (P)AFU continued to use Long Newnton through into 1943, although experiencing some problems with waterlogging.

Airspeed Oxfords were a common sight in the circuit at Long Newnton. (Aeroplane)

North American Mitchell, of the type that came to grief at Long Newnton in August 1944. (Aeroplane)

Training carried on through that summer, with only one flying accident, albeit a serious one. On 11 July, an Oxford of 3(P)AFU crashed near the airfield, killing its crew, Flying Officer Schurman and Sergeant Southwall.

In August 1943, No 3 (P)AFU handed over the airfield to No 15 (P)AFU, which had its HQ at Ramsbury (later moved to Castle Coombe), and they brought in several of their flights from Greenham Common. Flying took place regularly until October, when heavy rain resulted in the airfield becoming waterlogged. This restricted movement on the ground and had an adverse affect on the flying programme. The airfield surface improved in the spring, and flying continued unabated through that summer. However, rain in August 1944 again caused problems. A Mitchell twin-engined bomber of No 320 (Dutch) Squadron landed at Long Newnton on the 31st, following a cross-county flight from its base at Dunsfold. The aircraft skidded across the slippery runway, crashed through the boundary hedge and came to a halt in a potato field with its back broken. Fortunately none of the crew was injured, but the seriously damaged aircraft was written off.

Bad weather during the remainder of the year restricted flying activities once more, and things hardly improved in the New Year. The airfield started to dry out again in March but the 15 (P)AFU flights only managed a couple of months of unhindered flying training before being transferred to Babdown Farm in June. This was not before Oxford V4061 overshot after landing at the airfield, and hit another Oxford, ED139, on 19 June. Flying then ended at the station and it was transferred to the control of 11 MU at Chilmark, which used it as a storage site.

Long Newnton reverted to its owners in about 1950, and was returned to agriculture. A few of the buildings remain today, including the control tower, T1 hangar and Maycrete huts, as reminders of the site's wartime past.

Northleach

10 miles north-east of Cirencester (SP 110155)

Northleach was planned as a Relief Landing Ground in 1940, but it was some time before the site was actually used. This was by 3 Glider Training School (GTS) based at Stoke Orchard, a detachment of which arrived on 2 November 1942. The unit trained glider pilots and flew Hotspur training gliders, Master glider tugs and Magister two-seat trainers. It was one of the Magisters, EM293, that was the first aircraft to be involved in a flying accident at Northleach, crashing just after take-off on 12 December (the pilot was uninjured).

Accommodation was fairly basic at Northleach and that, coupled

Student pilot about to fly solo in an Airspeed Hotspur. (Aeroplane)

235

Hotspur coming in to land. (Aeroplane)

with the fact that the airfield's surface was muddy and waterlogged, causing it to become rutted very easily, encouraged the detachment to return to its base. No 3 GTS returned the following March when the weather and the surface had improved.

Several aircraft were involved in accidents at Northleach during the year. Three of these involved Masters that either landed with their undercarriage up, or it collapsed on landing. Another Master hit a boundary wall on landing. There were also three glider accidents, all involving landings – one Hotspur undershot and hit a wall, and another crashed during the landing, injuring the pilot. The worst accident of the year was on 8 April 1943, to a Hotspur that was being flown with heavy ballast to simulate a load of cargo. The aircraft stalled from 15 feet while on the approach, its starboard wing hit the ground and it broke up, killing the Instructor, Sergeant Holme and injuring the second pilot, Corporal Kennedy.

The waterlogging problems returned the following winter. It was therefore decided to upgrade the airfield, and two Blister hangars and several Nissen huts were erected, Northleach then being raised to Satellite Landing Ground status.

However, during the winter of 1944/45, bad weather again intervened and the flying training programme was disrupted because of the airfield's waterlogged and rutted surface. Only one accident was recorded during 1944, when on 5 June Master DL544 hit a tractor while taxiing. On 21 October 1944 the 3 GTS detachment started to leave, and within a couple of days all aeroplanes, equipment and staff had been transferred to Zeals in north-west Wiltshire. There being no further requirement for the airfield, Northleach was closed shortly afterwards and soon returned to agriculture. Very little remains there today to indicate that an airfield occupied the spot.

Overley
4½ miles north-west of Cirencester (SO 965046)

The site for an airfield near Overley Wood was selected by personnel from 20 Maintenance Unit (MU) in late 1940. They were seeking more Satellite Landing Grounds (SLG) on which to store aircraft on dispersal from the unit's main base at Aston Down. A suitable landing field was identified near to woodland, in which aircraft could be stored under the tree canopy. Once the site was approved, work started on grading the surface of the landing ground and laying out dispersals on which to park the aircraft. These activities continued throughout most of the following year, and Overley airfield was eventually opened as No 14 SLG on 1 March 1942.

Aircraft soon arrived for storage from Aston Down and the dispersals started to fill up. As with most of the SLGs, security was a problem, and Army guards were deployed at Overley to protect the aircraft. Guard dogs were also used for a while. The airfield soon attracted the attention of the flying training organisation, and in June the Oxfords of 3 Service Flying Training School (SFTS), South Cerney started using it as a Relief Landing Ground (RLG). The instructors and student pilots used the airfield for circuit planning, landing and take-off practice.

Overley was approved for the storage of four-engined aircraft in mid-1942. In October work began on extending the runway, which had

Four-engined bombers such as the Lancaster were stored at Overley. (Aeroplane)

a surface consisting of steel Sommerfield tracking. Eventually some 16,000 square yards of the mesh were laid on the airfield's runway, taxiways and dispersals. Buildings were also erected, including a Super Robin hangar and a combined HQ and security building. These were designed to look like civilian buildings – the HQ resembled a bungalow and the Super Robin hangar looked like a large farm machinery shed anyway.

Other MUs used Overley for a period during 1944, including 10 MU Hullavington from April, and 27 MU Shawbury from July, but these were gone by September. There was a gradual flow of aircraft arriving for storage and departing on issue for the rest of 1944 and into 1945, but this slowed down after May 1945. The airfield was still used for flying training at least until 23 March 1945, when Oxford AS894 of 3 (P)AFU, overshot on landing at Overley and crashed. When the war ended aircraft were transferred to Aston Down for storage or dispersal. The site at Overley was then cleared and returned to its owners in October 1945. Today little can be seen at the former airfield, apart from the remains of the HQ building.

Southrop
3 miles north-west of Lechlade (SP 190035)

An area for a flying training Relief Landing Ground (RLG) was identified to the south-west of the Cotswold village of Southrop in 1939. With the site having been prepared and basic accommodation provided, it was opened for use by 2 Service Flying Training School (SFTS), Brize Norton in August 1940. (The school had in fact used the airfield before this, one of its Harvards having had the dubious distinction of being the first aircraft to have an accident there, with its undercarriage up on 19 November 1939.)

The School's Audaxes and Harvards were soon in evidence at Southrop, although the main activity at the RLG would be night flying using Oxford twin-engined trainers. Goose-neck flare-paths were laid initially, but these were later replaced by electric lamps. The two runways were reinforced in steel planking, known as Army Track, and a perimeter track was added.

Other developments took place over the next few years, so that Southrop eventually became extremely well-equipped for an RLG. There were two sites on the airfield, the main servicing area in the south-west corner (which included two Blister hangars and a large aviation bulk fuel tank) and the operational area in the south-east which consisted of seven Over-type Blister hangars. A technical site was constructed to the north of the airfield, including a large T1 hangar, and alongside it was an instructional site of classrooms, photographic and armament training rooms, etc in Laing huts. A large domestic site was built in Macaroni Woods nearby, capable of accommodating over 700 personnel to a reasonable level of comfort.

No 2 SFTS used Southrop successfully for day and night training for a couple of years, having only one accident there (apart from the Harvard which came to grief before the school officially took over!) when an Oxford crashed during a landing at night. One of the more unusual arrivals was a Wellington twin-engined bomber of 2 Operational Training Unit (OTU) that force-landed on 28 May 1941. The aircraft had been flying on a navigational exercise from its base at Moreton-in-Marsh when its port engine developed an oil leak, and the pilot made a precautionary landing at Southrop.

On 14 March 1942 No 2 SFTS was re-roled and redesignated as No 2 (Pilots) Advanced Flying Unit ((P)AFU). Although the unit retained Southrop as its RLG, this was not to be for long as 2 (P)AFU was disbanded at Brize Norton on 13 July 1942. Southrop then passed to No 3 (P)AFU, which was based at South Cerney. This unit operated mainly Ansons and Oxfords, and it was one of the latter that was involved in the unit's first accident at Southrop just over a week after taking over the RLG. On 21 July Oxford AT603 struck trees just after take-off from Southrop and crashed into nearby buildings at

Ansons flew with 3 (P)AFU from Southrop. (Aeroplane)

Substantial parts of the buildings remained at Southrop, such as these accommodation blocks, until at least 1996. (Steve Lawrence)

Homeleigh Farm. Unfortunately the two pilots aboard were killed. No 3(P)AFU flew from Southrop for almost a further two and a half years. During that time another three Oxfords were to be lost there, one undershooting and crashing before it reached the runway in May 1943, another following an engine failure two months later and the third catching fire while taxiing in May 1944. Given the high level of flying activity at the airfield, this was not a bad accident rate.

It was decided that Southrop was no longer needed as a RLG by 3 (P)AFU by 1945 and the unit moved its detachment to South Cerney on 22 January. The last flying accident to occur at Southrop was on 1 April 1945 when Mosquito MM328 of the Photographic Reconnaissance Development Unit based at Benson was being flown over the airfield. The aircraft was put into a high-speed dive, but unfortunately broke up and crashed.

The airfield was used briefly as a RLG by two South Cerney-based units towards the end of 1945. These were No 6 Service Flying Training School flying Harvards and Oxfords and No 27 Group Communications Flight, which flew Ansons. Although Southrop closed in 1946, and the area returned to agriculture, many of the airfield buildings were used as industrial units for many years afterwards.

240

20

CIVILIANS AT WAR

On the morning of 3 September 1939, at 11.15, Neville Chamberlain, the British Prime Minister announced to the nation in a radio broadcast that Britain was at war with Germany. Although this may have been a shock to the population, it was not really a surprise, as war had been expected for some time. Only a few months before, in July, four Public Information leaflets had been issued to every household. These were entitled *Some things you should know if war should come*; *Your gas mask*; *Your food in wartime*; and *Evacuation, when and how*. The leaflets were all endorsed with the words: 'This does not mean that war is expected now.'

However, the international situation had been deteriorating for some time before this. During the Munich Crisis of September 1938, hostilities were felt to be so close that an Air Raid Precautions Act had been invoked. This resulted in the formation of a Civil Defence Corps, and the recruitment and training of air raid wardens, auxiliary firemen, ambulance drivers and other volunteers. Millions of respirators (or gas masks as they were popularly known) had been issued to the civilian population as well as to the armed forces and it was decreed that they were to be carried at all times should war come. Anderson shelters had been manufactured and during 1939 thousands were being made available to families throughout Britain. Public air raid shelters were also built in towns, and public buildings took on a new appearance as sandbags were piled up against their walls to protect them from blast damage.

Other air raid precautions included the blacking out of windows, either with heavy black-out curtains or by painting the glass, and putting tape across the windows to prevent the glass shattering and causing injury if it was broken. White paint was used liberally to assist movement in the blackout. With car headlights and torches masked, it was difficult to see at night, so white lines were painted down the

241

The author's father and his work colleague trying on their newly-issued gas masks during the Munich Crisis of September 1938. (DGB)

centre of the roads and at junctions (and remain with us today). Some kerbs, particularly those on corners, were also painted white. White bands were painted around trees, lamp-posts and other hazards so that they would stand out. The edges of the front and rear mudguards of road vehicles were similarly outlined so that they could be seen by other road-users.

The Air Raid Precautions (ARP) organisation's main function was to protect the public, and warn them of impending air raids, then to co-ordinate any rescue or emergency measures that might be required. Each county was split into divisions and areas for administrative purposes (Gloucestershire, for example, had 15 ARP areas arranged into four divisions). Wardens were appointed to patrol each area and ensure that the blackout regulations were being observed. Should an air raid warning be given it would be issued to the areas affected, so that the alarms could be sounded and people shepherded to their shelters. In smaller towns, until sirens could be installed, the wardens had to cycle round, blowing short blasts on a whistle (if a gas attack was suspected, the warning would be given by a rattle).

The ARP wardens worked with the local police, the Civil Defence Organisation and also the Auxiliary Fire Service, that had been formed to assist the County Fire Brigades. Blackout exercises were held during the summer of 1938, and their effectiveness was often tested by RAF aircraft flying overhead. Fire and rescue exercises were also held to practise the control and co-ordination of the emergency services, as well as providing excellent training. During such exercises in Cheltenham in January 1939, three aircraft from RAF Little Rissington simulated a bombing attack. Two cottages that were due to be demolished were set on fire to add realism to the exercise, mock incendiary bombs were scattered about and a gas attack simulated.

The Observer Corps had also been ordered to 'stand to' during the Munich Crisis, their role being to identify and track enemy aircraft in their vicinity. There was an expansion of the AA defences in April 1939, marked in Gloucestershire with the formation of the 98th Heavy Anti-Aircraft Regiment, a Territorial Army unit within 46 AA Brigade. With its HQ at Horfield Barracks in Bristol, batteries of 3.7 inch AA guns were to be sited in Gloucester, Cheltenham and Moreton-in-Marsh. Despite all these preparations for war, the Empire Air Day optimistically took place as planned on Saturday, 20 May 1939, with 78 RAF airfields opened to the public including South Cerney and Little Rissington. As part of the celebrations, a massed formation of 72 Fairey Battles flew over the West of England and South Wales.

On 24 August 1939 the Emergency Powers (Defence) Bill was passed in Parliament because of the 'imminent peril of war'. The new Act gave the authorities far reaching powers. Houses could be entered and searched without reason or warning, property and land could be requisitioned for war use at will, people could be evacuated from certain areas, the ports and railways were taken over by the Government, and bus and train services severely cut back.

One of the most ominous signs of the impending conflict was the mass evacuation of children from London and other major cities thought to be likely targets for enemy bombers. The evacuation plan was actually initiated on the morning of 1 September, and resulted in tens of thousands of children, with name-tags, gas masks and a few treasured possessions, being assembled ready to be moved to towns and villages in the country. More than 7,000 evacuees arrived in Gloucestershire during the first two days of September. Although their Cockney and Brummie accents caused amusement and some misunderstandings the children were generally welcomed. Volunteers, such as members of the Women's Voluntary Service, ensured that the evacuees' reception went as smoothly as possible.

The first arrivals in Cirencester were 450 schoolchildren from Barking in Essex, along with a few of their teachers and some mothers. At the railway station they were put aboard buses which took them to the Cornhall, where they were allocated accommodation, being 'billeted' with local householders who had available room. Within a few weeks over 2,000 youngsters were found new homes in the town. Similarly in Stroud, thousands of children arrived from the Edgbaston and Handsworth districts of Birmingham and were all found local

Air Raid Precautions exercise at the end of June 1939. (DGB)

accommodation. Although some of the evacuees returned home within a year, many stayed until the end of the war.

The passing of the National Service (Armed Forces) Act within days of the declaration of war made all fit men between the ages of 18 and 41 liable for military call-up. In late September a National Register was established, which was a comprehensive census of every household in the country. This enabled the issue of identity cards to everyone, to be shown on demand to 'anyone in authority'. Petrol rationing also started in September, followed two months later by the first food rationing. There were also shortages of fuel, sorely felt by the public during the extremely cold winter of 1939/40. This was a far from easy time for the civilian population.

One of the greatest successes of the wartime period was the National Savings Movement. This had started in November 1939 as the War Savings Scheme, with the aim of raising £475 million in one year to contribute towards the Defence Budget. It fell narrowly short of this target by just £8 million, but National Savings became popular, as people could save money and help the war effort. Savings groups were set up in offices, factories, schools and streets, and it was estimated that at least 25% of weekly incomes were put into savings during this time (this was despite 'an unprecedented level of income tax' of 7s 6d in the £1 introduced in late September 1939).

In addition national drives were mounted such as the Spitfire Fund in the Summer of 1940, War Weapons Week in 1941, Warship Week in 1942 and Wings for Victory in 1943. Every county, city, town and village took part in these drives, and they were given financial targets to achieve. Gloucestershire's target for Warship Week, for example was £700,000, but it was exceeded by £125,000. During the Wings for Victory campaign, Cheltenham generously raised a figure of £1.5 million, which was enough to buy 25 Lancaster bombers. The drives were accompanied by carnivals, concerts and military parades, and this did much to brighten life in wartime Britain. That National Savings made an important contribution to the country's war effort can be judged by the fact that in one year alone (1944), the war cost Britain £4.8 billion.

Winston Churchill became Prime Minister on 10 May 1940, at the head of a coalition government. The plight of Britain at this time was demonstrated on 14 May by Anthony Eden, the new Secretary of State for War. He broadcast an appeal for men between the ages of 17 and 65 to come forward and offer their services to defend the country against invasion. These volunteers would not be paid, but they would be issued with uniforms and weapons. It was hoped that a force of 150,000 men would be raised, but within two weeks 400,000 had come forward, and a month later this had risen to one million. Known as the Local Defence Volunteers, they received just armbands to start with, the initials LDV being printed on them (which were jokingly said to stand for 'Look, Duck and Vanish!'). Later known as the Home Guard, almost every village had its own platoon of volunteers, and soon the organisation covered the whole country.

Their primary task was to act as defence against invading forces, and they took their duties very seriously. They manned roadblocks and patrolled their home territory, which of course they knew well. Initially the Home Guard had no uniforms or weapons, but made do with the armbands, as well as pitchforks and shotguns. Later they were organised into military formations and issued with British army uniforms and weapons. The Home Guard in Gloucestershire consisted of several battalions across the county, divided into companies in the larger towns, and platoons in smaller towns or villages. In some areas, Auxiliary Units were formed. These were volunteers prepared to go into hiding if the Germans did successfully invade, and act as resistance squads to operate in enemy-held territory, attacking arms dumps, lines of communication, airfields and military headquarters. By mid 1942 the Home Guard numbered 1.2 million troops. They developed into a well-trained force that was used as a reserve army, freeing up regular units for other military duties, until they were disbanded in 1944.

As the war went on, further sacrifices had to be made by the British population. With the decrease in arrivals of shipping in British ports due to the U-boat offensive, rationing increased and soon covered most food items. Every member of the civilian population was issued with a ration book to show and monitor their weekly food allowances, and each shopkeeper was only allowed to have a certain number of registered customers on his books. These were then audited to ensure that his supplies balanced with his sales to customers. There were severe penalties for irregularities, but despite this there was a thriving 'black market' and almost anything could be obtained so long as payment was made and no questions were asked!

Everyone was expected to supplement their rations wherever possible by growing food in their gardens. Under the 'Dig for Victory' campaign the population was encouraged to turn their lawns and flower gardens into vegetable patches and to use all available land for allotments. The scheme was also extended to army camps and RAF stations, some actually becoming self-sufficient for some crops. Clothing was rationed and people had to 'make do and mend'. 'Save' became another watchword and everyone was encouraged to support campaigns for saving scrap metal, saucepans, rags, bones, rubber and waste paper. Towards the end of 1941, when railings were cut down for their metal, towns such as Cheltenham lost their ornamental Crimean War cannon, and First World War tanks that had been set up as war memorials (such as the one in Gloucester Park) were taken away, all for scrap to help the war effort.

As an acceptance of the difficulties presented by the clothing ration, in November 1941 the Church of England relaxed its rule requiring that women had to wear hats in church. A year later soap rationing was introduced (one tablet per person per month) and the bath depth was restricted to five inches of water! In view of food rationing, the Government was worried that the population was not eating well enough, and housewives were bombarded with nutritional information, such as in pamphlets on *Food Facts* and *Food and Hints*. Concerned that people should get at least one cooked and nourishing meal per day, Community Feed Centres, or 'British Restaurants' as they were renamed by Winston Churchill, were set up in most towns and cities. Breakfast cost 4d and a good hot mid-day meal was available for one shilling. By 1943 the Restaurants had became an established part of British urban life with over 2,000 then in operation, serving over half a million mid-day meals. In rural villages there was the Rural Pie Scheme, set up in 1942 by the Women's Voluntary Service, and providing over a million pies and snacks per week to some 5,000 villages.

The war brought new construction, much of which caused disruption to local communities. However, it also brought employment and one of the first projects, the installation of local defence positions, gave work to many building companies across the country. Remnants of these exist today, mainly in the form of pillboxes, which appear to have been placed randomly across the fields. They were in fact carefully positioned according to a master plan developed by General Sir Edmund Ironside, Commander-in-Chief Home Forces.

With the fall of France imminent, the invasion of Britain seemed next; Ironside's plan called for defence – ie coastal defences, backed up by layers of further installations inland. London and the Midlands were to be protected by a line of defences known as the GHQ line, with a series of Command, Corps and Divisional stop-lines between it and the coast. There were also a series of local lines of defence that incorporated roads, villages, railway embankments, rivers and canals. Pillboxes and road-blocks within these lines were to be manned by locally-based troops and the Home Guard, to prevent enemy troops making a breakthrough into the country's interior. Mobile columns would be brought up to reinforce areas threatened, and should the enemy break through, he would be harried by the Home Guard Auxiliary units.

The plans were approved on 25 June 1940, and work began immediately by hundreds of local authorities and civilian contractors across the country on the building of thousands of pillboxes, fire positions and anti-tank obstacles. Pillboxes were built in several sizes according to standard designs, although there were also local variations to blend in with particular locations – they were disguised as beach huts or ice cream booths at the seaside, for instance, or as line-side sheds or farm out-houses further inland. Anti-tank obstacles included concrete 'dragon's teeth' or more prosaic ones made out of steel rails.

From the end of June 1940 construction teams worked twelve-hour days, seven days per week for five weeks, then worked normal hours for a further six weeks until the defences were complete. The lines used natural topography to produce a continuous anti-tank obstacle, with pillboxes overlooking strategic points and providing cover for each other. The defences were impressive – part of the GHQ stop-line (codename Green) went from Highbridge on the Somerset coast to Freshford, south of Bath, then to Stroud and on to a point six miles south-west of Gloucester (covering a distance of 91 miles, with 319 pillboxes and 20 miles of anti-tank ditches). It was also known as the Bristol Outer Defence Line.

The first bomb to drop on Gloucestershire fell near the Bristol Aircraft Works at Filton on 18 June 1940. This heralded a massive air offensive by Germany on Britain's industrial, commercial and population centres that was to continue with increased ferocity until many Luftwaffe bomber units were transferred to the Russian Front in June 1941. Bristol was seen as an important centre, and bombs were dropped on the city on about 70 occasions between 19 June and 5 July 1941. One of the first heavy raids was on Wednesday, 25 September when 60 Heinkel He 111s of KG53 approached the city from the south

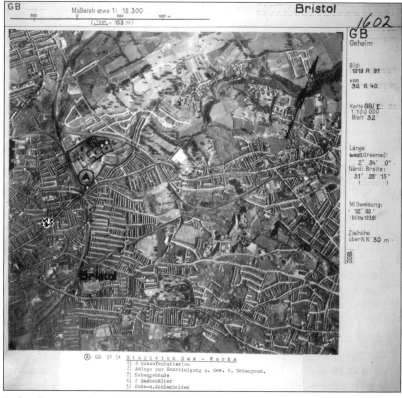

Luftwaffe target photograph of Bristol. (Nigel J. Clarke Publications)

Heinkel He 111 brought down by AA fire during a daylight raid. (Aeroplane)

and dropped 300 bombs over the northern suburbs – 141 houses were destroyed or damaged beyond repair and a further 756 badly damaged. The Filton aircraft works was hit by over 150 bombs; six air raid shelters were hit, resulting in the deaths of 91 people and the injury of 166 more. Eight aircraft in production were destroyed and another 20 others damaged.

Sunday, 24 November marked the first of a further series of heavy raids that month. Pathfinder He 111 bombers of KG100 appeared over Bristol at 18.30 hours, dropping flares. These were followed by a four-hour raid, during which successive waves of German bombers dropped over 1,000 high explosive (HE) bombs on the city. Over 200 people were killed, and 700 injured. Some 10,000 houses were destroyed or badly damaged, and many historic buildings in the old centre of the city were destroyed.

Cheltenham was raided for the first time on Wednesday, 11 December 1940 when pathfinders dropped flares at 19.20 hours. Bombers followed, dropping over 100 HE and oil bombs and several hundred incendiaries onto the city. Extensive damage was done to factories and housing, and twelve people were killed.

Another heavy raid on Bristol occurred on the evening of Sunday, 16 March 1941 when the Luftwaffe attacked Avonmouth Docks, but the bombs fell short into the nearby residential areas. The casualties were heavy – 229 men, women and children were killed and a further 422 injured. Over 416 houses were destroyed and 8,000 more damaged.

The war must have seemed all-encompassing to the civilian population of the country during 1939 to 1945. However, this was a period of total war for Britain, and everyone was involved. Women volunteered to 'do their bit', and many joined the Women's Voluntary Service (WVS). This organisation had been formed in 1938, to encourage women into Civil Defence. They made a vital contribution to the Home Front throughout the war. Often operating under difficult circumstances, the 'women in green' (as they were known from their uniforms) performed a variety of tasks. These included aiding the victims of air raids, operating rest and reception centres for war workers and service personnel, organising the collection of salvage and running canteens.

Other female war-workers included the girls of the Women's Land Army (WLA). Formed by Lady Denham in June 1939, WLA strength had risen to 17,000 by the outbreak of war. Attracted by the healthy outdoor life, many WLA volunteers found the work to be hard, long and exhausting. Most stuck it out, and eventually won the respect of a sceptical farming community. At its peak in 1943 the organisation was 87,000 strong and provided a vital resource for the farming industry, enabling it to make a valuable contribution to the nation's survival.

Although many women were already involved in the war effort, the gravity of Britain's situation was shown at the end of 1942 when the British Government introduced conscription for women. During the course of the war, Britain was the only combatant nation to do this and even Germany never felt the need to introduce this measure. All unmarried women between the ages of 20 and 30 years were 'called up', and given the choice of joining one of the three Women's Armed Services, the Civil Defence or working in Industry. Many women went to work for the first time. Coupled to this was the Essential Work Order that was invoked by the Government to bring workers into the factories. This involved transferring workers from what were regarded as non-essential jobs into those that were essential for the war effort.

Coming from all walks of life, from milkmen and salesmen to waitresses and librarians, people were uprooted from their houses, friends and families to be sent off to unfamiliar parts of the country. There they would live in lodgings and work in strange factories. However, this workforce, of which over half were women, produced supplies and equipment that kept the services fighting, and without them ultimate victory would not have been possible. Such workers were employed at aircraft and armament factories across Gloucestershire, including Filton, Hucclecote, Yate, Bristol and Gloucester, as well as at essential manufacturing and food processing companies.

With the involvement of the USA in the war in late 1941, the fate of the Axis forces was sealed. So long as the USA remained committed to the war effort, with its massive resources, large population and huge production capacity, it was not a question of whether the Allies would win the war, but when. One of the first US actions was to send troops to Britain in order to threaten Germany, which was Japan's main ally in Europe.

This 'friendly invasion' of the UK took place from the spring of 1942, and came as a culture shock to the population of the UK. The Americans were generally well received by the British population. However, there were more than a few who resented the sudden appearance of these well-fed, well-dressed and often boastful strangers in their midst, after over two years of suffering, bombing and blockade, and standing alone against the Third Reich. This, and the Americans' popularity with many of the Hollywood-influenced younger women, soon led to the complaint that they were 'overpaid, oversexed and over here'. Fortunately the US Supreme Commander, General Dwight D. Eisenhower, was pro-British and encouraged his troops to get along with the local population. Amongst other measures, he made his commanders personally responsible for the behaviour of their GIs in the street (GI was a term originating from the First World War, when US troops appeared in Britain with the letters 'GI' prominently stamped on their equipment, which stood for 'Government Issue').

There was also a cultural invasion of Britain by the Americans. As part of their campaign of friendly relations with the locals they established contacts with local dignitaries and councils, as well as inviting local people (mainly women!) to dances at their camps. The US bases soon became 'Little Americas' as the troops made themselves at home. American supplies were imported in vast quantities, and much found its way to the local communities. British people saw varieties of food, such as canned fruit, that had not been available for years.

As part of the process of making their troops feel at home the US Army set up the American Forces Network, a radio station which broadcast the latest baseball and American football results as well as the shows of such popular entertainers as Bob Hope and Jack Benny.

The station also played jazz and swing music that was not only popular with the GIs, but also with the British public who soon became regular listeners. The larger US camps also had theatres, where the troops could see the latest movies, or shows put on by visiting stars such as Bing Crosby, Bob Hope, James Cagney and Cab Calloway. The composer Irving Berlin also visited the US bases, and starred in a show at Bristol's Victoria Rooms. Major Glenn Miller was another popular artist, who toured camps and air stations with his Army Air Force Band (he appeared, for example, at the US General Hospital in Cirencester on 7 August 1944).

Although they were established at other locations in Gloucestershire (e.g. a Logistics HQ at Ben Hill Farm near Cheltenham), the US Army had a particularly heavy presence in the Bristol area. The city was the HQ of the 1st US Army (later replaced by the 9th Army). One of the main US Ordnance Depots was G-38, which was established on 14 sites in and around Bristol. Camps and other depots were also set up at other locations in the city, including Brislington, Bedminster and Shirehampton. Several hospitals were set up in the area, one of the largest being at Frenchay. Here three large medical units took over a former auxiliary hospital that had been set up in Frenchay Park and enlarged it with extra wards, technical, stores and other support facilities. Eventually 27 wards were to be built, and the hospital treated many casualties, including those evacuated to the UK after the D-Day landings. After the war, Frenchay Hospital was handed over to the Bristol Health Committee, and remains in operation today.

The British public suffered air raids, the blackout, the rationing of food, fuel and clothing, along with shortages of all kinds and the total disruption of their lives for six long years. The surrender of the German armed forces on 8 May 1945 marked the beginning of the end of the war, and when the Japanese finally surrendered in August 1945, there was rejoicing in the streets. People then tried to get their lives back together.

Many of the airfields across Gloucestershire were closed shortly afterwards and most of their personnel returned to civilian life. Some of the airfields were to carry on for years afterwards and several are still in use today. However, the majority were disposed of, and are now forgotten by most people. It is only the occasional memorial and monument, and accounts such as this that remain to remind and inform coming generations of the part that the airfields, and the people, of Gloucestershire played in the momentous events of the Second World War.

BIBLIOGRAPHY

During the preparation of this book I consulted many sources, including documents (both published and unpublished), books and magazines. The following is a list of the main publications that I have used:

Action Stations, nos 5 and 9, C. Ashworth, PSL, 1982

Action Stations Revisited, no 2, M. J. F. Bowyer, Crecy, 2004

Adolf Hitler's Holiday Snaps, Nigel J. Clarke Publications, 1995

Aircraft of the RAF since 1918, O. Thetford, Putnam, 1995

Bomber Command 1939-45, R. Overy, Harper Collins, 1997

Bomber Squadrons of the RAF and their Aircraft, P. Moyes, McDonald, 1974

Bristol Aircraft since 1910, C. H. Barnes, Putnam, 1995

Britain's Military Airfields 1939-45, D. J. Smith, PSL, 1989

British Aircraft at War 1939-45, G. Swanborough, HPC, 1997

British-built Aircraft Vol 2, R. Smith, Tempus, 2003

British VCs of World War 2, J. Laffin, Budding Books, 1997

Coastal, Support and Special Squadrons of the RAF and their Aircraft, J. D. R. Rawlings, Janes, 1982

Fields of Deception, C. Robinson, Methuen, 2000

Fighter Squadrons of the RAF and their Aircraft, J. D. R. Rawlings, McDonald Janes, 1975

Flying Units of the RAF, A. Lake, Airlife, 1999

Gloster Aircraft Since 1917, D. N. James, Putnam, 1971

Hawker Aircraft Since 1920, F. K. Mason, Putnam, 1995

Operation Bolero, K. Wakefield, Crecy, 1994

Pillboxes, H. Wills, Leo Cooper, 1985

RAF Squadrons, C. G. Jefford, Airlife, 1994

Royal Air Force – the Aircraft in Service since 1918, M. Turner and C. Bowyer, Hamlyn, 1981

Six of the Best, J. Edwards, Robson Books, 1984

The Source Book of the RAF, K. Delve, Airlife, 1994

The Squadrons of the Fleet Air Arm, R. Sturtivant, Air Britain, 1984

The Squadrons of the Royal Air Force and Commonwealth 1918-1988, J. J. Halley, Air Britain, 1988

U.K. Flight Testing Accidents 1940-71, D. Collier Webb, Air Britain, 2002

War Over the West, E. Walford, Amigo Books, 1989

Wings Over Gloucestershire, John Rennison, Piccadilly Publishing, 1988

Various issues of magazines, including the following:

Aeromilitaria (Air Britain), *Aeroplane, Air Pictorial, Airfield Review* (Airfield Research Group), *After the Battle, Flypast*

INDEX

RAF Squadrons and Units

USAAF and Other Units